Unreal Engine 4 Scripting with C++ Cookbook

Get the best out of your games by scripting them using UE4

William Sherif

Stephen Whittle

BIRMINGHAM - MUMBAI

Unreal Engine 4 Scripting with C++ Cookbook

First published: October 2016

Production reference: 1171016

Published by Packt Publishing Ltd.
Livery Place
35 Livery Street
Birmingham B3 2PB, UK.

ISBN 978-1-78588-554-9

www.packtpub.com

Credits

Authors

William Sherif

Stephen Whittle

Reviewer

John Doran

Commissioning Editor

Amarabha Banerjee

Acquisition Editor

Smeet Thakkar

Content Development Editor

Prashanth G

Technical Editor

Sunith Shetty

Copy Editor

Sonia Mathur

Project Coordinator

Ulhas Kambali

Proofreader

Safis Editing

Indexer

Hemangini Bari

Graphics

Jason Monteiro

Abhinash Sahu

Production Coordinator

Melwyn Dsa

Cover Work

Melwyn Dsa

About the Authors

William Sherif is a C++ programmer with more than eight years of experience in the programming world, ranging from game programming to web programming. He also worked as a university course instructor (sessional) for seven years. Additionally, he released several apps on the iTunes store, including Strum and MARSHALL OF THE ELITE SQUADRON. In the past, he has won acclaim for delivering course material in an easy-to-understand manner.

Stephen Whittle is a game developer and educator with nearly 10 years of development experience, most of which has been done using Unreal Engine. He is a community contributor to the engine, with features or bug fixes included in almost every major version of the engine since its public release.

I'd like to thank God; my partner, Nichelle; and my family and colleagues for their constant support while I wrote this book. Epic Games, in particular Mike Fricker and Alex Paschall, have also provided invaluable assistance.

About the Reviewer

John Doran is a technical game designer who has been creating games for over 10 years. He has worked on an assortment of games in teams from just himself to over 70 in student, mod, and professional projects in different roles from game designer to lead UI programmer. He previously worked at LucasArts on Star Wars 1313 as a game designer. He later graduated from DigiPen Institute of Technology in Redmond, WA, with a bachelor of science in game design.

In addition to working at DigiPen Game Studios, John is currently a part of DigiPen's research and development branch in Singapore. He is also the lead instructor of the DigiPen-Ubisoft campus game programming program, instructing graduate-level students in an intensive, advanced game-programming curriculum. He also tutors and assists students on various subjects, including C#, C++, Unreal, Unity, and game design.

He has authored *Unity 5.x Game Development Blueprints, Unreal Engine Game Development Cookbook, Building an FPS Game in Unity, Unity Game Development Blueprints, Getting Started with UDK, UDK Game Development, Mastering UDK Game Development*, and coauthored *UDK iOS Game Development Beginner's Guide*, all by Packt Publishing. You can find more about him at http://johnpdoran.com.

www.PacktPub.com

eBooks, discount offers, and more

Did you know that Packt offers eBook versions of every book published, with PDF and ePub files available? You can upgrade to the eBook version at www.PacktPub.com and as a print book customer, you are entitled to a discount on the eBook copy. Get in touch with us at customercare@packtpub.com for more details.

At www.PacktPub.com, you can also read a collection of free technical articles, sign up for a range of free newsletters and receive exclusive discounts and offers on Packt books and eBooks.

https://www.packtpub.com/mapt

Get the most in-demand software skills with Mapt. Mapt gives you full access to all Packt books and video courses, as well as industry-leading tools to help you plan your personal development and advance your career.

Why subscribe?

- ▸ Fully searchable across every book published by Packt
- ▸ Copy and paste, print, and bookmark content
- ▸ On demand and accessible via a web browser

Table of Contents

Preface

Unreal Engine 4 (UE4) is a complete suite of game development tools made by game developers for game developers. With more than 80 practical recipes, this book is a guide that showcases techniques to use the power of C++ scripting while developing games with UE4. We will start by adding and editing C++ classes from within the Unreal Editor. Then we will delve into one of Unreal's primary strengths—the ability for designers to customize programmer-developed actors and components. This will help you understand the benefits of when and how to use C++ as a scripting tool. With a blend of task-oriented recipes, this book will provide actionable information about scripting games with UE4 and manipulating the game and the development environment using C++. Toward the end of this book, you will be empowered to become a top-notch developer with UE4 using C++ as the scripting language.

What this book covers

Chapter 1, UE4 Development Tools, outlines basic recipes to get you started with UE4 game development and the basic tools used to create the code that makes your game.

Chapter 2, Creating Classes, focuses on how to create C++ classes and structs that integrate well with the UE4 Blueprints Editor. These classes will be graduated versions of regular C++ classes called UCLASSES.

Chapter 3, Memory Management and Smart Pointers, takes the reader through using all three types of pointer and mentions some common pitfalls regarding automatic garbage collection. This chapter also shows readers how to use Visual Studio or XCode to interpret crashes or confirm that the functionality is implemented correctly.

Chapter 4, Actors and Components, deals with creating custom actors and components, what purpose each serves, and how they work together.

Chapter 5, Handling Events and Delegates, describes delegates, events, and event handlers, and guides you through creating their own implementations.

Chapter 6, Input and Collision, shows how to connect user input to C++ functions and how to handle collisions in C++ from UE4. It will also provide default handling of game events such as user input and collision, allowing designers to override when necessary, using Blueprint.

Chapter 7, Communication between Classes and Interfaces, shows you how to write your own UInterfaces, and demonstrates how to take advantage of them within C++ to minimize class coupling and help keep your code clean.

Chapter 8, Integrating C++ and the Unreal Editor, shows you how to customize the editor by creating custom Blueprint and animation nodes from scratch. We will also implement custom editor windows and custom detail panels to inspect types created by users.

Chapter 9, User Interfaces – UI and UMG, demonstrates that displaying feedback to the player is one of the most important elements within game design, and this will usually involve some sort of HUD, or at least menus, within your game.

Chapter 10, AI for Controlling NPCs, covers recipes to control your NPC characters with a bit of Artificial Intelligence (AI).

Chapter 11, Custom Materials and Shaders, talks about creating custom materials and audio graph nodes used in the UE4 editor.

Chapter 12, Working with UE4 APIs, explains that the application programming interface (API) is the way in which you, as the programmer, can instruct the engine (and so the PC) on what to do. Each module has an API for it. To use an API, there is a very important linkage step where you must list all APIs that you will use in your build in `ProjectName.Build.cs` file.

What you need for this book

Creating a game is an elaborate task that will require a combination of assets and code. To create assets and code, we'll need some pretty advanced tools, including art tools, sound tools, level-editing tools, and code-editing tools. Assets include any visual artwork (2D sprites, 3D models), audio (music and sound effects), and game levels. To perform that, we'll set up a C++ coding environment to build our UE4 applications. We'll download Visual Studio 2015, install it, and set it up for UE4 C++ coding. (Visual Studio is an essential package for code editing when editing the C++ code for your UE4 game.)

Who this book is for

This book is intended for game developers who understand the fundamentals of game design and C++ and would like to incorporate native code into the games they make with Unreal. They will be programmers who want to extend the engine or implement systems and actors that allow designers control and flexibility when building levels.

Sections

In this book, you will find several headings that appear frequently (Getting ready, How to do it, How it works, There's more, and See also).

To give clear instructions on how to complete a recipe, we use these sections as follows:

Getting ready

This section tells you what to expect in the recipe, and describes how to set up any software or any preliminary settings required for the recipe.

How to do it...

This section contains the steps required to follow the recipe.

How it works...

This section usually consists of a detailed explanation of what happened in the previous section.

There's more...

This section consists of additional information about the recipe in order to make the reader more knowledgeable about the recipe.

See also

This section provides helpful links to other useful information for the recipe.

Conventions

In this book, you will find a number of text styles that distinguish between different kinds of information. Here are some examples of these styles and an explanation of their meaning.

Code words in text, database table names, folder names, filenames, file extensions, pathnames, dummy URLs, user input, and Twitter handles are shown as follows: "The parameters passed to the UPROPERTY() macro specify a couple of important pieces of information regarding the variable."

A block of code is set as follows:

```
#include<stdio.h>

int main()
{
    puts("Welcome to Visual Studio 2015 Community Edition!");
}
```

When we wish to draw your attention to a particular part of a code block, the relevant lines or items are set in bold:

```
int intVar = 5;
float floatVar = 3.7f;
FString fstringVar = "an fstring variable";
UE_LOG(LogTemp, Warning, TEXT("Text, %d %f %s"), intVar,
floatVar, *fstringVar );
```

New terms and **important words** are shown in bold. Words that you see on the screen, for example, in menus or dialog boxes, appear in the text like this: "After you select the tools you'd like to add on to Visual Studio, click the **Next** button."

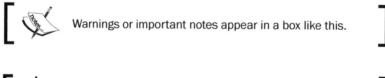

Warnings or important notes appear in a box like this.

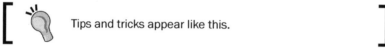

Tips and tricks appear like this.

Reader feedback

Feedback from our readers is always welcome. Let us know what you think about this book— what you liked or disliked. Reader feedback is important for us as it helps us develop titles that you will really get the most out of.

To send us general feedback, simply e-mail feedback@packtpub.com, and mention the book's title in the subject of your message.

If there is a topic that you have expertise in and you are interested in either writing or contributing to a book, see our author guide at www.packtpub.com/authors.

Customer support

Now that you are the proud owner of a Packt book, we have a number of things to help you to get the most from your purchase.

Downloading the example code

You can download the example code files for this book from your account at `http://www.packtpub.com`. If you purchased this book elsewhere, you can visit `http://www.packtpub.com/support` and register to have the files e-mailed directly to you.

You can download the code files by following these steps:

1. Log in or register to our website using your e-mail address and password.
2. Hover the mouse pointer on the **SUPPORT** tab at the top.
3. Click on **Code Downloads & Errata**.
4. Enter the name of the book in the **Search** box.
5. Select the book for which you're looking to download the code files.
6. Choose from the drop-down menu where you purchased this book from.
7. Click on **Code Download**.

You can also download the code files by clicking on the **Code Files** button on the book's webpage at the Packt Publishing website. This page can be accessed by entering the book's name in the **Search** box. Please note that you need to be logged in to your Packt account.

Once the file is downloaded, please make sure that you unzip or extract the folder using the latest version of:

- WinRAR / 7-Zip for Windows
- Zipeg / iZip / UnRarX for Mac
- 7-Zip / PeaZip for Linux

The code bundle for the book is also hosted on GitHub at `https://github.com/PacktPublishing/Unreal-Engine-4-Scripting-with-CPlusPlus-Cookbook`. We also have other code bundles from our rich catalog of books and videos available at `https://github.com/PacktPublishing/`. Check them out!

Downloading the color images of this book

We also provide you with a PDF file that has color images of the screenshots/diagrams used in this book. The color images will help you better understand the changes in the output. You can download this file from `https://www.packtpub.com/sites/default/files/downloads/UnrealEngine4ScriptingwithC_Cookbook_ColorImages.pdf`.

Errata

Although we have taken every care to ensure the accuracy of our content, mistakes do happen. If you find a mistake in one of our books—maybe a mistake in the text or the code—we would be grateful if you could report this to us. By doing so, you can save other readers from frustration and help us improve subsequent versions of this book. If you find any errata, please report them by visiting `http://www.packtpub.com/submit-errata`, selecting your book, clicking on the **Errata Submission Form** link, and entering the details of your errata. Once your errata are verified, your submission will be accepted and the errata will be uploaded to our website or added to any list of existing errata under the Errata section of that title.

To view the previously submitted errata, go to `https://www.packtpub.com/books/content/support` and enter the name of the book in the search field. The required information will appear under the **Errata** section.

Piracy

Piracy of copyrighted material on the Internet is an ongoing problem across all media. At Packt, we take the protection of our copyright and licenses very seriously. If you come across any illegal copies of our works in any form on the Internet, please provide us with the location address or website name immediately so that we can pursue a remedy.

Please contact us at `copyright@packtpub.com` with a link to the suspected pirated material.

We appreciate your help in protecting our authors and our ability to bring you valuable content.

Questions

If you have a problem with any aspect of this book, you can contact us at `questions@packtpub.com`, and we will do our best to address the problem.

UE4 Development Tools

1

In this chapter, we will outline basic recipes for getting started in UE4 game development, and the basic tools that we use for creating the code that makes your game. This will include the following recipes:

- ▶ Installing Visual Studio
- ▶ Creating and building your first C++ project in Visual Studio
- ▶ Changing the code font and color in Visual Studio
- ▶ Extension – changing the color theme in Visual Studio
- ▶ Formatting your code (Autocomplete settings) in Visual Studio
- ▶ Shortcut keys in Visual Studio
- ▶ Extended mouse usage in Visual Studio
- ▶ UE4 – installation
- ▶ UE4 – first project
- ▶ UE4 – creating your first level
- ▶ UE4 – logging with `UE_LOG`
- ▶ UE4 – making an `FString` from `FStrings` and other variables
- ▶ Project management on GitHub – getting your Source Control
- ▶ Project management on GitHub – using the Issue Tracker
- ▶ Project management on VisualStudio.com – managing the tasks in your project
- ▶ Project management on VisualStudio.com – constructing user stories and tasks

Introduction

Creating a game is an elaborate task that will require a combination of **assets** and **code**. To create assets and code, we'll need some pretty advanced tools including *art tools, sound tools, level editing tools,* and *code editing tools*. In this chapter, we'll discuss finding suitable tools for asset creation and coding. Assets include any visual artwork (2D sprites, 3D models), audio (music and sound effects), and game levels. Code is the text (usually C++) that instructs the computer on how to tie these assets together to make a game world and level, and how to make that game world "play." There are dozens of very good tools for each task; we will explore a couple of each, and make some recommendations. Game editing tools, especially, are hefty programs that require a powerful CPU and lots of memory, and very good, ideal GPUs for good performance.

Protecting your assets and work is also a necessary practice. We'll explore and describe source control, which is how you back up your work on a remote server. An introduction to *Unreal Engine 4 Programming* is also included, along with exploring basic logging functions and library use. Significant planning is also required to get the tasks done, so we'll use a task-planner software package to do so.

Installing Visual Studio

Visual Studio is an essential package for code editing when editing the C++ code for your UE4 game.

Getting ready

We're going to set up a C++ coding environment to build our UE4 applications. We'll download Visual Studio 2015, install it, and set it up for UE4 C++ coding.

How to do it...

1. Begin by visiting https://www.visualstudio.com/en-us/products/visual-studio-community-vs.aspx. Click on **Download Community 2015**. This downloads the ~200 KB loader/installer.

You can compare editions of Visual Studio at `https://www.visualstudio.com/en-us/products/compare-visual-studio-2015-products-vs.aspx`. The Community Edition of Visual Studio is fully adequate for UE4 development purposes in this book.

2. Launch the installer, and select the components of Visual Studio 2015 that you want to add to your PC. Keep in mind that the more features you select, the larger your installation will be.

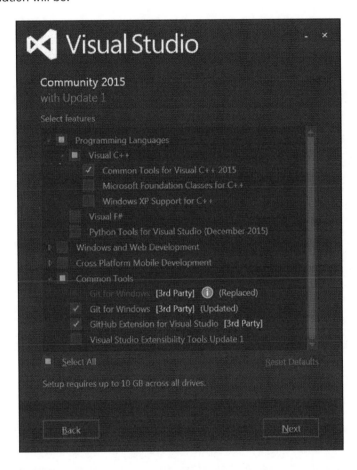

The preceding screenshot shows a recommended minimum installation, with **Common Tools for Visual C++ 2015**, **Git for Windows**, and **GitHub Extension for Visual Studio** all checked. We will use the **Git for Windows** features in a later section in this chapter.

3. After you have selected the tools you'd like to add onto Visual Studio, click the **Next** button. The installer tool will download the required components, and continue setup. Installation should take 20-40 minutes, depending on your option selections and connection speed.

4. After you download and install Visual Studio 2015, launch it. You will be presented with a **Sign in** dialog box.

You can **Sign in** with your Microsoft account (the one you use to sign into Windows 10), or **Sign up** for a new account. After you've signed in or signed up, you will be able to sign into Visual Studio itself. It may seem odd to sign into a desktop code editing program, but your sign-in will be used for source control commits to your repositories. On first signing in to Visual Studio, you can select (one time only) a unique URL for your source code repositories as hosted on Visualstudio.com.

How it works...

Visual Studio is an excellent editor, and you will have a fantastic time coding within it. In the next recipe, we'll discuss how to create and compile your own code.

Creating and building your first C++ project in Visual Studio

In order to compile and run code from Visual Studio, it must be done from within a project.

Getting ready

In this recipe, we will identify how to create an actual executable running program from Visual Studio. We will do so by creating a project in Visual Studio to host, organize, and compile the code.

How to do it...

In Visual Studio, each group of code is contained within something called a **Project**. A Project is a buildable conglomerate of code and assets that produce either an executable (`.exe` runnable) or a library (`.lib`, or `.dll`). A group of Projects can be collected together into something called a **Solution**. Let's start by constructing a Visual Studio Solution and Project for a console application, followed by constructing a UE4 sample Project and Solution.

1. Open Visual Studio, and go to **File | New | Project...**
2. You will see a dialog as follows:

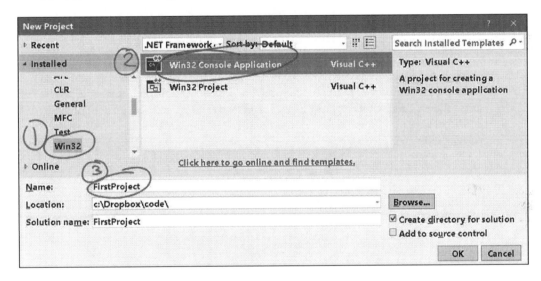

Select **Win32** in the pane on the left-hand side. In the right-hand pane, hit **Win32 Console Application**. Name your project in the lower box, then hit **OK**.

3. In the next dialog box, we specify the properties of our console application. Read the first dialog box and simply click **Next**. Then, in the **Application Settings** dialog, choose the **Console Application** bullet, then under **Additional options**, choose **Empty project**. You can leave **Security Development Lifecycle (SDL) checks** unchecked.

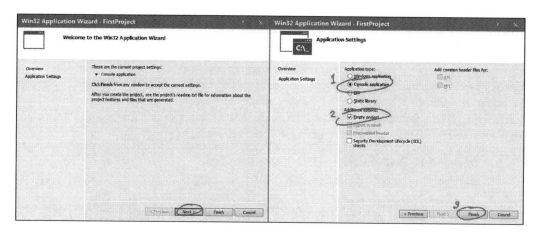

4. Once the application wizard completes, you will have created your first project. Both a Solution and a Project are created. To see these, you need **Solution Explorer**. To ensure that **Solution Explorer** is showing, go to **View | Solution Explorer** (or press *Ctrl + Alt + L*). **Solution Explorer** is a window that usually appears docked on the left-hand side or right-hand side of the main editor window as shown in the following screenshot:

Solution Explorer also displays all the files that are part of the project. Using **Solution Explorer**, we will also add a code file into the editor. Right click on your Project `FirstProject`, and select **Add | New Item...**

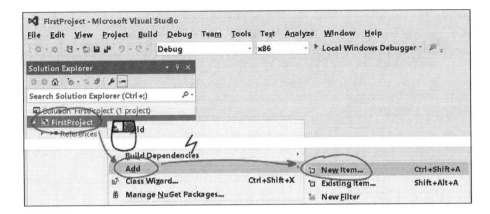

5. In the next dialog, simply select **C++ File (.cpp)**, and give the file any name you'd like. I called mine `Main.cpp`.

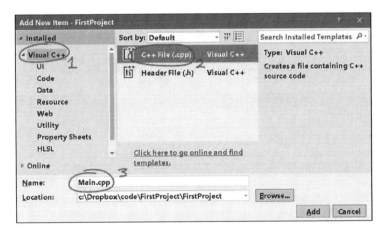

6. Once you have added the file, it will appear in **Solution Explorer** under your `FirstProject`'s source file filter. As your Project grows, more and more files are going to be added to your project. You can compile and run your first C++ program using the following text:

```cpp
#include<stdio.h>

int main()
{
    puts("Welcome to Visual Studio 2015 Community Edition!");
}
```

7. Press *Ctrl + Shift + B* to build the project, then *Ctrl + F5* to run the project.

8. Your executable will be created, and you will see a small black window with the results of your program's run:

How it works...

Building an executable involves translating your C++ code from text language to a binary file. Running the file runs your game program, which is just the code text that occurs in the `main()` function between { and }.

There's more...

Build configurations are **styles** of build that we should discuss them here. There are at least two important build configurations you should know about: **Debug** and **Release**. The Build configuration selected is at the top of the editor, just below the toolbar in the default position.

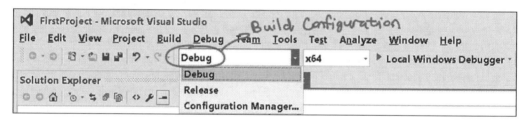

Depending on which configuration you select, different compiler options are used. A **Debug** configuration typically includes extensive debug information in the build as well as turning off optimizations to speed up compilation. **Release** builds are often optimized (either for size or for speed), take a bit longer to build, and result in smaller or faster executables. Behavior stepping through with the debugger is often better in the **Debug** mode than the **Release** mode.

Changing the code font and color in Visual Studio

Customizing the font and color in Visual Studio is not only extremely flexible, you will also find it very necessary if your monitor resolution is quite high or quite low.

Getting ready

Visual Studio is a highly customizable code editing tool. You might find the default fonts too small for your screen. You may want to change your code's font size and color. Or you may want to completely customize the coloration of keywords and the text background colors. The **Fonts and Colors** dialog box, which we'll show you how to use in this section, allows you to completely customize every aspect of the code editor's font and color.

```c
#include <stdio.h>

int main()
{
    puts( "Welcome to Visual Studio 2015 Community Edition!" );
}
```

How to do it...

1. From within Visual Studio, go to **Tools | Options...**

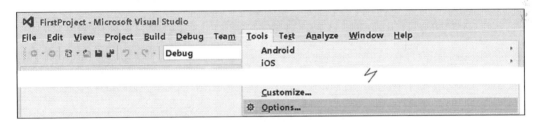

2. Select **Environment | Fonts and Colors** from the dialog that appears. It will look like the following screenshot:

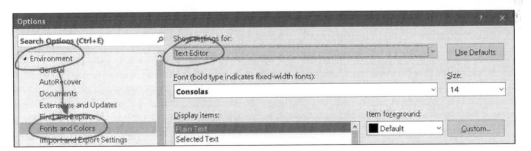

3. Play around with the font and font size of **Text Editor/Plain Text**. Click **OK** on the dialog, and see the results in the code-text editor.

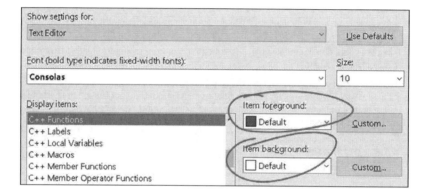

```
#include <stdio.h>
```
```
int main()
{
    puts( "Welcome!" );
}
```

Text Editor/Plain Text describes the font and size used for all code text within the regular code editor. If you change the size of the font, the size changes for any text entered into the coding window (for all languages, including C, C++, C#, and others).

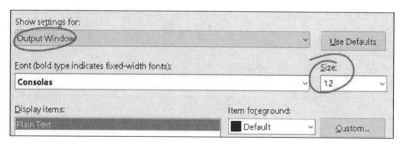

The color (foreground and background) is completely customizable for each item. Try this for the **Text Editor/Keyword** setting (affects all languages), or for C++-specific items, such as **Text Editor/C++ Functions**. Click **OK**, and you will see the changed color of the item reflected in the code editor.

You may also want to configure the font size of the **Output Window**—choose **Show settings for** => **Output Window** as seen in the following screenshot:

The **Output Window** is the little window at the bottom of the editor that displays build results and compiler errors.

You can't save-out (export) or bring in (import) your changes to the **Fonts and Colors** dialog. But you can use something called the *Visual Studio Theme Editor Extension,* learn more refer to *Extension – changing the color theme in Visual Studio* to export and import customized color themes.

For this reason, you may want to avoid changing font colors from this dialog. You must use this dialog to change the font and font-size, however, for any setting (at the time of writing).

How it works...

The **Fonts and Colors** dialog simply changes the appearance of code in the text editor as well as for other windows such as the output window. It is very useful for making your coding environment more comfortable.

There's more...

Once you have customized your settings, you'll find that you may want to save your customized **Fonts and Colors** settings for others to use, or to put into another installation of Visual Studio, which you have on another machine. Unfortunately, by default, you won't be able to save-out your customized **Fonts and Colors** settings. You will need something called the Visual Studio Theme Editor extension to do so. We will explore this in the next recipe.

See also

▶ The *Extension – changing the color theme in Visual Studio* section describes how to import and export color themes

Extension – changing the color theme in Visual Studio

By default, you cannot save the changes you make to the font colors and background settings that you make in the **Fonts and Colors** dialog. To fix this issue, Visual Studio 2015 has a feature called **Themes**. If you go to **Tools | Options | Environment | General**, you can change the theme to one of the three pre-installed stock themes (**Light**, **Blue**, and **Dark**).

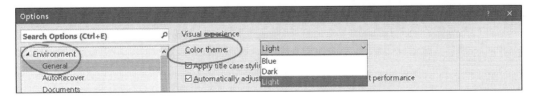

A different theme completely changes the look of Visual Studio—from the colors of the title bars to the background color of the text editor window.

You can also customize the theme of Visual Studio completely, but you'll need an extension to do so. Extensions are little programs that can be installed into Visual Studio to modify its behavior.

By default, your customized color settings cannot be saved or reloaded into another Visual Studio installation without the extension. With the extension, you will also be able to save your own color theme to share with others. You can also load the color settings made by another person or by yourself into a fresh copy of Visual Studio.

How to do it...

1. Go to **Tools | Extensions and Updates...**

2. From the dialog that appears, choose **Online** in the panel on the left-hand side. Start typing Theme Editor into the search box at the right. The **Visual Studio 2015 Color Theme Editor** dialog will pop up in your search results.

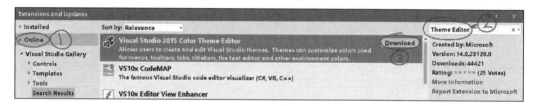

3. Click the small **Download** button in the top right-hand corner of the entry. Click through the installation dialog prompts, allowing the plugin to install. After installation, Visual Studio will prompt you to restart.

 Alternatively, visit https://visualstudiogallery.msdn. microsoft.com/6f4b51b6-5c6b-4a81-9cb5-f2daa560430b and download/install the extension by double-clicking the .vsix that comes from your browser.

4. Click **Restart Now** to ensure the plugin is loaded.

You must restart Microsoft Visual Studio in order for the changes to take effect.   Restart Now   Close

5. After restarting, go to **Tools | Customize Colors** to open the **Color Themes** editor page.

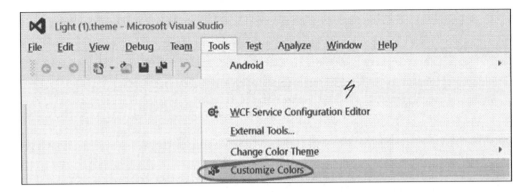

6. From the **Color Themes** dialog that appears, click on the little palette-shaped icon on the upper-right corner of the theme that you want to use as your base or starting theme (I've clicked on the palette for the **Light** theme here, as you can see in the following screenshot).

7. A copy of the theme will appear in the **Custom Themes** section in the lower part of the **Color Themes** window. Click on **Edit Theme** to modify the theme. When you are editing the theme, you can change everything from the font text color to the C++ keyword color.

8. The main area you are interested in is the C++ Text Editor section. To gain access to all the C++ Text Editor options, be sure to select the **Show All Elements** option at the top of the Theme Editor window, as shown in the following screenshot:

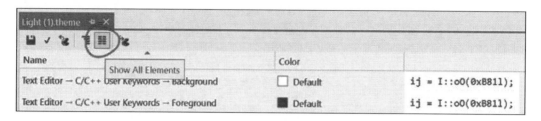

 Be sure to select the **Show All Elements** option in the Theme Editor window to show C++-specific text editor settings. Otherwise, you'll be left with Chrome/GUI type modifications being possible only.

9. Note that, while most of the settings you are interested in will be under **Text Editor | C/C++**, some will not have that **C++** subheading. For example, the setting for the main/plain text inside the editor window (for all languages) is under **Text Editor | Plain Text** (without the **C++** subheading).

10. Select the theme to use from **Tools | Options | Environment | General**. Any new themes you have created will appear automatically in the drop-down menu.

How it works...

Once we load the plugin, it integrates into Visual Studio quite nicely. Exporting and uploading your themes to share with others is quite easy too.

Adding a theme to your Visual Studio installs it as an extension in **Tools | Extensions and Updates...**, To remove a theme, simply **Uninstall** its Extension.

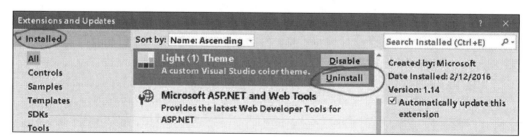

Formatting your code (Autocomplete settings) in Visual Studio

Code-writing formatting with Visual Studio is a pleasure. In this recipe, we'll discuss how to control the way Visual Studio lays out the text of your code.

Getting ready

Code has to be formatted correctly. You and your co-programmers will be able to better understand, **grok**, and keep your code bug-free if it is consistently formatted. This is why Visual Studio includes a number of auto-formatting tools inside the editor.

How to do it...

1. Go to **Tools | Options | Text Editor | C/C++**. This dialog displays a window that allows you to toggle **Automatic brace completion**.

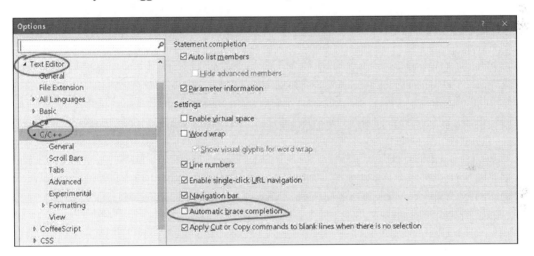

Automatic brace completion is the feature where, when you type { , a corresponding } is automatically typed for you. This feature may irk you if you don't like the text editor inserting characters for you unexpectedly.

You generally want **Auto list members** on, as that displays a nice dialog with the complete names of data members listed for you as soon as you start typing. This makes it easy to remember variable names, so you don't have to memorize them:

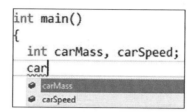

```
int main()
{
    int carMass, carSpeed;
    car
```
carMass	
carSpeed	

 If you press *Ctrl + Spacebar* inside the code editor at any time, the auto list pops up.

2. Some more autocomplete behavior options are located under **Text Editor | C/C++ | Formatting**:

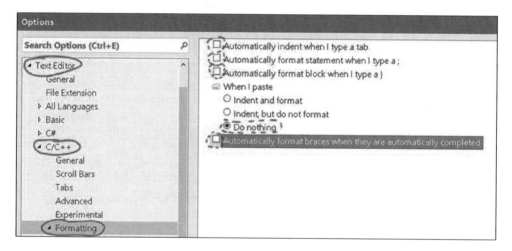

Autoformat section: Highlight a section of text and select **Edit | Advanced | Format Selection** (*Ctrl + K, Ctrl + F*).

How it works...

The default autocomplete and autoformat behaviors may irk you. You need to converse with your team on how you want your code formatted (spaces or tab indents, size of indent, and so on), and then configure your Visual Studio settings accordingly.

Shortcut keys in Visual Studio

Shortcut keys really save you time when coding. Knowing shortcut keys offhand is always good.

Getting ready

There are a number of shortcut keys that will make coding and project navigation much faster and more efficient for you. In this recipe, we describe how to use some of the common shortcut keys that will really enhance your coding speed.

How to do it...

The following are some very useful keyboard shortcuts for you to try:

1. Click on one page of the code, then click somewhere else, at least 10 lines of code away. Now press *Ctrl + -* [navigate backwards]. Navigation through different pages of source code (the last place you were at, and the place you are at now) is done by pressing *Ctrl + -* and *Ctrl + Shift + -* respectively.

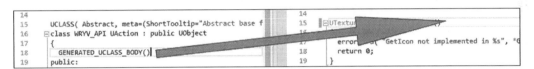

```
14                                                          14
15    UCLASS( Abstract, meta=(ShortTooltip="Abstract base f  15    ⊟UTextu
16  ⊟class WRYV_API UAction : public UObject                 16
17    {                                                      17        erro       "GetIcon not implemented in %s", *G
18        GENERATED_UCLASS_BODY()                            18        return 0;
19    public:                                                19    }
```

 Warping around in the text editor using *Ctrl + -*. The cursor will jump back to the last location it was in that is more than 10 lines of code away, even if the last location was in a separate file.

Say, for example, you're editing code in one place, and you want to go back to the place you've just been (or go back to the section in the code you came from). Simply press *Ctrl + -*, and that will warp you back to the location in the code you were at last. To warp forward to the location you were at before you pressed *Ctrl + -*, press *Ctrl + Shift + -*. To warp back, the previous location should be more than 10 lines away, or in a different file. These correspond to the Forward and Back menu buttons in the toolbar:

The Back and Forward navigation buttons in the toolbar, which correspond to the *Ctrl + -* and *Ctrl + Shift + -* shortcuts respectively.

2. Press *Ctrl + W* to highlight a single word.

3. Press and hold *Ctrl + Shift* + right arrow (or left arrow) (not *Shift* + right arrow) just to move to the right and left of the cursor, selecting entire words.

4. Press *Ctrl + C* to copy text, *Ctrl + X* to cut text, and *Ctrl + V* to paste text.

5. **Clipboard ring**: The clipboard ring is a kind of a reference to the fact that Visual Studio maintains a stack of the last copy operations. By pressing *Ctrl + C*, you push the text that you are copying into an effective stack. Pressing *Ctrl + C* a second time on different text pushes that text into the **Clipboard Stack**. For example, in the following diagram, we pressed *Ctrl + C* on the word **cyclic** first, then *Ctrl + C* on the word **paste** afterwards.

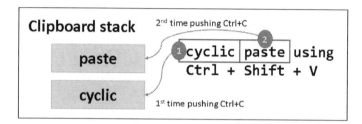

As you know, pressing *Ctrl + V* pastes the top item in the stack. Pressing *Ctrl + Shift + V* accesses a very long history of all the items ever copied in that session, that is, items underneath the top item in the stack. After you exhaust the list of items, the list wraps back to the top item in the stack. This is an odd feature, but you may find it useful occasionally.

6. *Ctrl + M, Ctrl + M* collapses a code section.

```
UTexture* UBuildAction::GetIcon()
{
    return Game->GetData( BuildingType ).Portrait;
}
```

```
UTexture* UBuildAction::GetIcon() { ... }
```

How it works...

Keyboard shortcuts allow you to speed up work in the code editor by reducing the number of mouse reaches that you have to perform in a coding session.

Extended mouse usage in Visual Studio

The mouse is a pretty handy tool for selecting text. In this section, we'll highlight how to use the mouse in an advanced way for quick edits to your code's text.

How to do it...

1. Hold down the *Ctrl* key while clicking to select an entire word.

```
FString::Printf( TEXT(
```

2. Hold down the *Alt* key to select a box of text (*Alt* + Left Click + Drag).

```
// initialize a bunch of cooldo
FString name = FString::Printf(
Clock* clock = new Clock( name,
```

You can then either cut, copy, or overwrite the box-shaped text area.

How it works...

Mouse clicking alone can be tedious, but with the help of *Ctrl* + *Alt*, it becomes quite cool. Try *Alt* + Left Click + Drag for selecting a row of text, then typing as well. The characters you type will be repeated in rows.

UE4 – installation

There are a number of steps to follow to install and configure UE4 properly. In this recipe, we'll walk through the correct installation and setup of the engine.

Getting ready

UE4 takes up quite a few GB of space, so you should have at least 20 GB or so free for the installation on the target drive.

How to do it...

1. Visit unrealengine.com and download it. Sign up for an account if required.

2. Run the installer for the Epic Games Launcher Program by double-clicking the `EpicGamesLauncherInstaller-x.x.x-xxx.msi` installer. Install it in the default location.

3. Once the Epic Games Launcher program is installed, open it by double-clicking its icon on your desktop or in the Start menu.

4. Browse the start page and take a look around. Eventually, you will need to install an engine. Click on the large orange **Install Engine** button on the top-left side from the **UE4** tab, as shown in the following image:

5. A pop-up dialog will show the components that can be installed. Select the components you'd like to install. The recommendation is to begin by installing the first three components (**Core Components**, **Starter Content**, and **Templates and Feature Packs**). You can leave out the **Editor symbols for debugging** component if you will not be using it.

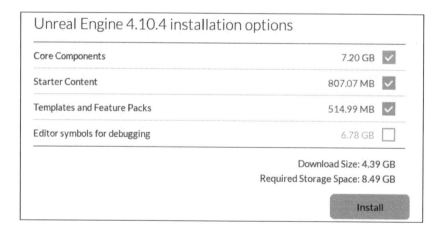

6. After the engine has installed, the **Install Engine** button will change to a **Launch Engine** button.

How it works...

The Epic Games Launcher is the program that you need to start up the engine itself. It keeps a copy of all your projects and libraries in the **Library** tab.

There's more...

Try downloading some of the free library packages in the **Library | Vault** section. For that, click the **Library** item on the left side, and scroll down until you see **Vault**, underneath **My Projects**.

UE4 – first project

Setting up a Project within UE4 takes a number of steps. It is important to get your options correct so that you can have the setup that you like, so carefully follow this recipe when constructing your first project.

Each project that you create within UE4 takes up at least 1 GB of space or so, so you should decide whether you want your created projects on the same target drive, or on an external or separate HDD.

How to do it...

1. From the Epic Games Launcher, click on the **Launch Unreal Engine 4.11.2** button. Once you are inside the engine, an option to create a new project or load an existing one will presents itself.
2. Select the **New Project** tab.
3. Decide whether you will be using C++ to code your project, or Blueprints exclusively.

    1. If using Blueprints exclusively, make your selection of a template to use from the **Blueprint** tab.

    2. If using C++ in addition to Blueprints to construct your project, select the project template to construct your project based on the **C++** tab.

    3. If you're not sure what template to base your code on, BASIC Code is an excellent starting point for any C++ project (or Blank for a Blueprint-exclusive project).

4. Take a look at the three icons that appear beneath the template listing. There are three options here to configure:

    1. You can choose to target Desktop or Mobile applications.

    2. You have an option to alter the quality settings (the picture of a plant with magic). But you probably don't need to alter these. The quality settings are reconfigurable under **Engine | Engine Scalability Settings** anyway.

    3. The last option is whether to include **Starter Content** with the project or not. You can probably use the **Starter Content** package in your project. It has some excellent materials and textures available within it.

> If you don't like the **Starter Content** package, try the packages in the UE4 Marketplace. There is some excellent free content there, including the **GameTextures Material Pack**.

5. Select the drive and folder in which you will save your project. Keep in mind that each project is roughly 1 GB in size, and you will need at least that much space on the destination drive.

6. Name your project. Preferably name it something unique and specific to what you are planning on creating.

7. Hit **Create**. Both the UE4 Editor and Visual Studio 2015 windows should pop up, enabling you to edit your project.

> In the future, keep in mind that you can open the Visual Studio 2015 Solution via one of the two following methods:
>
> ▸ Via your local file explorer. Navigate to the root of where your project is stored, and double-click on the `ProjectName.sln` file.
> ▸ From UE4, click on **File | Open Visual Studio**.

UE4 – creating your first level

Creating levels in UE4 is easy and facilitated by a great UI all around. In this recipe, we'll outline basic editor use and describe how to construct your first level once you have your first project launched.

Getting ready

Complete the previous recipe, *UE4 – First Project*. Once you have a project constructed, we can proceed with creating a level.

How to do it...

1. The default level that gets set up when you start a new project will contain some default geometry and scenery. You don't need to start with this starter stuff, however. If you don't want to build from it, you can delete it, or create a new level.

2. To create a new level, click **File | New Level...** and select to create a level with a background sky (**Default**), or without a background sky (**Empty Level**).

> If you choose to create a level without a background sky, keep in mind that you must add a **light** to it to see the geometry you add to it effectively.

3. If you loaded the **Starter Content** on your project's creation (or some other content), then you can use the **Content Browser** to pull content into your level. Simply drag and drop instances of your content from the **Content Browser** into the level, save, and launch them.

4. Add some geometry to your level using the **Modes** panel (**Window | Modes**). Be sure to click on the picture of a light bulb and cube to access the placeable geometry. You can also add lights via the **Modes** tab by clicking on the **Lights** subtab on the left-hand side of the **Modes** tab.

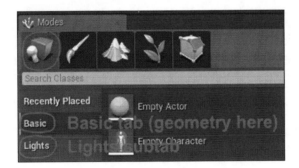

>
> The **Modes** panel contains two useful items for level construction: some sample geometry to add (cubes and spheres and the like) as well as a panel full of lights. Try these out and experiment to begin laying out your level.

UE4 – logging with UE_LOG

Logging is extremely important for outputting internal game data. Using log tools lets you print information into a handy little **Output Log** window in the UE4 editor.

Getting ready

When coding, we may sometimes want to send some debug information out to the UE log window. This is possible using the UE_LOG macro. Log messages are an extremely important and convenient way to keep track of information in your program as you are developing it.

How to do it...

1. In your code, enter a line of code using the form:

    ```
    UE_LOG(LogTemp, Warning, TEXT("Some warning message") );
    ```

2. Turn on the **Output Log** inside the UE4 editor to see your log messages printed in that window as your program is running.

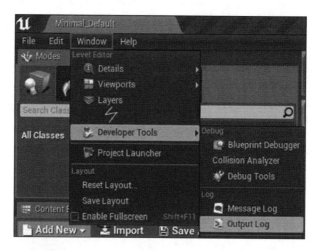

How it works...

The UE_LOG macro accepts a minimum of three parameters:

▸ The Log category (we used LogTemp here to denote a log message in a temporary log)

▸ The Log level (we used a warning here to denote a log message printed in yellow warning text)

▸ A string for the actual text of the log message itself

Do not forget the TEXT () macro around your log message text! It promotes the enclosed text to Unicode (it prepends an L) when the compiler is set to run with Unicode on.

UE_LOG also accepts a variable number of arguments, just like `printf()` from the C programming language.

```
int intVar = 5;
float floatVar = 3.7f;
FString fstringVar = "an fstring variable";
UE_LOG(LogTemp, Warning, TEXT("Text, %d %f %s"), intVar,
floatVar, *fstringVar );
```

There will be an asterisk * just before `FString` variables when using `UE_LOG` to **dereference** the `FString` to a regular C-style `TCHAR` pointer.

TCHAR is usually defined as a variable type `where`, if Unicode is being used in the compile, the `TCHAR` resolves to `wchar_t`. If Unicode is off (compiler switch `_UNICODE` not defined), then `TCHAR` resolves to simply char.

Don't forget to clear your log messages after you no longer need them from the source!

UE4 – making an FString from FStrings and other variables

When coding in UE4, you often want to construct a string from variables. This is pretty easy using the `FString::Printf` or `FString::Format` functions.

Getting ready

For this, you should have an existing project into which you can enter some UE4 C++ code. Putting variables into a string is possible via **printing**. It may be counterintuitive to print into a string, but you can't just concatenate variables together, and hope that they will automatically convert to string, as in some languages such as JavaScript.

How to do it...

1. Using `FString::Printf()`:
    1. Consider the variables you'd like printed into your string.
    2. Open and take a look at a reference page of the `printf` format specifiers, such as `http://en.cppreference.com/w/cpp/io/c/fprintf`.

3. Try code such as the following:

```
FString name = "Tim";
int32 mana = 450;
FString string = FString::Printf( TEXT( "Name = %s Mana =
%d" ), *name, mana );
```

Notice how the preceding code block uses the format specifiers precisely as the traditional `printf` function does. In the preceding example, we used `%s` to place a string in the formatted string, and `%d` to place an integer in the formatted string. Different format specifiers exist for different types of variables, and you should look them up on a site such as cppreference.com.

2. Using `FString::Format()`. Write code in the following form:

```
FString name = "Tim";
int32 mana = 450;
TArray< FStringFormatArg > args;
args.Add( FStringFormatArg( name ) );
args.Add( FStringFormatArg( mana ) );
FString string = FString::Format( TEXT( "Name = {0} Mana =
{1}" ), args );
UE_LOG( LogTemp, Warning, TEXT( "Your string: %s" ),
*string );
```

With `FString::Format()`, instead of using correct format specifiers, we use simple integers and a TArray of `FStringFormatArg` instead. The `FstringFormatArg` helps `FString::Format()` deduce the type of variable to put in the string.

Project management on GitHub – getting your Source Control

A very important thing to do for your project as you're developing it is to generate a timeline history as you're working. To do so, you need to back up your source code periodically. A great tool for doing so is Git. Git allows you to park changes (commits) into a repository online on a remote server so that your code's development history is documented and preserved on that remote server. If your local copy gets damaged somehow, you can always recover from the online backups. This timeline-history of your codebase's development is called **Source Control**.

Getting ready

There are a couple of free services that offer online source backups. Some of the free alternatives for storing your data include:

- ▶ **Visualstudio.com**: limited/private sharing of your repository
- ▶ **github.com**: unlimited public sharing of your repositories

Visualstudio.com is great for when you want some privacy for your project for free, while GitHub is great when you want to share your project with lots of users for free. Visualstudio. com also offers some very good workboarding and planning features, which we will use later in this text (GitHub also offers a competing Issue Tracker, which we'll discuss later on as well).

The website you choose depends mostly on how you plan on sharing your code. In this text, we will use GitHub for source code storage, since we need to share our code with a large number of users (you!)

How to do it...

1. Sign up for a GitHub account at `https://github.com`. Sign into your GitHub account using the **Team Explorer** menu (**View | Team Explorer**).

2. Once you have the **Team Explorer** open, you can sign into your GitHub account using the button that appears in the **Team Explorer** window.

3. After you've signed in, you should gain the capability to **Clone** and **Create** repositories. These options will appear right underneath the GitHub menu in the **Team Explorer**.

4. From here, we want to create our first repository. Hit the **Create** button, and name your repository in the window that comes up.

 When creating your project, take care to select the **VisualStudio** option from the `.gitignore` options menu. This will cause Git to ignore the Visual Studio-specific files that you don't want included in your repository, such as the Build and Release directories.

5. Now you have a repository! The repository is initialized on GitHub. We just have to put some code into it.

6. Open up the Epic Games Launcher, and create a project to put into the repository.

7. Open the C++ project in Visual Studio 2015, and right-click on Solution. Select **Add Solution to Source Control** from the context menu that appears. The dialog that appears will ask whether you want to use **Git** or **TFVC**.

 If you use **Git** for your source control, then you can host on either github.com or Visualstudio.com.

8. After you add Git Source Control to the project, take a look at **Team Explorer** again. From that window, you should enter a brief message, then click on the **Commit** button.

How it works...

Git repositories are important for backing up copies of your code and project files as your project evolves. There are many commands within Git to browse the project history (try the Git GUI tool), see what changes you've made since the last commit (`git diff`), or move backward and forward through the Git history (`git checkout commit-hash-id`).

Project management on GitHub – using the Issue Tracker

Keeping track of you project's progress, features, and bugs is extremely important. The GitHub Issue Tracker will enable you to do this.

Getting ready

Keeping track of your project's planned features and running issues is important. GitHub's Issue Tracker can be used to create lists of features you'd like to add to your project as well as bugs you need to fix at some time in the future.

How to do it...

1. To add an issue to your Issue Tracker, first select the repository that you'd like to edit by going to the front page of GitHub and selecting the **Repositories** tab:

2. From your repository's homepage, select the **Issues** tab under your repository. To add an issue to track, click the **New Issue** button in the lower-right corner of the screen, as seen in the following screenshot:

3. When adding your issue, it is good practice to detail it as much as possible. Including screenshots and diagrams in the features or bugs you post is highly recommended, as it documents the issue much better, and parks important information and a good description into your **Issue Tracker**. Dragging and dropping images into the text editor window automatically uploads a copy of the image to GitHub's own cloud server, and the image will appear inline in the issue, as shown in the following screenshot:

4. The box into which you enter the description of your bug or feature supports **Markdown**. Markdown is a simplified HTML-like markup language that lets you quickly write HTML-like syntax with ease. Examples of some markdown syntax are as follows:

```
# headings
## sub-headings
### sub-sub-headings
_italics_, __bold__, ___bold-italics___
[hyperlinks](http://towebsites.com/)


code (indented by 4 spaces), preceded by a blank line


* bulleted
* lists
```

```
    - sub bullets
      - sub sub bullets


>quotations
```

 If you want to learn more about Markdown's syntax, check out `https://daringfireball.net/projects/markdown/syntax`.

5. You can further mark the issue as either a bug, enhancement (feature), or any other label you like. Customizing labels is possible via the **Issues | Labels** link:

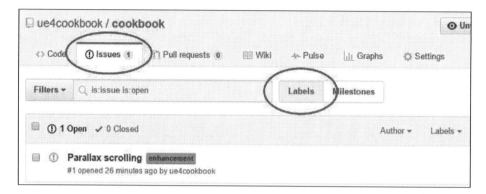

6. From there, you can edit, change the color of, or delete your labels. I deleted all the stock labels, and replaced the word **enhancement** with `feature`, as seen in the following two screenshots:

7. Once you've fully customized your labels, your GitHub **Issue Tracker** is much easier to navigate. Prioritize issues by tagging with the appropriate labels.

How it works...

GitHub's Issue Tracker is a fantastic way to track bugs and features in your project. Using it not only organizes your workflow, but also maintains an excellent history of the work done on the project.

See also

▶ You should also check out the Wiki feature, which allows you to document your source code

Project management on VisualStudio.com – managing the tasks in your project

High-level management of your project is usually done using a planning tool. GitHub's **Issue Tracker** may meet your needs, but if you're looking for more, Microsoft's Visual Studio Team Services offers planning tools for **Scrum** and **Kanban** style programming assignment of tasks (Features, Bugs, and so on).

Using this tool is a great way to organize your tasks to make sure things get done on time, and to get used to an industrial-standard workflow. When you sign up for Visual Studio's Community Edition during setup, your account includes free use of these tools.

How to do it...

In this section, we'll describe how to use the **Workboard** feature on Visualstudio.com to plan a few simple tasks.

1. To create your own project Workboard, go to your account at Visualstudio.com. Log in, and then select the **Overview** tab. Under **Recent projects & teams title**, select the **New** link.

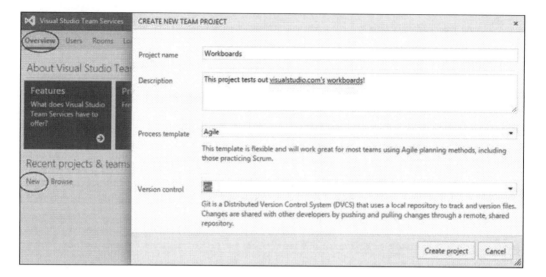

2. Add a **Project name** and **Description** to your project. After you've named your project (I've named mine Workboards), click on **Create project**. You will wait a second or two for project creation to complete, then hit the **Navigate to project** button in the next dialog.

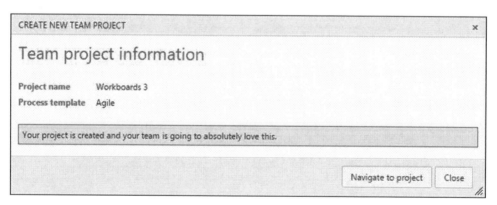

3. The next screen that is shown allows you to navigate to the **Workboards** area. Click on **Manage Work**.

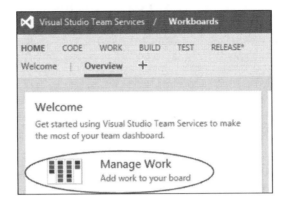

4. The **Manage Work** screen is a Kanban styled (read: prioritized) task queue of things to do in your project. You can hit the **New item** button to add new items to your list of things to do.

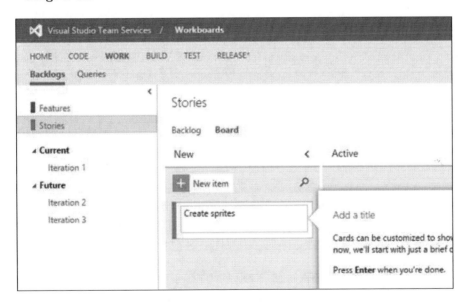

 As soon as you add something to your to-do list, it is called being part of your backlog. In Kanban, you're always behind! If you're a manager, you never want an empty backlog.

How it works...

Each item on your Board's backlog is called a **User Story**. A User Story is an Agile software development term, and each User Story is supposed to describe a need of a particular end user. For example, in the preceding User Story, the need is to have visual graphics, and the User Story describes that graphics (sprites) must be created to satisfy this user requirement.

User stories will often have a specific format:

[As a <someone>, I want <this> so that <advantage>.]

For example:

[As a <player of the game> I want to <reorganize items> so that I can <set hotkeys to slots that I desire>.]

On the Workboard, you'll have a bunch of user stories. I have placed a few user stories earlier so we can play with them.

Once your board is filled with user stories, they will all sit in the New vertical column. As you start work on or make progress on a particular User Story, you can drag it horizontally from **New** to **Active**, then finally to **Resolved** and **Closed** when the User Story is complete.

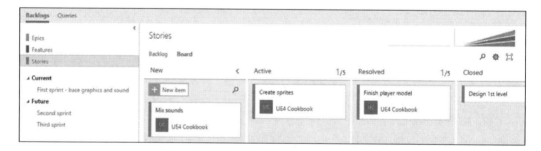

Project management on VisualStudio.com – constructing user stories and tasks

From the Scrum point of view, a User Story is grouping of tasks that need to be done. A group of user stories can be collected into a **Feature**, and a group of Features can be gathered together into what is called an **Epic**. VisualStudio.com organizes User Story creation very well so that it's easy to construct and plan the completion of any particular task (user story). In this recipe, we'll describe how to assemble and put together user stories.

Getting ready

Every item entered into VisualStudio.com's project management suite should always be a feature that somebody wants to be in the software. User story creation is a fun, easy, and exciting way to group together and mete out bunches of tasks to your programmers as work to be done. Log in to your VisualStudio.com account now, edit one of your projects, and begin using this feature.

How to do it...

1. From the VisualStudio.com **Team Services** landing page, navigate to the project into which you want to enter some new work to be done. All of your Projects can be found if you click on **Browse** under the **Recent projects & teams** heading.

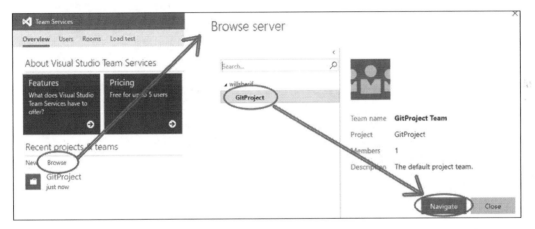

2. Select the project that you want to work with and hit **Navigate**.

3. Tasks inside Visualstudio.com take place inside of one of the three categories of super task:

   - User Story

   - Features

   - Epics

User Stories, Features, and Epics are just organizational units for work. An Epic contains many Features. A Feature contains many User Stories, and a User Story contains many Tasks.

By default, **Epics** are not shown. You can display **Epics** by going to Settings (the gear icon on the right side of the screen). Then navigate to **General | Backlogs**. Under the section that says **See only the backlogs your team manages**, select to display all three flavors of Backlog: **Epics, Features**, and **Stories**.

4. There are now four navigation steps to perform before you can enter your first task (User Story) into the **Backlog**:

    1. From the menu bar at the top, select **WORK**.

    2. Then, in the submenu that appears on the **WORK** page, select **Backlogs**.

    3. On the sidebar that appears, click on **Stories**.

    4. From the panel on the right-hand side, select **Board**.

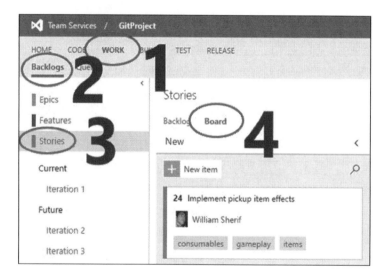

 Backlog is the set of User Stories and Tasks that we have yet to complete. You might think, "Are brand new tasks really entered into a Backlog?" That's right! You're already behind! The implications of Scrum's terminology seem to imply "overflowing with work".

5. From the panel on the right-hand side, hit **New item**, and fill in the text for your new **User Story** item.

6. Click on the text of the **User Story** card, and fill in the fields for **Assignee**, the **Iteration** that it's a part of, **Description**, **tags**, and any other fields of the **Details** tab that you want to explore.

7. Next we break down the overall **User Story** into a series of achievable tasks. Hover over your new **User Story** item until the ellipsis (three dots...) appears. Click on the ellipsis, and select **+ Add Task**.

8. List the details of completing the **User Story** in the series of Tasks.

9. Assign each Task to:

   ❏ An Assignee

   ❏ An Iteration

Simply put, an Iteration is really just a time period. At the end of each iteration, you should have a deliverable, testable piece of software completed. Iteration is a time period that refers to producing yet another version of your amazing software (for testing and possible release).

10. Continue adding Tasks to the project as the project develops features to complete and bugs to fix.

How it works...

Epics contain a number of Features. Features contain a number of User Stories, and User Stories contain a number of Tasks and Tests.

All of these items are assignable to a User (an actual human), and to an Iteration (time period), for both assigning responsibility and scheduling a task. Once these are assigned, the task should appear in the **Queries** tab.

Detailed steps to download the code bundle are mentioned in the Preface of this book. Please have a look.

The code bundle for the book is also hosted on GitHub at `https://github.com/PacktPublishing/Unreal-Engine-4-Scripting-with-CPlusPlus-Cookbook`. We also have other code bundles from our rich catalog of books and videos available at `https://github.com/PacktPublishing/`. Check them out!

2

Creating Classes

This chapter focuses on how to create C++ classes and structs that integrate well with the UE4 Blueprints editor. These classes are graduated versions of the regular C++ classes, and are called UCLASS.

A UCLASS is just a C++ class with a whole lot of UE4 macro decoration on top. The macros generate additional C++ header code that enables integration with the UE4 Editor itself.

Using UCLASS is a great practice. The UCLASS macro, if configured correctly, can possibly make your UCLASS Blueprintable. The advantage of making your UCLASS Blueprintable is that it can enable your custom C++ objects to have Blueprints visually editable properties (UPROPERTY) with handy UI widgets such as text fields, sliders, and model selection boxes. You can also have functions (UFUNCTION) that are callable from within a Blueprints diagram. Both of these are shown in the following screenshots:

On the left, two UPROPERTY decorated class members (a UTexture reference and an FColor) show up for editing in a C++ class's Blueprint. On the right, a C++ function GetName marked as BlueprintCallable UFUNCTION shows up as callable from a Blueprints diagram.

Code generated by the UCLASS macro will be located in a `ClassName.generated.h` file, which will be the last `#include` required in your UCLASS header file, `ClassName.h`.

The following are the topics that we will cover in this chapter:

▸ Making a UCLASS – deriving from UObject

▸ Creating a user-editable UPROPERTY

▸ Accessing a UPROPERTY from Blueprints

▸ Specifying a UCLASS as the type of a UPROPERTY

▸ Creating a Blueprint from your custom UCLASS

▸ Instantiating UObject-derived classes (`ConstructObject <>` and `NewObject <>`)

▸ Destroying UObject-derived classes

▸ Creating a USTRUCT

▸ Creating a UENUM()

▸ Creating a UFUNCTION

 You will notice that the sample objects we create in this class, even when Blueprintable, will not be placed in levels. That is because in order to be placed in levels, your C++ class must derive from the `Actor` base class, or below it. See *Chapter 4, Actors and Components* for further details.

Introduction

The UE4 code is, typically, very easy to write and manage once you know the patterns. The code we write to derive from another UCLASS, or to create a UPROPERTY or UFUNCTION, is very consistent. This chapter provides recipes for common UE4 coding tasks revolving around basic UCLASS derivation, property and reference declaration, construction, destruction, and general functionality.

Making a UCLASS – deriving from UObject

When coding with C++, you can have your own code that compiles and runs as native C++ code, with appropriate calls to `new` and `delete` to create and destroy your custom objects. Native C++ code is perfectly acceptable in your UE4 project as long as your `new` and `delete` calls are appropriately paired so that no leaks are present in your C++ code.

You can, however, also declare custom C++ classes, which behave like UE4 classes, by declaring your custom C++ objects as UCLASS. UCLASS use UE4's Smart Pointers and memory management routines for allocation and deallocation according to Smart Pointer rules, can be loaded and read by the UE4 Editor, and can optionally be accessed from Blueprints.

> Note that when you use the UCLASS macro, your UCLASS object's creation and destruction must be completely managed by UE4: you must use ConstructObject to create an instance of your object (not the C++ native keyword new), and call UObject::ConditionalBeginDestroy() to destroy the object (not the C++ native keyword delete). How to create and destroy your UObject-derivative classes is outlined in the *Instantiating UObject-derived classes (ConstructObject <> and NewObject <>)* and *Destroying UObject-derived classes* sections later in this chapter.

Getting ready

In this recipe, we will outline how to write a C++ class that uses the UCLASS macro to enable managed memory allocation and deallocation as well as to permit access from the UE4 Editor and Blueprints. You need a UE4 project into which you can add new code to use this recipe.

How to do it...

To create your own UObject derivative class, follow the steps below:

1. From your running project, select **File | Add C++ Class** inside the UE4 Editor.

2. In the **Add C++ Class** dialog that appears, go to the upper-right side of the window, and tick the **Show All Classes** checkbox:

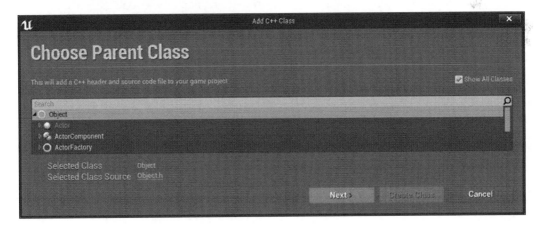

3. Create a UCLASS by choosing to derive from the `Object` parent class. UObject is the root of the UE4 hierarchy. You must tick the **Show All Classes** checkbox in the upper-right corner of this dialog for the `Object` class to appear in the list view.

4. Select `Object` (top of the hierarchy) as the parent class to inherit from, and then click on **Next**.

> Note that although `Object` will be written in the dialog box, in your C++ code, the C++ class you will deriving from is actually `UObject` with a leading uppercase `U`. This is the naming convention of UE4:
>
> UCLASS deriving from `UObject` (on a branch other than `Actor`) must be named with a leading `U`.
>
> UCLASS deriving from `Actor` must be named with a leading `A` (*Chapter 4, Actors and Components*).
>
> C++ classes (that are not UCLASS) deriving from nothing do not have a naming convention, but can be named with a leading `F` (for example, `FAssetData`), if preferred.
>
> Direct derivatives of `UObject` will not be level placeable, even if they contain visual representation elements such as `UStaticMeshes`. If you want to place your object inside a UE4 level, you must at least derive from the `Actor` class or beneath it in the inheritance hierarchy. See *Chapter 4, Actors and Components* for how to derive from the `Actor` class for a level-placeable object.
>
> This chapter's example code will not be placeable in the level, but you can create and use Blueprints based on the C++ classes that we write in this chapter in the UE4 Editor.

5. Name your new `Object` derivative something appropriate for the object type that you are creating. I call mine `UserProfile`. This comes off as `UUserObject` in the naming of the class in the C++ file that UE4 generates to ensure that the UE4 conventions are followed (C++ UCLASS preceded with a leading `U`).

6. Go to Visual Studio, and ensure your class file has the following form:

```
#pragma once

#include "Object.h" // For deriving from UObject
#include "UserProfile.generated.h" // Generated code

// UCLASS macro options sets this C++ class to be
// Blueprintable within the UE4 Editor
UCLASS( Blueprintable )
```

```
class CHAPTER2_API UUserProfile : public UObject
{
  GENERATED_BODY()
};
```

7. Compile and run your project. You can now use your custom UCLASS object inside Visual Studio, and inside the UE4 Editor. See the following recipes for more details on what you can do with it.

How it works...

UE4 generates and manages a significant amount of code for your custom UCLASS. This code is generated as a result of the use of the UE4 macros such as UPROPERTY, UFUNCTION, and the UCLASS macro itself. The generated code is put into UserProfile.generated.h. You must #include the UCLASSNAME.generated.h file with the UCLASSNAME.h file for compilation to succeed. Without including the UCLASSNAME.generated.h file, compilation would fail. The UCLASSNAME.generated.h file must be included as the last #include in the list of #include in UCLASSNAME.h:

Right	Wrong

`#pragma once`
 	
`#include "Object.h"`
`#include "Texture.h"`
`// CORRECT: .generated.h last file`
`#include "UserProfile.generated.h"`
	`#pragma once`
	
	`#include "Object.h"`
	`#include "UserProfile.generated.h"`
	`// WRONG: NO INCLUDES AFTER`
	`// .GENERATED.H FILE`
	`#include "Texture.h"`

The error that occurs when a UCLASSNAME.generated.h file is not included last in a list of includes is as follows:

```
>> #include found after .generated.h file - the .generated.h file
should always be the last #include in a header
```

There's more...

There are a bunch of keywords that we want to discuss here, which modify the way a UCLASS behaves. A UCLASS can be marked as follows:

▶ Blueprintable: This means that you want to be able to construct a Blueprint from the **Class Viewer** inside the UE4 Editor (when you right-click, **Create Blueprint Class...** becomes available). Without the Blueprintable keyword, the **Create Blueprint Class...** option will not be available for your UCLASS, even if you can find it from within the **Class Viewer** and right-click on it:

▶ The **Create Blueprint Class...** option is only available if you specify Blueprintable in your UCLASS macro definition. If you do not specify Blueprintable, then the resultant UCLASS will not be Blueprintable.

▶ BlueprintType: Using this keyword implies that the UCLASS is usable as a variable from another Blueprint. You can create Blueprint variables from the **Variables** group in the left-hand panel of any Blueprint's **EventGraph**. If NotBlueprintType is specified, then you cannot use this Blueprint variable type as a variable in a Blueprints diagram. Right-clicking the UCLASS name in the **Class Viewer** will not show **Create Blueprint Class...** in its context menu:

Any UCLASS that have BlueprintType specified can be added as variables to your Blueprint class diagram's list of variables.

You may be unsure whether to declare your C++ class as a UCLASS or not. It is really up to you. If you like Smart Pointers, you may find that UCLASS not only make for safer code, but also make the entire code base more coherent and more consistent.

See also

> ► To add additional programmable UPROPERTY to the Blueprints diagrams, see the *Creating a user-editable UPROPERTY* section below. For details on referring to instances of your UCLASS using appropriate Smart Pointers, refer to *Chapter 3, Memory Management and Smart Pointers*.

Creating a user-editable UPROPERTY

Each UCLASS that you declare can have any number of UPROPERTY declared for it within it. Each UPROPERTY can be a visually editable field, or some Blueprints accessible data member of the UCLASS.

There are a number of qualifiers that we can add to each UPROPERTY, which change the way it behaves from within the UE4 Editor, such as EditAnywhere (screens from which the UPROPERTY can be changed), and BlueprintReadWrite (specifying that Blueprints can both read and write the variable at any time in addition to the C++ code being allowed to do so).

Getting ready

To use this recipe, you should have a C++ project into which you can add C++ code. In addition, you should have completed the preceding recipe, *Making a UCLASS – deriving from UObject*.

How to do it...

1. Add members to your UCLASS declaration as follows:

```
UCLASS( Blueprintable )
class CHAPTER2_API UUserProfile : public UObject
{
  GENERATED_BODY()
  public:
  UPROPERTY(EditAnywhere, BlueprintReadWrite, Category =
  Stats)
```

```
      float Armor;
      UPROPERTY(EditAnywhere, BlueprintReadWrite, Category =
      Stats)
      float HpMax;
  };
```

2. Create a Blueprint of your UObject class derivative, and open the Blueprint in the UE4 editor by double-clicking it from the object browser.

3. You can now specify values in Blueprints for the default values of these new UPROPERTY fields:

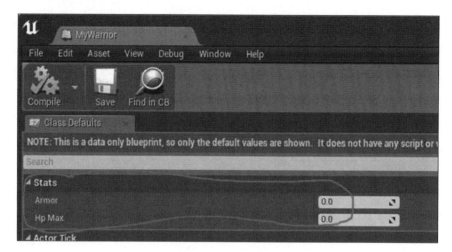

4. Specify per-instance values by dragging and dropping a few instances of the Blueprint class into your level, and editing the values on the object placed (by double-clicking on them).

How it works...

The parameters passed to the UPROPERTY() macro specify a couple of important pieces of information regarding the variable. In the preceding example, we specified the following:

►   EditAnywhere: This means that the UPROPERTY() macro can be edited either directly from the Blueprint, or on each instance of the UClass object as placed in the game level. Contrast this with the following:

  ❑   EditDefaultsOnly: The Blueprint's value is editable, but it is not editable on a per-instance basis

  ❑   EditInstanceOnly: This would allow editing of the UPROPERTY() macro in the game-level instances of the UClass object, and not on the base blueprint itself

- ▶ BlueprintReadWrite: This indicates that the property is both readable and writeable from Blueprints diagrams. UPROPERTY() with BlueprintReadWrite must be public members, otherwise compilation will fail. Contrast this with the following:
  - ❑ BlueprintReadOnly: The property must be set from C++ and cannot be changed from Blueprints

- ▶ Category: You should always specify a Category for your UPROPERTY(). The Category determines which submenu the UPROPERTY() will appear under in the property editor. All UPROPERTY() specified under Category=Stats will appear in the same Stats area in the Blueprints editor.

See also

- ▶ A complete UPROPERTY listing is located at https://docs.unrealengine.com/latest/INT/Programming/UnrealArchitecture/Reference/Properties/Specifiers/index.html. Give it a browse.

Accessing a UPROPERTY from Blueprints

Accessing a UPROPERTY from Blueprints is fairly simple. The member must be exposed as a UPROPERTY on the member variable that you want to access from your Blueprints diagram. You must qualify the UPROPERTY in your macro declaration as being either BlueprintReadOnly or BlueprintReadWrite to specify whether you want the variable to be either readable (only) from Blueprints, or even writeable from Blueprints.

You can also use the special value BlueprintDefaultsOnly to indicate that you only want the default value (before the game starts) to be editable from the Blueprints editor. BlueprintDefaultsOnly indicates the data member cannot be edited from Blueprints at runtime.

How to do it...

1. Create some UObject-derivative class, specifying both Blueprintable and BlueprintType, such as the following:

```
UCLASS( Blueprintable, BlueprintType )
class CHAPTER2_API UUserProfile : public UObject
{
  GENERATED_BODY()
  public:
  UPROPERTY(EditAnywhere, BlueprintReadWrite, Category =
  Stats)
  FString Name;
};
```

The `BlueprintType` declaration in the `UCLASS` macro is required to use the `UCLASS` as a type within a Blueprints diagram.

2. Within the UE4 Editor, derive a Blueprint class from the C++ class, as shown in *Creating a Blueprint from your custom UCLASS*.

3. Create an instance of your Blueprint-derived class in the UE4 Editor by dragging an instance from the **Content Browser** into the main game world area. It should appear as a round white sphere in the game world unless you've specified a model mesh for it.

4. In a Blueprints diagram which allows function calls (such as the **Level Blueprint**, accessible via **Blueprints | Open Level Blueprint**), try printing the **Name** property of your Warrior instance, as seen in the following screenshot:

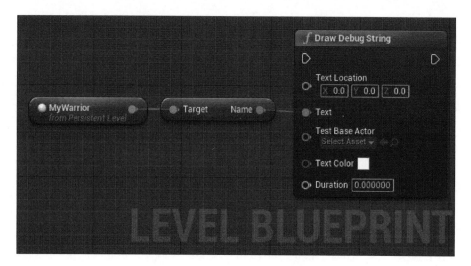

 Navigating Blueprints diagrams is easy. Right-click and drag to pan a Blueprints diagram; *Alt* + Right-Click + Drag to zoom.

How it works...

`UPROPERTY` are automatically written `Get/Set` methods for UE4 classes. They must not be declared as `private` variables within the `UCLASS`, however. If they are not declared as `public` or `protected` members, you will get a compiler error of the form:

```
>> BlueprintReadWrite should not be used on private members
```

Specifying a UCLASS as the type of a UPROPERTY

So, you've constructed some custom UCLASS intended for use inside UE4. But how do you instantiate them? Objects in UE4 are reference-counted and memory-managed, so you should not allocate them directly using the C++ keyword new. Instead, you'll have to use a function called ConstructObject to instantiate your UObject derivative. ConstructObject doesn't just take the C++ class of the object you are creating, it also requires a Blueprint class derivative of the C++ class (a UClass* reference). A UClass* reference is just a pointer to a Blueprint.

How do we instantiate an instance of a particular Blueprint from C++ code? C++ code does not, and should not, know concrete UCLASS names, since these names are created and edited in the UE4 Editor, which you can only access after compilation. We need a way to somehow hand back the Blueprint class name to instantiate to the C++ code.

The way we do this is by having the UE4 programmer select the UClass that the C++ code is to use from a simple drop-down menu listing all the Blueprints available (derived from a particular C++ class) inside the UE4 Editor. To do this, we simply have to provide a user-editable UPROPERTY with a TSubclassOf<C++ClassName>-typed variable. Alternatively, you can use FStringClassReference to achieve the same objective.

This makes selecting the UCLASS in the C++ code is exactly like selecting a texture to use. UCLASS should be considered as resources to the C++ code, and their names should never be hardcoded into the code base.

Getting ready

In your UE4 code, you're often going to need to refer to different UCLASS in the project. For example, say you need to know the UCLASS of the player object so that you can use SpawnObject in your code on it. Specifying a UCLASS from C++ code is extremely awkward, because the C++ code is not supposed to know about the concrete instances of the derived UCLASS that were created in the Blueprints editor at all. Just as we don't want to bake specific asset names into the C++ code, we don't want to hardcode derived Blueprints class names into the C++ code.

So, we use a C++ variable (for example, UClassOfPlayer), and select that from a Blueprints dialog in the UE4 editor. You can do so using a TSubclassOf member or an FStringClassReference member, as shown in the following screenshot:

How to do it...

1. Navigate to the C++ class that you'd like to add the UCLASS reference member to. For example, decking out a class derivative with the UCLASS of the player is fairly easy.

2. From inside a UCLASS, use code of the following form to declare a UPROPERTY that allows selection of a UClass (Blueprint class) that derives from UObject in the hierarchy:

```
UCLASS()
class CHAPTER2_API UUserProfile : public UObject
{
  UPROPERTY(EditAnywhere, BlueprintReadWrite, Category =
  Unit)
  TSubclassOf<UObject> UClassOfPlayer; // Displays any
  UClasses
  // deriving from UObject in a dropdown menu in Blueprints

  // Displays string names of UCLASSes that derive from
  // the GameMode C++ base class
  UPROPERTY( EditAnywhere, meta=(MetaClass="GameMode"),
  Category = Unit )
  FStringClassReference UClassGameMode;
};
```

3. Blueprint the C++ class, and then open that Blueprint. Click on the drop-down menu beside your UClassOfPlayer menu.

4. Select the appropriate UClassOfPlayer member from the drop-down menu of the listed UClass.

How it works...

TSubclassOf

The TSubclassOf< > member will allow you to specify a UClass name using a drop-down menu inside the UE4 editor when editing any Blueprints that have TSubclassOf< > members.

FStringClassReference

The MetaClass tag refers to the base C++ class from which you expect the UClassName to derive. This limits the drop-down menu's contents to only the Blueprints derived from that C++ class. You can leave the MetaClass tag out if you wish to display all the Blueprints in the project.

Creating a Blueprint from your custom UCLASS

Blueprinting is just the process of deriving a Blueprint class for your C++ object. Creating Blueprint-derived classes from your UE4 objects allows you to edit the custom UPROPERTY visually inside the editor. This avoids hardcoding any resources into your C++ code. In addition, in order for your C++ class to be placeable within the level, it must be Blueprinted first. But this is only possible if the C++ class underlying the Blueprint is an Actor class-derivative.

There is a way to load resources (such as textures) using FStringAssetReferences and StaticLoadObject. These pathways to loading resources (by hardcoding path strings into your C++ code) are generally discouraged, however. Providing an editable value in a UPROPERTY(), and loading from a proper concretely typed asset reference is a much better practice.

Getting ready

You need to have a constructed UCLASS that you'd like to derive a Blueprint class from (see the *Making a UCLASS – deriving from UObject* section earlier in this chapter) in order to follow this recipe. You must have also marked your UCLASS as Blueprintable in the UCLASS macro for Blueprinting to be possible inside the engine.

Any UObject-derived class with the meta keyword Blueprintable in the UCLASS macro declaration will be Blueprintable.

How to do it...

1. To Blueprint your UserProfile class, first ensure that UCLASS has the Blueprintable tag in the UCLASS macro. This should look as follows:

```
UCLASS( Blueprintable )
class CHAPTER2_API UUserProfile : public UObject
```

2. Compile and run your code.

3. Find the `UserProfile` C++ class in the **Class Viewer** (**Window | Developer Tools | Class Viewer**). Since the previously created UCLASS does not derive from `Actor`, to find your custom UCLASS, you must turn off **Filters | Actors Only** in the **Class Viewer** (which is checked by default):

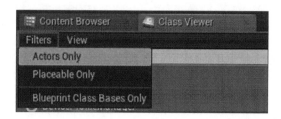

Turn off the **Actors Only** check mark to display all the classes in the **Class Viewer**. If you don't do this, then your custom C++ class may not show!

 Keep in mind that you can use the small search box inside the **Class Viewer** to easily find the `UserProfile` class by starting to type it in:

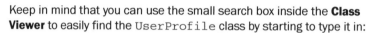

4. Find your `UserProfile` class in the **Class Viewer**, right-click on it, and create a Blueprint from it by selecting **Create Blueprint...**

5. Name your Blueprint. Some prefer to prefix the Blueprint class name with `BP_`. You may choose to follow this convention or not, just be sure to be consistent.

6. Double-click on your new Blueprint as it appears in the **Content Browser**, and take a look at it. You will be able to edit the **Name** and **Email** fields for each `UserProfile` Blueprint instance you create.

How it works...

Any C++ class you create that has the `Blueprintable` tag in its UCLASS macro can be Blueprinted within the UE4 editor. A Blueprint allows you to customize properties on the C++ class in the visual GUI interface of UE4.

Instantiating UObject-derived classes (ConstructObject < > and NewObject < >)

Creating class instances in C++ is traditionally done using the keyword new. However, UE4 actually creates instances of its classes internally, and requires you to call special factory functions to produce copies of any UCLASS that you want to instantiate. You produce instances of the UE4 Blueprints classes, not the C++ class alone. When you create UObject-derived classes, you will need to instantiate them using special UE4 Engine functions.

The factory method allows UE4 to exercise some memory management on the object, controlling what happens to the object when it is deleted. This method allows UE4 to track all references to an object so that on object destruction, all references to the object can be easily unlinked. This ensures that no dangling pointers with references to invalidated memory exist in the program.

Getting ready

Instantiating UObject-derived classes that are not AActor class derivatives does not use UWorld::SpawnActor< >. Instead, we have to use special global functions named ConstructObject< >, or NewObject< >. Note that you should not use the bare C++ keyword new to allocate new instances of your UE4 UObject class derivatives.

You will need at least two pieces of information to properly instantiate your UCLASS instance:

▶ A C++ typed UClass reference to the class type that you would like to instantiate (Blueprint class)

▶ The original C++ base class from which the Blueprint class derives

How to do it...

1. In a globally accessible object (like your GameMode object), add a TSubclassOf< YourC++ClassName > UPROPERTY() to specify and supply the UCLASS name to your C++ code. For example, we add the following two lines to our GameMode object:

   ```
   UPROPERTY( EditAnywhere, BlueprintReadWrite, Category =
   UClassNames )
   TSubclassOf<UUserProfile> UPBlueprintClassName;
   ```

2. Enter the UE4 editor, and select your UClass name from the drop-down menu so that you can see what it does. Save, and exit the editor.

3. In your C++ code, find the section where you want to instantiate the UCLASS instance.

4. Instantiate the object using ConstructObject< > with the following formula:

```
ObjectType* object = ConstructObject< ObjectType >(
UClassReference );
```

For example, using the UserProfile object that we specified in the last recipe, we would get code like this:

```
// Get the GameMode object, which has a reference to
// the UClass name that we should instantiate:
AChapter2GameMode *gm = Cast<AChapter2GameMode>(
GetWorld()->GetAuthGameMode() );
if( gm )
{
  UUserProfile* object = ConstructObject<UUserProfile>(
  gm->UPBlueprintClassName );
}
```

If you prefer, you can also use the NewObject function as follows:

```
UProfile* object = NewObject<UProfile>(
GetTransientPackage(),
uclassReference );
```

How it works...

Instantiating a UObject class using ConstructObject or NewObject is simple. NewObject and ConstructObject do nearly the same thing: instantiate an object of Blueprint class type, and return a C++ pointer of the correct type.

Unfortunately, NewObject has a nasty first parameter which requires you to pass GetTransientPackage() with each call. ConstructObject does not require this parameter with each call. In addition, ConstructObject provides you with more construction options.

Do not use the keyword new when constructing your UE4 UObject derivative! It will not be properly memory-managed.

There's more...

NewObject and ConstructObject are what the OOP world calls factories. You ask the factory to make you the object—you don't go about constructing it by yourself. Using a factory pattern enables the engine to easily track objects as they are created.

Destroying UObject-derived classes

Removing any UObject derivative is simple in UE4. When you are ready to delete your UObject-derived class, we will simply call a single function (ConditionalBeginDestroy()) on it to begin teardown. We do not use the native C++ delete command on UObject derivatives. We show this in the following recipe.

Getting ready

You need to call ConditionalBeginDestroy() on any unused UObject-derived classes so that they get removed from memory. Do not call delete on a UObject-derived class to recoup the system memory. You must use the internal engine-provided memory management functions instead. The way to do this is shown next.

How to do it...

1. Call objectInstance->ConditionalBeginDestroy() on your object instance.

2. Null all your references to objectInstance in your client code, and do not use objectInstance again after ConditionalBeginDestroy() has been called on it.

How it works...

The ConditionalBeginDestroy() function begins the destruction process by removing all internal engine linkages to it. This marks the object for destruction as far as the engine is concerned. The object is then destroyed some time later by destroying its internal properties, followed by actual destruction of the object.

After ConditionalBeginDestroy() has been called on an object, your (client) code must consider the object to be destroyed, and must no longer use it.

Actual memory recovery happens some time later than when ConditionalBeginDestroy() has been called on an object. There is a garbage collection routine that finishes clearing the memory of objects that are no longer referenced by the game program at fixed time intervals. The time interval between garbage collector calls is listed in C:\Program Files (x86)\Epic Games\4.11\Engine\Config \BaseEngine.ini, and defaults to one collection every 60 seconds:

```
gc.TimeBetweenPurgingPendingKillObjects=60
```

If memory seems low after several `ConditionalBeginDestroy()` calls, you can trigger memory cleanup by calling `GetWorld()->ForceGarbageCollection(true)` to force an internal memory cleanup.

Usually, you do not need to worry about garbage collection or the interval unless you urgently need memory cleared. Do not call garbage collection routines too often, as this may cause unnecessary lag in the game.

Creating a USTRUCT

You may want to construct a Blueprints editable property in UE4 that contains multiple members. The `FColoredTexture` struct that we will create in this chapter will allow you to group together a texture and its color inside the same structure for inclusion and specification in any other `UObject` derivative, `Blueprintable` class:

The `FColoredTexture` structure does have the visual within Blueprints appearance as shown in the figure above.

This is for good organization and convenience of your other UCLASS UPROPERTIES(). You may want to construct a C++ structure in your game using the keyword `struct`.

Getting ready

A `UObject` is the base class of all UE4 class objects, while an `FStruct` is just any plain old C++ style struct. All objects that use the automatic memory management features within the engine must derive from this class.

If you' recall from the C++ language, the only difference between a C++ class and a C++ struct is that C++ classes have default `private` members, while structs default to `public` members. In languages like C#, this isn't the case. In C#, a struct is value-typed, while a class is reference-typed.

How to do it...

We'll create a structure `FColoredTexture` in C++ code to contain a texture and a modulating color:

1. Create a file `ColoredTexture.h` in your project folder (not `FColoredTexture`).

2. `ColoredTexture.h` contains the following code:

```cpp
#pragma once

#include "Chapter2.h"
#include "ColoredTexture.generated.h"

USTRUCT()
struct CHAPTER2_API FColoredTexture
{
  GENERATED_USTRUCT_BODY()
  public:
  UPROPERTY( EditAnywhere, BlueprintReadWrite, Category =
  HUD )
  UTexture* Texture;
  UPROPERTY( EditAnywhere, BlueprintReadWrite, Category =
  HUD )
  FLinearColor Color;
};
```

3. Use `ColoredTexture.h` as a `UPROPERTY()` in some Blueprintable `UCLASS()`, using a `UPROPERTY()` declaration like this:

```cpp
UPROPERTY( EditAnywhere, BlueprintReadWrite, Category = HUD
)
FColoredTexture* Texture;
```

How it works...

The `UPROPERTY()` specified for the `FColoredTexture` will show up in the editor as editable fields when included as `UPROPERTY()` fields inside another class, as shown in step 3.

There's more...

The main reason for making a struct a `USTRUCT()` instead of just a plain old C++ struct is to interface with the UE4 Engine functionality. You can use plain C++ code (without creating `USTRUCT()` objects) for quick small structures that don't ask the engine to use them directly.

Creating a UENUM( )

C++ enum are very useful in typical C++ code. UE4 has a custom type of enumeration called UENUM(), which allows you to create an enum that will show up in a drop-down menu inside a Blueprint that you are editing.

How to do it...

1. Go to the header file that will use the UENUM() you are specifying, or create a file EnumName.h.

2. Use code of the form:

```
UENUM()
enum Status
{
   Stopped      UMETA(DisplayName = "Stopped"),
   Moving       UMETA(DisplayName = "Moving"),
   Attacking    UMETA(DisplayName = "Attacking"),
};
```

3. Use your UENUM() in a UCLASS() as follows:

```
UPROPERTY(EditAnywhere, BlueprintReadWrite, Category =
Status)
TEnumAsByte<Status> status;
```

How it works...

UENUM() show up nicely in the code editor as drop-down menus in the Blueprints editor from which you can only select one of a few values.

Creating a UFUNCTION

UFUNCTION() are useful because they are C++ functions that can be called from both your C++ client code as well as Blueprints diagrams. Any C++ function can be marked as a UFUNCTION().

How to do it...

1. Construct a `UClass` with a member function that you'd like to expose to Blueprints. Decorate that member function with `UFUNCTION( BlueprintCallable, Category=SomeCategory)` to make it callable from Blueprints. For example, the following is the `Warrior` class again:

```
// Warrior.h
class WRYV_API AWarrior : public AActor
{
  GENERATED_BODY()
  public:
  UPROPERTY(EditAnywhere, BlueprintReadWrite, Category =
  Properties)
  FString Name;
  UFUNCTION(BlueprintCallable, Category = Properties)
  FString ToString();
};

// Warrior.cpp
FString UProfile::ToString()
{
  return FString::Printf( "An instance of UProfile: %s",
  *Name );
}
```

2. Create an instance of your `Warrior` class by dragging an instance on to your game world.

3. From Blueprints, call the `ToString()` function on that `Warrior` instance by clicking on your `Warrior` instance. Then, in a Blueprints diagram, type in `ToString()`. It should look like in the following screenshot:

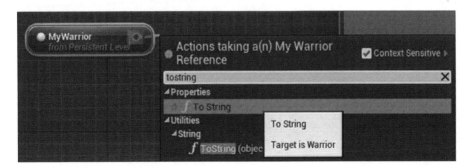

In order to call a function on an instance, the instance must be selected in the **World Outliner** when you start to type into the autocomplete menu in the Blueprints diagram, as shown in the following screenshot:

How it works...

UFUNCTION() are really C++ functions, but with additional metadata that make them accessible to Blueprints.

3

Memory Management and Smart Pointers

In this chapter, we are going to cover the following topics:

- ▶ Unmanaged memory – using `malloc()`/`free()`
- ▶ Unmanaged memory – using `new`/`delete`
- ▶ Managed memory – using `NewObject< >` and `ConstructObject< >`
- ▶ Managed memory – deallocating memory
- ▶ Managed memory – smart pointers (`TSharedPtr`, `TWeakPtr`, `TAutoPtr`) to track an object
- ▶ Using `TScopedPointer` to track an object
- ▶ Unreal's garbage collection system and `UPROPERTY()`
- ▶ Forcing garbage collection
- ▶ Breakpoints and stepping through code
- ▶ Finding bugs and using call stacks
- ▶ Using the Profiler to identify hot spots

Introduction

Memory management is always one of the most important things to get right in your computer program to ensure stability and good, bug-free operation of your code. A dangling pointer (pointer referring to something that has been removed from memory) is an example of a bug that is hard to track if it occurs.

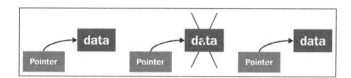

In any computer program, memory management is extremely important. UE4's `UObject` reference counting system is the default way that memory is managed for Actors and `UObject` derivatives. This is the default way that your memory will be managed within your UE4 program.

If you write custom C++ classes of your own, which do not derive from `UObject`, you may find the `TSharedPtr` / `TWeakPtr` reference counted classes useful. These classes provide reference counting and automatic deletion for 0 reference objects.

This chapter provides recipes for memory management within UE4.

Unmanaged memory – using malloc( )/free( )

The basic way to allocate memory for your computer program in C (and C++) is by using `malloc()`. `malloc()` designates a block of the computer system's memory for your program's use. Once your program is using a segment of memory, no other program can use or access that segment of memory. An attempt to access a segment of memory not allocated to your program will generate a "segmentation fault", and represents an illegal operation on most systems.

How to do it...

Let's look at an example code that allocates a pointer variable `i`, then assigns memory to it using `malloc()`. We allocate a single integer behind an `int *` pointer. After allocation, we store a value inside `int`, using the dereferencing operator `*`:

```
// CREATING AND ALLOCATING MEMORY FOR AN INT VARIABLE i
int* i; // Declare a pointer variable i
```

```
i = ( int* )malloc( sizeof( int ) ); // Allocates system memory
*i = 0; // Assign the value 0 into variable i
printf( "i contains %d", *i ); // Use the variable i, ensuring to
// use dereferencing operator * during use
// RELEASING MEMORY OCCUPIED BY i TO THE SYSTEM
free( i ); // When we're done using i, we free the memory
// allocated for it back to the system.
i = 0;// Set the pointer's reference to address 0
```

How it works...

The preceding code does what is shown in the diagram that follows:

1. The first line creates an `int*` pointer variable `i`, which starts as a dangling pointer referring to a segment of memory that probably won't be valid for your program to reference.

2. In the second diagram, we use a `malloc()` call to initialize the variable `i` to point to a segment of memory precisely the size of an `int` variable, which will be valid for your program to refer to.

3. We then initialize the contents of that memory segment to the value `0` using the command `*i = 0;`.

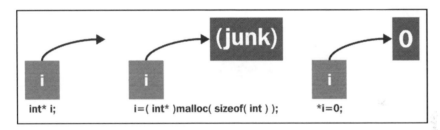

 Note the difference between assignment to a pointer variable (`i =`), which tells the pointer what memory address to refer to, and assignment to what is inside the memory address that the pointer variable refers to (`*i =`).

When the memory in the variable i needs to be released back to the system, we do so using a free() deallocation call, as shown in the following diagram. i is then assigned to point to memory address 0, (diagrammed by the **electrical grounding** symbol reference ⏚).

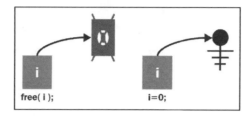

The reason we set the variable i to point to the NULL reference is to make it clear that the variable i does not refer to a valid segment of memory.

Unmanaged memory – using new/delete

The new operator is almost the same as a malloc call, except that it invokes a constructor call on the object created immediately after the memory is allocated. Objects allocated with the operator new should be deallocated with the operator delete (and not free()).

Getting ready

In C++, use of malloc() was replaced, as best practice, by use of the operator new. The main difference between the functionality of malloc() and the operator new is that new will call the constructor on object types after memory allocation.

malloc	new
Allocates a zone of contiguous space for use.	Allocates a zone of contiguous space for use.
	Calls constructor as object type used as an argument to the operator new.

How to do it...

In the following code, we declare a simple Object class, then construct an instance of it using the operator new:

```
class Object
{
  Object()
  {
    puts( "Object constructed" );
```

```
  }
  ~Object()
  {
    puts( "Object destructed" );
  }
};
Object* object= new Object(); // Invokes ctor
delete object; // Invokes dtor
object = 0; // resets object to a null pointer
```

How it works...

The operator `new` works by allocating space just as `malloc()` does. If the type used with the operator `new` is an object type, the constructor is invoked automatically with the use of the keyword `new`, whereas the constructor is never invoked with the use of `malloc()`.

There's more...

You should avoid using naked heap allocations with the keyword `new` (or `malloc` for that matter). Managed memory is preferred within the engine so that all memory use is tracked and clean. If you allocate a `UObject` derivative, you definitely need to use `NewObject< >` or `ConstructObject< >` (outlined in subsequent recipes).

Managed memory – using NewObject< > and ConstructObject< >

Managed memory refers to memory that is allocated and deallocated by some programmed subsystem above the `new`, `delete`, `malloc`, and `free` calls in C++. These subsystems are commonly created so that the programmer does not forget to release memory after allocating it. Unreleased, occupied, but unused memory chunks are called memory leaks. For example:

```
for( int i = 0; i < 100; i++ )
int** leak = new int[500]; // generates memory leaks galore!
```

In the preceding example, the memory allocated is not referenceable by any variable! So you can neither use the allocated memory after the `for` loop, nor can you free it. If your program allocates all available system memory, then what will happen is that your system will run out of memory entirely, and your OS will flag your program and close it for using up too much memory.

Memory management prevents forgetting to release memory. In memory-managed programs, it is commonly remembered by objects that are dynamically allocated the number of pointers referencing the object. When there are zero pointers referencing the object, it is either automatically deleted immediately, or flagged for deletion on the next run of the **garbage collector**.

Use of managed memory is automatic within UE4. Any allocation of an object to be used within the engine must be done using `NewObject< >()` or `SpawnActor< >()`. The release of objects is done by removing the reference to the object, then occasionally calling the garbage cleanup routine (listed further in this chapter).

Getting ready

When you need to construct any `UObject` derivative that is not a derivative of the `Actor` class, you should always use `NewObject< >`. `SpawnActor< >` should be used only when the object is an `Actor` or its derivative.

How to do it...

Say we are trying to construct an object of type `UAction`, which itself derives from `UObject`. For example, the following class:

```
UCLASS(BlueprintType, Blueprintable, meta=(ShortTooltip="Base
class for any Action type") )
Class WRYV_API UAction : public UObject
{
  GENERATED_UCLASS_BODY()
  public:
  UPROPERTY(EditAnywhere, BlueprintReadWrite, Category=Properties)
  FString Text;
  UPROPERTY(EditAnywhere, BlueprintReadWrite, Category=Properties)
  FKey ShortcutKey;
};
```

To construct an instance of the `UAction` class, we'd do the following:

```
UAction* action = NewObject<UAction>( GetTransientPackage(),
UAction::StaticClass() /* RF_* flags */ );
```

How it works...

Here, `UAction::StaticClass()` gets you a base `UClass*` for the `UAction` object. The first argument to `NewObject< >` is `GetTransientPackage()`, which simply retrieves the transient package for the game. A package (`UPackage`) in UE4 is just a data conglomerate. Here we use the **Transient Package** to store our heap-allocated data. You could also use `UPROPERTY()` `TSubclassOf<AActor>` from Blueprints to select a `UClass` instance.

The third argument (optional) is a combination of parameters that indicate how `UObject` is treated by the memory management system.

There's more...

There is another function very similar to `NewObject< >` called `ConstructObject< >`. `ConstructObject< >` provides more parameters in construction, and you may find it useful if you need to specify these parameters. Otherwise, `NewObject` works just fine.

See also

▸ You may also want to see the documentation for `RF_*` flags at `https://docs.unrealengine.com/latest/INT/Programming/UnrealArchitecture/Objects/Creation/index.html#objectflags`

Managed memory – deallocating memory

`UObjects` are reference-counted and garbage-collected when there are no more references to the `UObject` instance. Memory allocated on a `UObject` class derivative using `ConstructObject<>` or `NewObject< >` can also be deallocated manually (before the reference count drops to 0) by calling the `UObject::ConditionalBeginDestroy()` member function.

Getting ready

You'd only do this if you were sure you no longer wanted `UObject` or the `UObject` class derivative instance in memory. Use the `ConditionalBeginDestroy()` function to release memory.

How to do it...

The following code demonstrates the deallocation of a `UObject class`:

```
UObject *o = NewObject< UObject >( ... );
o->ConditionalBeginDestroy();
```

How it works...

The command `ConditionalBeginDestroy()` begins the deallocation process, calling the `BeginDestroy()` and `FinishDestroy()` overrideable functions.

There's more...

Be careful not to call `UObject::ConditionalBeginDestroy()` on any object still being referenced in memory by other objects' pointers.

Managed memory – smart pointers (TSharedPtr, TWeakPtr, TAutoPtr) to track an object

When people are afraid that they'll forget the `delete` call for standard C++ objects they create, they often use smart pointers to prevent memory leaks. `TSharedPtr` is a very useful C++ class that will make any custom C++ object reference-counted—with the exception of `UObject` derivatives, which are already reference-counted. An alternate class `TWeakPtr` is also provided for pointing to a reference-counted object with the strange property of being unable to prevent deletion (hence, "weak").

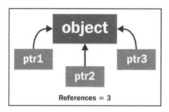

 `UObject` and it's derivative classes (anything created with `NewObject` or `ConstructObject`) cannot use `TSharedPtr`!

Getting ready

If you don't want to use raw pointers and manually track deletes into your C++ code that does not use `UObject` derivatives, then that code is a good candidate for using smart pointers such as `TSharedPtr`, `TSharedRef,` and the like. When you use a dynamically allocated object (created using the keyword `new`), you can wrap it up in a reference-counted pointer so that deallocation happens automatically. The different types of smart pointers determine the smart pointer behavior and deletion call time. They are as follows:

- `TSharedPtr`: A thread-safe (provided you supplied `ESPMode::ThreadSafe` as the second argument to the template) reference-counted pointer type that indicates a shared object. The shared object will be deallocated when there are no more references to it.

- `TAutoPtr`: Non-thread-safe shared pointer.

How to do it...

We can demonstrate use of the four types of smart pointers referred to previously using a short code segment. In all of this code, the starting pointer can either be a raw pointer, or a copy of another smart pointer. All you have to do is take the C++ raw pointer and wrap it in a constructor call to any of `TSharedPtr`, `TSharedRef`, `TWeakPtr`, or `TAutoPtr`.

For example:

```
// C++ Class NOT deriving from UObject
class MyClass { };
TSharedPtr<MyClass>sharedPtr( new MyClass() );
```

How it works...

There are some differences between weak pointers and shared pointers. Weak pointers do not have the capability to keep the object in memory when the reference count drops to 0.

The advantage of using a weak pointer (over a raw pointer) is that when the object underneath the weak pointer is manually deleted (using `ConditionalBeginDestroy()`), the weak pointer's reference becomes a `NULL` reference. This enables you to check if the resource underneath the pointer is still allocated properly by checking a statement of the form:

```
if( ptr.IsValid() ) // Check to see if the pointer is valid
{
}
```

There's more...

Shared pointers are thread-safe. This means that the underlying object can safely be manipulated on separate threads. Always remember that you cannot use `TSharedRef` with `UObjects` or `UObject` derivatives—only on your custom C++ classes, or on your `FStructures` can you use any of the `TSharedPtr`, `TSharedRef`, `TWeakPtr` classes to wrap up a raw pointer. You must use `TWeakObjectPointer` or `UPROPERTY()` as a starting point to point to an object using a smart pointer.

You can use `TAutoPtr` if you do not need the thread-safety guarantee of `TSharedPtr`. `TAutoPtr` will automatically delete an object when the number of references to it drops to 0.

Using TScopedPointer to track an object

A scoped pointer is a pointer that is auto-deleted at the end of the block in which it was declared. Recall that a scope is just a section of code during which a variable is "alive". A scope will last until the first closing brace, }, that occurs.

For example, in the following block, we have two scopes. The outer scope declares an integer variable x (valid for the entire outer block), while the inner scope declares an integer variable y (valid for the inner block, after the line on which it is declared):

```
{
  int x;
  {
    int y;
  } // scope of y ends
} // scope of x ends
```

Getting ready

Scoped pointers are useful when it is important that a reference-counted object (which is in danger of going out of scope) is retained for the duration of usage.

How to do it...

To declare a scoped pointer, we simply use the following syntax:

```
TScopedPointer<AWarrior> warrior(this );
```

This declares a scoped pointer referencing an object of the type declared within the angle brackets: < AWarrior >.

How it works...

The TScopedPointer variable type automatically adds a reference count to the variable pointed to. This prevents deallocation of the underlying object for at least the life of the scoped pointer.

Unreal's garbage collection system and UPROPERTY( )

When you have an object (such as TArray< >) as a UPROPERTY () member of UCLASS (), you need to declare that member as UPROPERTY () (even if you won't edit it in blueprints), otherwise TArray will not stay allocated properly.

How to do it...

Say we have a UCLASS() macro as follows:

```
UCLASS()
class MYPROJECT_API AWarrior : public AActor
{
  //TArray< FSoundEffect > Greets; // Incorrect
  UPROPERTY() TArray< FSoundEffect > Greets; // Correct
};
```

You'd have to list the `TArray` member as `UPROPERTY()` for it to be properly reference counted. If you don't do so, you'll get an unexpected memory error type bug sitting about in the code.

How it works...

The `UPROPERTY()` declaration tells UE4 that `TArray` must be properly memory managed. Without the `UPROPERTY()` declaration, your `TArray` won't work properly.

Forcing garbage collection

When memory fills up, and you want to free some of it, garbage collection can be forced. You seldom need to do this, but you can do it in the case of having a very large texture (or set of textures) that are reference-counted that you need to clear.

Getting ready

Simply call `ConditionalBeginDestroy()` on all `UObjects` that you want deallocated from memory, or set their reference counts to 0.

How to do it...

Garbage collection is performed by calling the following:

```
GetWorld()->ForceGarbageCollection( true );
```

Breakpoints and stepping through code

Breakpoints are how you pause your C++ program to temporarily stop the code from running, and have a chance to analyze and inspect your program's operation. You can peer at variables, step through code, and change variable values.

Getting ready

Breakpoints are easy to set in Visual Studio. All you have to do is press *F9* on the line of code that you want operation to pause at, or click in the grey margin to the left of the line of code that you want to pause operation at. The code will pause when operation reaches the line indicated.

How to do it...

1. Press *F9* on the line you want execution to pause at. This will add a breakpoint to the code, indicated by a red dot, as shown in the screenshot below. Clicking on the red dot toggles it.

```
8      UObject *o = NewObject<UObject>( GetTransientPackage(),
9          UObject::StaticClass() );
```

2. Set **Build Configuration** to any of the configurations with **Debug** in the title (**DebugGame** Editor or simply **DebugGame** if you will launch without the editor).

3. Launch your code by pressing *F5* (without holding *Ctrl*), or select the **Debug | Start Debugging** menu option.

4. When the code reaches the red dot, the code's execution will pause.

5. The paused view will take you to the code editor in **Debug mode**. In this mode, the windows may appear rearranged, with **Solution Explorer** possibly moved to the right, and new windows appearing at the bottom, including **Locals**, **Watch 1**, and **Call Stack**. If these windows do not appear, find them under the **Debug | Windows** submenu.

6. Check out your variables under the **Locals** window (**Debug | Windows | Locals**).

7. Press *F10* to step over a line of code.

8. Press *F11* to step into a line of code.

How it works...

Debuggers are powerful tools that allow you to see everything about your code as it is running, including variable states.

Stepping over a line of code (*F10*) executes the line of code in its entirety, and then pauses the program again, immediately, at the next line. If the line of code is a function call, then the function is executed without pausing at the first line of code of the function call. For example:

```
void f()
{
  // F11 pauses here
  UE_LOG( LogTemp, Warning, TEXT( "Log message" ) );
}
int main()
{
  f(); // Breakpoint here: F10 runs and skips to next line
}
```

Stepping into a line of code (*F11*) will pause execution at the very next line of code run.

Finding bugs and using call stacks

When you have a bug in your code, Visual Studio halts and allows you to inspect the code. The place at which Visual Studio halts won't always be the exact location of the bug, but it can be close. It will at least be at a line of code that doesn't execute properly.

Getting ready

In this recipe, we'll describe **Call Stack,** and how to trace where you think an error may come from. Try adding a bug to your code, or add a breakpoint somewhere interesting that you'd like to pause for inspection.

How to do it...

1. Run the code to a point where a bug occurs by pressing *F5,* or selecting the **Debug | Start Debugging** menu option. For example, add these lines of code:

    ```
    UObject *o = 0; // Initialize to an illegal null pointer
    o->GetName(); // Try and get the name of the object (has
    bug)
    ```

2. The code will pause at the second line (`o->GetName()`).

3. When the code pauses, navigate to the **Call Stack** window (**Debug | Windows | Call Stack**).

How it works...

The **Call Stack** is a list of function calls that were executed. When a bug occurs, the line on which it occurred is listed at the top of the **Call Stack**.

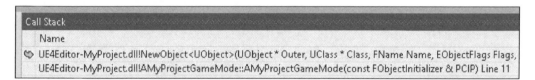

Using the Profiler to identify hot spots

The C++ Profiler is extremely useful for finding sections of code that require a high amount of processing time. Using the Profiler can help you find sections of code to focus on during optimization. If you suspect that a region of code runs slowly, then you can actually confirm that it isn't slow if it doesn't appear highlighted in the Profiler.

How to do it...

1. Go to **Debug | Start Diagnostic Tools Without Debugging...**

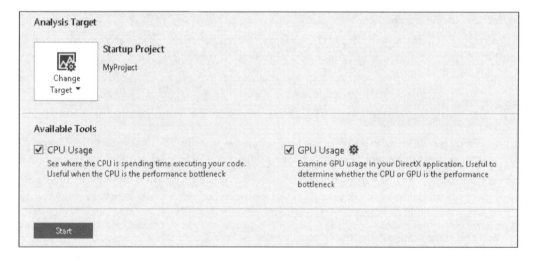

2. In the dialog shown in the preceding screenshot, select the type of analysis you'd like displayed. You can choose to analyze **CPU Usage**, **GPU Usage**, **Memory Usage**, or step through a **Performance Wizard** to assist you in selecting what you want to see.

3. Click on the **Start** button at the bottom of the dialog.

4. Stop the code after a brief time (less than a minute or two) to halt sample collection.

 Do not collect too many samples or the Profiler will take a really long time to start up.

5. Inspect the results that appear in the `.diagsession` file. Be sure to browse all available tabs that open up. Available tabs will vary depending on the type of analysis performed.

How it works...

The C++ Profiler samples and analyzes the running code, and presents to you a series of diagrams and figures about how the code performed.

4

Actors and Components

In this chapter, we will cover following recipes:

- ▶ Creating a custom `Actor` in C++
- ▶ Instantiating an `Actor` using `SpawnActor`
- ▶ Destroying an `Actor` using `Destroy` and a Timer
- ▶ Destroying an `Actor` after a delay using `SetLifeSpan`
- ▶ Implementing the `Actor` functionality by composition
- ▶ Loading assets into components using `FObjectFinder`
- ▶ Implementing the `Actor` functionality by inheritance
- ▶ Attaching components to create a hierarchy
- ▶ Creating a custom `Actor` Component
- ▶ Creating a custom `Scene` Component
- ▶ Creating a custom `Primitive` Component
- ▶ Creating an `InventoryComponent` for an RPG
- ▶ Creating an `OrbitingMovement` Component
- ▶ Creating a building that spawns units

Introduction

Actors are classes which have some presence in the game world. Actors gain their specialized functionality by incorporating Components. This chapter deals with creating custom Actors and Components, the purpose that they serve, and how they work together.

Creating a custom Actor in C++

While there are a number of different types of Actors that ship with Unreal as part of the default installation, you will find yourself needing to create custom Actors at some point during your project's development. This might happen when you need to add functionality to an existing class, combine Components in a combination not present in the default subclasses, or add additional member variables to a class. The next two recipes demonstrate how to use either composition or inheritance to customize Actors.

Getting ready

Make sure you have installed Visual Studio and Unreal 4 as per the recipe in *Chapter 1, UE4 Development Tools.* You'll also need to have either an existing project, or create a new one using the Unreal-provided wizard.

How to do it...

1. Open up your project within the Unreal Editor, then click on the **Add New** button in **Content Browser**:

2. Select **New C++ Class...**

3. In the dialog that opens, select **Actor** from the list:

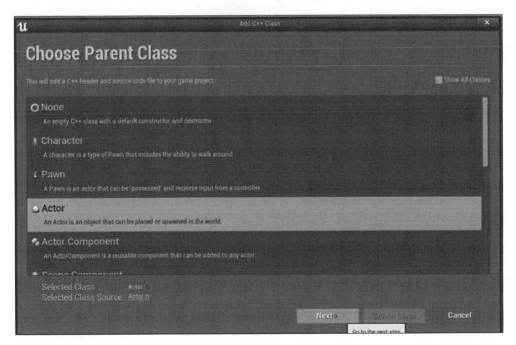

4. Give your Actor a name, such as `MyFirstActor`, then click on **OK** to launch Visual Studio.

By convention, class names for `Actor` subclasses begin with an `A`. When using this class creation wizard, make sure you don't prefix your class with `A`, as the engine automatically adds the prefix for you.

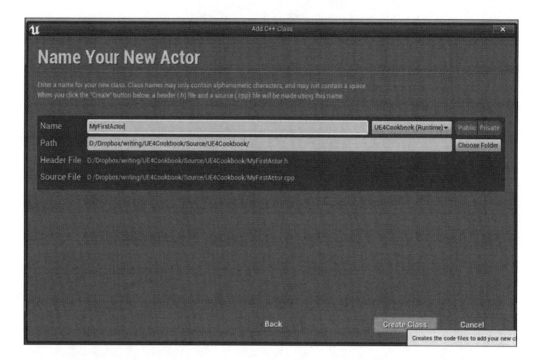

5. When Visual Studio loads, you should see something very similar to the following listing:

```
MyFirstActor.h
#pragma once

#include "GameFramework/Actor.h"
#include "MyFirstActor.generated.h"

UCLASS()
class UE4COOKBOOK_API AMyFirstActor : public AActor
{
  GENERATED_BODY()
  public:
```

```
    AMyFirstActor();
};
MyFirstActor.cpp
#include "UE4Cookbook.h"
#include "MyFirstActor.h"
AMyFirstActor::AMyFirstActor()
{
    PrimaryActorTick.bCanEverTick = true;
}
```

How it works...

In time, you'll become familiar enough with the standard code, so you will be able to just create new classes from Visual Studio without using the Unreal wizard.

- ▶ `#pragma once`: This preprocessor statement, or `pragma`, is Unreal's expected method of implementing include guards—pieces of code that prevent an `include` file from causing errors by being referenced multiple times.

- ▶ `#include "GameFramework/Actor.h"`: We're going to create an `Actor` subclass, so naturally, we need to include the `header` file for the class we are inheriting from.

- ▶ `#include "MyFirstActor.generated.h"`: All actor classes need to include their `generated.h` file. This file is automatically created by **Unreal Header Tool (UHT)** based on the macros that it detects in your files.

- ▶ `UCLASS()`: UCLASS is one such macro, which allows us to indicate that a class will be exposed to Unreal's reflection system. Reflection allows us to inspect and iterate object properties during runtime as well as manage references to our objects for garbage collection.

- ▶ `class UE4COOKBOOK_API AMyFirstActor : public AActor`: This is the actual declaration of our class. The `UE4COOKBOOK_API` macro is created by UHT, and is necessary to help our project compile properly on Windows by ensuring that our project module's classes are exported correctly in the DLL. You will also notice that both `MyFirstActor` and `Actor` have the prefix A—this is the naming convention that Unreal requires for native classes that are inherited from `Actor`.

- ▶ `GENERATED_BODY()`: GENERATED_BODY is another UHT macro that has been expanded to include the automatically generated functions that the underlying UE type system requires.

- ▶ `PrimaryActorTick.bCanEverTick = true;`: Inside the constructor implementation, this line enables ticking for this `Actor`. All Actors have a function called `Tick`, and this Boolean variable means that the `Actor` will have that function called once per frame enabling the actor to perform actions in every frame as necessary. As a performance optimization, this is disabled by default.

Instantiating an Actor using SpawnActor

For this recipe, you'll need to have an `Actor` subclass ready to instantiate. You can use a built-in class such as `StaticMeshActor`, but it would help to practice with the custom `Actor` you made in the previous recipe.

How to do it...

1. Create a new C++ class, like in the previous recipe. This time, select `GameMode` as your base class, giving it a name such as `UE4CookbookGameMode`.

2. Declare a function override in your new `GameMode` class:

```
virtual void BeginPlay() override;
```

3. Implement `BeginPlay` in the `.cpp` file:

```
void AUE4CookbookGameMode::BeginPlay()
{
  Super::BeginPlay();
  GEngine->AddOnScreenDebugMessage(-1, -1, FColor::Red,
  TEXT("Actor Spawning"));

  FTransform SpawnLocation;
  GetWorld()->SpawnActor<AMyFirstActor>(
  AMyFirstActor::StaticClass(), &SpawnLocation);
}
```

4. Compile your code, either through Visual Studio or by clicking on the **Compile** button in Unreal Editor.

5. Open the **World Settings** panel for the current level by clicking on the **Settings** toolbar icon, then pick **World Settings** from the drop-down menu. In the **GameMode Override** section, change the game mode to the GameMode subclass you just created as shown in the following two screenshots:

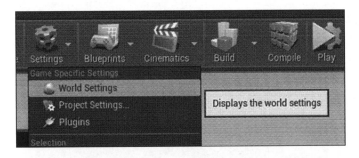

6. Start the level, and verify that `GameMode` spawns a copy of your `Actor` in the world by looking at the **World Outliner** panel. You can verify that the `BeginPlay` function is being run by viewing the **Actor Spawning** text being displayed on screen. If it doesn't spawn, make sure there are no obstructions at the world origin to prevent the `Actor` from being spawned. You can search the list of objects in the world by typing in the search bar at the top of the **World Outliner** panel to filter the entities shown.

How it works...

1. `GameMode` is a special type of actor which is part of the Unreal Game Framework. Your map's `GameMode` is instantiated by the engine automatically when the game starts.

2. By placing some code into the `BeginPlay` method of our custom `GameMode`, we can run it automatically when the game begins.

3. Inside `BeginPlay`, we create an `FTransform` to be used by the `SpawnActor` function. By default, `FTransform` is constructed to have zero rotation and a location at the origin.

4. We then get a reference to the current level's `UWorld` instance using `GetWorld`, then call its `SpawnActor` function. We pass in `FTransform`, which we created earlier, to specify that the object should be created at its location, that is, the origin.

Destroying an Actor using Destroy and a Timer

This recipe will reuse the GameMode from the previous recipe, so you should complete it first.

How to do it...

1. Make the following changes to the GameMode declaration:

```
UPROPERTY()
AMyFirstActor* SpawnedActor;
UFUNCTION()
void DestroyActorFunction();
```

2. Add #include "MyFirstActor.h" to the implementation file's includes.

3. Assign the results of SpawnActor to the new SpawnedActor variable:

```
SpawnedActor = GetWorld()->SpawnActor<AMyFirstActor>
(AMyFirstActor::StaticClass(), SpawnLocation);
```

4. Add the following to the end of the BeginPlay function:

```
FTimerHandle Timer;
GetWorldTimerManager().SetTimer(Timer, this,
&AUE4CookbookGameMode::DestroyActorFunction, 10);
```

5. Lastly, implement DestroyActorFunction:

```
void AUE4CookbookGameMode::DestroyActorFunction()
{
  if (SpawnedActor != nullptr)
  {
    SpawnedActor->Destroy();
  }
}
```

6. Load the level you created in the previous recipe, which had the game mode set to your custom class.

7. Play your level, and use the Outliner to verify that your SpawnedActor gets deleted after 10 seconds.

How it works...

▶ We declare a UPROPERTY to store our spawned Actor instance, and a custom function to call so that we can call Destroy() on a timer:

```
UPROPERTY()
AMyFirstActor* SpawnedActor;
UFUNCTION()
void DestroyActorFunction();
```

▶ In BeginPlay, we assign the spawned Actor to our new UPROPERTY:

```
SpawnedActor = GetWorld()->SpawnActor<AMyFirstActor>
(AMyFirstActor::StaticClass(), SpawnLocation);
```

▶ We then declare a TimerHandle object, and pass it to GetWorldTimerManager::SetTimer. SetTimer calls DestroyActorFunction on the object pointed to by this pointer after 10 seconds. SetTimer returns an object—a handle—to allow us to cancel the timer if necessary. The SetTimer function takes the TimerHandle object in as a reference parameter, hence, we declare it in advance so that we can pass it into the function properly:

```
FTimerHandle Timer;
GetWorldTimerManager().SetTimer(Timer, this,
&AUE4CookbookGameMode::DestroyActorFunction, 10);
```

▶ The DestroyActorFunction checks if we have a valid reference to a spawned Actor:

```
void AUE4CookbookGameMode::DestroyActorFunction()
{
  if (SpawnedActor != nullptr)
}
```

▶ If we do, it calls Destroy on the instance, so it will be destroyed, and eventually, garbage collected:

```
SpawnedActor->Destroy();
```

Destroying an Actor after a delay using SetLifeSpan

Let's look at how we can destroy an Actor.

How to do it...

1. Create a new C++ class using the wizard. Select `Actor` as your base class.
2. In the implementation of `Actor`, add the following code to the `BeginPlay` function:

   `SetLifeSpan(10);`
3. Drag a copy of your custom `Actor` into the viewport within the Editor.
4. Play your level, and look at the Outliner to verify that your `Actor` instance disappears after 10 seconds, having destroyed itself.

How it works...

1. We insert our code into the `BeginPlay` function so that it executes when the game starts.
2. `SetLifeSpan(10);`: The `SetLifeSpan` function allows us to specify a duration in seconds, after which the `Actor` calls its own `Destroy()` method.

Implementing the Actor functionality by composition

Custom Actors without components don't have a location, and can't be attached to other Actors. Without a root Component, an Actor doesn't have a base transform, and so it has no location. Most Actors, therefore, require at least one Component to be useful.

We can create custom Actors through composition—adding a number of components to our `Actor`, where each component provides some of the functionality required.

Getting ready

This recipe will use the `Actor` class created in the *Creating a custom Actor in C++* recipe.

How to do it...

1. Add a new member to your custom class in C++ by making the following changes in the `public` section:

   ```
   UPROPERTY()
   UStaticMeshComponent* Mesh;
   ```
2. Add the following line to the constructor inside the cpp file:

   ```
   Mesh =
   CreateDefaultSubobject<UStaticMeshComponent>("BaseMeshCompo
   nent");
   ```

3. Verify your code looks like the following snippet, and compile it by using the **Compile** button in the editor, or building the project in Visual Studio:

```
UCLASS()
class UE4COOKBOOK_API AMyFirstActor : public AActor
{
  GENERATED_BODY()
  public:
  AMyFirstActor();

  UPROPERTY()
  UStaticMeshComponent* Mesh;
};

#include "UE4Cookbook.h"
#include "MyFirstActor.h"
AMyFirstActor::AMyFirstActor()
{
  PrimaryActorTick.bCanEverTick = true;

  Mesh = CreateDefaultSubobject<UStaticMeshComponent>
  ("BaseMeshComponent");
}
```

4. Once you've compiled this code, drag an instance of your class from the **Content Browser** out into the game environment, and you will be able to verify that it now has a transform and other properties, such as a Static Mesh, which comes from the `StaticMeshComponent` that we added.

How it works...

1. The UPROPERTY `macro` we added to the class declaration is a pointer to hold the component we are using as a subobject of our `Actor`.

```
UPROPERTY()
UStaticMeshComponent* Mesh;
```

2. Using the UPROPERTY() macro ensures that the object declared in the pointer is considered to be referenced, and won't be garbage-collected (that is, deleted) out from under us, leaving the pointer dangling.

3. We're using a Static Mesh component, but any of the `Actor` Component subclasses would work. Note the asterisk is connected to the variable type in accordance with Epic's style guide.

4. In the constructor, we initialize the pointer to a known valid value by using a `template` function, `template<class TReturnType> TReturnType* CreateDefaultSubobject(FName SubobjectName, bool bTransient = false)`.

5. This function is responsible for calling the engine code to appropriately initialize the component, and return a pointer to the newly constructed object so that we can give our component pointer a default value. This is important, obviously, to ensure that the pointer has a valid value at all times, minimizing the risk of dereferencing uninitialized memory.

6. The function is templated based on the type of object to create, but also takes two parameters—the first one is the name of the subobject, which ideally should be human-readable, and the second is whether the object should be transient (that is—not saved along with the parent object).

See also

▶ The following recipe shows you how to reference a mesh asset in your Static Mesh Component so that it can be displayed without requiring a user to specify a mesh in the Editor

Loading assets into components using FObjectFinder

In the last recipe, we created a Static Mesh Component, but we didn't try to load a mesh for the Component to display. While it's possible to do this in the Editor, sometimes it is helpful to specify a default in C++.

Getting ready

Follow the previous recipe so you have a custom `Actor` subclass with a Static Mesh Component ready.

In your **Content Browser**, click on the **View Options** button, and select **Show Engine Content**:

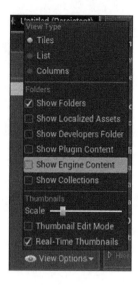

Browse to **Engine Content**, then **BasicShapes** to see the **Cube** we will be using in this recipe.

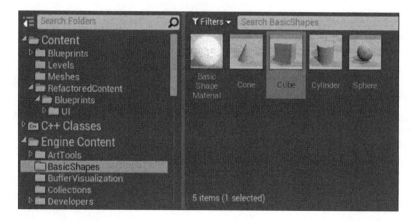

How to do it...

1. Add the following code to the constructor of your class:

```
auto MeshAsset =
ConstructorHelpers::FObjectFinder<UStaticMesh>(TEXT("Static
Mesh'/Engine/BasicShapes/Cube.Cube'"));
if (MeshAsset.Object != nullptr)
{
  Mesh->SetStaticMesh(MeshAsset.Object);
}
```

2. Compile, and verify in the Editor that an instance of your class now has a mesh as its visual representation.

How it works...

▸ We create an instance of the `FObjectFinder` class, passing in the type of asset that we are trying to load as a template parameter.

▸ `FObjectFinder` is a class template that helps us to load assets. When we construct it, we pass in a string that contains a path to the asset that we are trying to load.

▸ The string is of the format `"{ObjectType}'/Path/To/Asset.Asset'"`. Note the use of single quotes in the string.

▸ In order to get the string for an asset that already exists in the editor, you can right-click on the asset in the **Content Browser** and select **Copy Reference**. This gives you the string so you can paste it into your code.

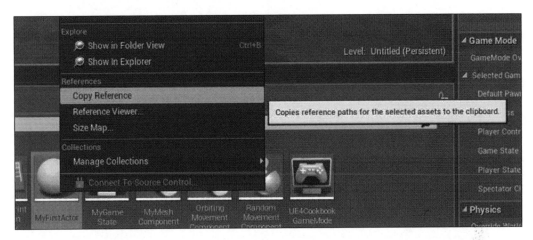

▸ We use the `auto` keyword, from C++11, to avoid typing out our whole object type in its declaration; the compiler deduces it for us. Without `auto`, we would have to use the following code instead:

```
ConstructorHelpers::FObjectFinder<UStaticMesh> MeshAsset =
ConstructorHelpers::FObjectFinder<UStaticMesh>(TEXT("Static
Mesh'/Engine/BasicShapes/Cube.Cube'"));
```

▸ The `FObjectFinder` class has a property called `Object` that will either have a pointer to the desired asset, or will be `NULL` if the asset could not be found.

▸ This means that we can check it against `nullptr`, and if it isn't null, assign it to `Mesh` using `SetStaticMesh`.

Implementing the Actor functionality by inheritance

Inheritance is the second way to implement a custom `Actor`. This is commonly done to make a new subclass, which adds member variables, functions, or a Component to an existing `Actor` class. In this recipe, we are going to add a variable to a custom `GameState` subclass.

How to do it...

1. In the Unreal Editor, click on **Add New** in the **Content Browser,** and then on **New C++ Class...** then select **GameState** as the base class, then give your new class a name.

2. Add the following code to the new class header:

```
AMyGameState();

UFUNCTION()
void SetScore(int32 NewScore);

UFUNCTION()
int32 GetScore();
private:
UPROPERTY()
int32 CurrentScore;
```

3. Add the following code to the cpp file:

```
AMyGameState::AMyGameState()
{
  CurrentScore = 0;
}

int32 AMyGameState::GetScore()
{
  return CurrentScore;
}

void AMyGameState::SetScore(int32 NewScore)
{
  CurrentScore = NewScore;
}
```

4. Confirm that your code looks like the following listing, and compile using the **Compile** button in the Unreal Editor:

```
MyGameState.h
#pragma once

#include "GameFramework/GameState.h"
#include "MyGameState.generated.h"

/**
 *
 */
UCLASS()
class UE4COOKBOOK_API AMyGameState : public AGameState
{
  GENERATED_BODY()
  public:
  AMyGameState();

  UPROPERTY()
  int32 CurrentScore;

  UFUNCTION()
  int32 GetScore();

  UFUNCTION()
  void SetScore(uint32 NewScore);
};
MyGameState.cpp
#include "UE4Cookbook.h"
#include "MyGameState.h"

AMyGameState::AMyGameState()
{
  CurrentScore = 0;
}

int32 AMyGameState::GetScore()
{
  return CurrentScore;
}

void AMyGameState::SetScore(uint32 NewScore)
{
  CurrentScore = NewScore;
}
```

How it works...

1. Firstly, we add the declaration of a default constructor:

```
AMyGameState();
```

2. This allows us to set our new member variable to a safe default value of 0 on object initialization:

```
AMyGameState::AMyGameState()
{
   CurrentScore = 0;
}
```

3. We use the `int32` type when declaring our new variable to ensure portability between the various compilers that Unreal Engine supports. This variable is going to be responsible for storing the current game score while it is running. As always, we will be marking our variable with `UPROPERTY` so that it is garbage collected appropriately. This variable is marked `private` so that the only way to change the value is through our functions:

```
UPROPERTY()
int32 CurrentScore;
```

4. The `GetScore` function will retrieve the current score, and return it to the caller. It is implemented as a simple accessor, which simply returns the underlying member variable.

5. The second function, `SetScore`, sets the value of the member variable allowing external objects to request a change to the score. Placing this request as a function ensures that the `GameState` can vet such requests, and only allow them when valid to prevent cheating. The specifics of such a check are beyond the scope of this recipe, but the `SetScore` function is the appropriate place to make it.

6. Our score functions are declared using the `UFUNCTION` macro for a number of reasons. Firstly, `UFUNCTION`, with some additional code, can be called or overridden by Blueprint. Secondly, `UFUNCTION` can be marked as `exec`—this means that they can be run as console commands by a player or developer during a play session, which enables debugging.

See also

► *Chapter 8, Integrating C++ and the Unreal Editor,* has a recipe, *Creating new console commands,* that you can refer to for more information regarding `exec` and the console command functionality

Attaching components to create a hierarchy

When creating custom Actors from components, it is important to consider the concept of **Attaching**. Attaching components together creates a relationship where transformations applied to the parent component will also affect the components that are attached to it.

How to do it...

1. Create a new class based on `Actor` using the editor, and call it `HierarchyActor`.

2. Add the following properties to your new class:

```
UPROPERTY()
USceneComponent* Root;
UPROPERTY()
USceneComponent* ChildSceneComponent;
UPROPERTY()
UStaticMeshComponent* BoxOne;
UPROPERTY()
UStaticMeshComponent* BoxTwo;
```

3. Add the following code to the class constructor:

```
Root = CreateDefaultSubobject<USceneComponent>("Root");
ChildSceneComponent =
CreateDefaultSubobject<USceneComponent>("ChildSceneComponen
t");
BoxOne =
CreateDefaultSubobject<UStaticMeshComponent>("BoxOne");
BoxTwo =
CreateDefaultSubobject<UStaticMeshComponent>("BoxTwo");

auto MeshAsset =
ConstructorHelpers::FObjectFinder<UStaticMesh>(TEXT("Static
Mesh'/Engine/BasicShapes/Cube.Cube'"));
if (MeshAsset.Object != nullptr)
{
  BoxOne->SetStaticMesh(MeshAsset.Object);
  BoxTwo->SetStaticMesh(MeshAsset.Object);
}
RootComponent = Root;
BoxOne->AttachTo(Root);
BoxTwo->AttachTo(ChildSceneComponent);
ChildSceneComponent->AttachTo(Root);
ChildSceneComponent->SetRelativeTransform
(FTransform(FRotator(0, 0, 0), FVector(250, 0, 0),
FVector(0.1f)));
```

4. Verify that your code looks like the following:

```
HierarchyActor.h
#pragma once

#include "GameFramework/Actor.h"
#include "HierarchyActor.generated.h"

UCLASS()
class UE4COOKBOOK_API AHierarchyActor : public AActor
{
  GENERATED_BODY()
  public:
  AHierarchyActor();
  virtual void BeginPlay() override;
  virtual void Tick( float DeltaSeconds ) override;
  UPROPERTY()
  USceneComponent* Root;
  UPROPERTY()
  USceneComponent* ChildSceneComponent;
  UPROPERTY()
  UStaticMeshComponent* BoxOne;
  UPROPERTY()
  UStaticMeshComponent* BoxTwo;
};
HierarchyActor.cpp

#include "UE4Cookbook.h"
#include "HierarchyActor.h"

AHierarchyActor::AHierarchyActor()
{
  PrimaryActorTick.bCanEverTick = true;
  Root = CreateDefaultSubobject<USceneComponent>("Root");
  ChildSceneComponent =
  CreateDefaultSubobject<USceneComponent>
  ("ChildSceneComponent");
  BoxOne =
  CreateDefaultSubobject<UStaticMeshComponent>("BoxOne");
  BoxTwo =
  CreateDefaultSubobject<UStaticMeshComponent>("BoxTwo");
  auto MeshAsset =
  ConstructorHelpers::FObjectFinder<UStaticMesh>
  (TEXT("StaticMesh'/Engine/BasicShapes/Cube.Cube'"));
  if (MeshAsset.Object != nullptr)
```

```
  {
    BoxOne->SetStaticMesh(MeshAsset.Object);
    BoxOne->SetCollisionProfileName
    (UCollisionProfile::Pawn_ProfileName);
    BoxTwo->SetStaticMesh(MeshAsset.Object);
    BoxTwo->SetCollisionProfileName
    (UCollisionProfile::Pawn_ProfileName);
  }
  RootComponent = Root;
  BoxOne->AttachTo(Root);
  BoxTwo->AttachTo(ChildSceneComponent);
  ChildSceneComponent->AttachTo(Root);
  ChildSceneComponent->SetRelativeTransform
  (FTransform(FRotator(0, 0, 0), FVector(250, 0, 0),
  FVector(0.1f)));
}
void AHierarchyActor::BeginPlay()
{
  Super::BeginPlay();
}
void AHierarchyActor::Tick( float DeltaTime )
{
  Super::Tick( DeltaTime );
}
```

5. Compile and launch the editor. Drag a copy of HierarchyActor into the scene.

6. Verify that `Actor` has components in a hierarchy, and that the second box has a smaller size.

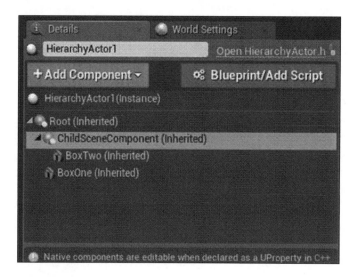

How it works...

1. As usual, we create some UPROPERTY-tagged Components for our actor. We create two Scene Components, and two Static Mesh components.

2. In the constructor, we create default subobjects for each component, as usual.

3. We then load the static mesh, and if loading is successful, assign it to the two static mesh components so that they have a visual representation.

4. We then construct a hierarchy within our `Actor` by attaching components.

5. We set the first Scene Component as the `Actor` root. This component will determine the transformations applied to all other components in the hierarchy.

6. We then attach the first box to our new root component, and parent the second scene component to the first one.

7. We attach the second box to our child scene component so as to demonstrate how changing the transform on that scene component affects its children, but no other components in the object.

8. Lastly, we set the relative transform of that scene component so that it moves a certain distance away from the origin, and is one-tenth of the scale.

9. This means that in the Editor, you can see that the `BoxTwo` component has inherited the translation and scaling of its parent component, `ChildSceneComponent`.

Creating a custom Actor Component

Actor components are an easy way to implement common functionality that should be shared between Actors. Actor components aren't rendered, but can still perform actions such as subscribing to events, or communicating with other components of the Actor that they are present within.

How to do it...

1. Create an `ActorComponent` named `RandomMovementComponent` using the Editor wizard. Add the following class specifiers to the `UCLASS` macro:

```
UCLASS( ClassGroup=(Custom),
meta=(BlueprintSpawnableComponent) )
```

2. Add the following `UPROPERTY` to the class header:

```
UPROPERTY()
float MovementRadius;
```

3. Add the following to the constructor's implementation:

```
MovementRadius = 0;
```

4. Lastly, add this to the implementation of `TickComponent( )`:

```
AActor* Parent = GetOwner();
if (Parent)
{
  Parent->SetActorLocation(
  Parent->GetActorLocation() +
  FVector(
  FMath::FRandRange(-1, 1) * MovementRadius,
  FMath::FRandRange(-1, 1) * MovementRadius,
  FMath::FRandRange(-1, 1) * MovementRadius));
}
```

5. Verify that your code looks like the following:

```
#pragma once
#include "Components/ActorComponent.h"
#include "RandomMovementComponent.generated.h"
UCLASS( ClassGroup=(Custom),
meta=(BlueprintSpawnableComponent) )
class UE4COOKBOOK_API URandomMovementComponent : public
UActorComponent
{
  GENERATED_BODY()
```

```
    public:
    URandomMovementComponent();
    virtual void BeginPlay() override;
    virtual void TickComponent( float DeltaTime, ELevelTick
    TickType, FActorComponentTickFunction* ThisTickFunction )
    override;
    UPROPERTY()
    float MovementRadius;
};


#include "UE4Cookbook.h"
#include "RandomMovementComponent.h"
URandomMovementComponent::URandomMovementComponent()
{
  bWantsBeginPlay = true;
  PrimaryComponentTick.bCanEverTick = true;
  MovementRadius = 5;
}


void URandomMovementComponent::BeginPlay()
{
  Super::BeginPlay();
}


void URandomMovementComponent::TickComponent( float
DeltaTime, ELevelTick TickType,
FActorComponentTickFunction* ThisTickFunction )
{
  Super::TickComponent( DeltaTime, TickType,
  ThisTickFunction );
  AActor* Parent = GetOwner();
  if (Parent)
  {
    Parent->SetActorLocation(
    Parent->GetActorLocation() +
    FVector(
    FMath::FRandRange(-1, 1)* MovementRadius,
    FMath::FRandRange(-1, 1)* MovementRadius,
    FMath::FRandRange(-1, 1)* MovementRadius));
  }
}
```

6. Compile your project. In the editor, create an empty `Actor`, and add your **Random Movement** Component to it. To do this, drag an **Empty Actor** from the **Placement** tab out into the level, then click on **Add Component** in the **Details** panel, and select **Random Movement**. Do the same thing to add a **Cube** Component so that you have something to visualize your actor's position with.

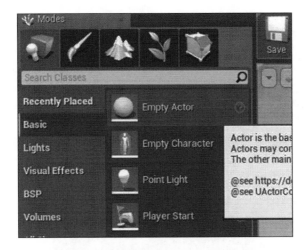

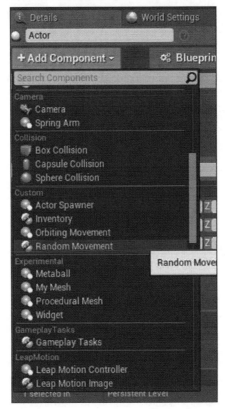

7. Play your level, and observe the actor randomly moving around as its location changes every time the `TickComponent` function is called.

How it works...

1. Firstly, we add a few specifiers to the UCLASS macro used in our component's declaration. Adding BlueprintSpawnableComponent to the class' meta values means that instances of the component can be added to blueprint classes in the editor. The ClassGroup specifier allows us to indicate what category of class our Component belongs to in the list of classes:

```
UCLASS( ClassGroup=(Custom),
meta=(BlueprintSpawnableComponent) )
```

2. Adding MovementRadius as a property to the new component allows us to specify how far the component will be allowed to wander in a single frame:

```
UPROPERTY()
float MovementRadius;
```

3. In the constructor, we initialize this property to a safe default value:

```
MovementRadius =5;
```

4. TickComponent is a function that is called every frame by the engine, just like Tick is for Actors. In its implementation, we retrieve the current location of the component's owner, that is, the Actor that contains our component, and we generate an offset in the world space:

```
AActor* Parent = GetOwner();
if (Parent)
{
  Parent->SetActorLocation(
  Parent->GetActorLocation() +
  FVector(
  FMath::FRandRange(-1, 1)* MovementRadius,
  FMath::FRandRange(-1, 1)* MovementRadius,
  FMath::FRandRange(-1, 1)* MovementRadius)
  );
}
```

5. We add the random offset to the current location to determine a new location, and move the owning actor to it. This causes the actor's location to randomly change from frame to frame and dance about.

Creating a custom Scene Component

Scene Components are a subclass of Actor Components that have a transform, that is, a relative location, rotation, and scale. Just like Actor Components, Scene Components aren't rendered themselves, but can use their transform for various things, such as spawning other objects at a fixed offset from an Actor.

How to do it...

1. Create a custom `SceneComponent` called `ActorSpawnerComponent`. Make the following changes to the header:

```
UFUNCTION()
void Spawn();
UPROPERTY()
TSubclassOf<AActor> ActorToSpawn;
```

2. Add the following function implementation to the cpp file:

```
void UActorSpawnerComponent::Spawn()
{
  UWorld* TheWorld = GetWorld();
  if (TheWorld != nullptr)
  {
    FTransform ComponentTransform(this-
    >GetComponentTransform());
    TheWorld->SpawnActor(ActorToSpawn,&ComponentTransform);
  }
}
```

3. Verify your code against this snippet:

```
ActorSpawnerComponent.h
#pragma once

#include "Components/SceneComponent.h"
#include "ActorSpawnerComponent.generated.h"

UCLASS( ClassGroup=(Custom),
meta=(BlueprintSpawnableComponent) )
class UE4COOKBOOK_API UActorSpawnerComponent : public
USceneComponent
{
  GENERATED_BODY()

  public:
  UActorSpawnerComponent();

  virtual void BeginPlay() override;

  virtual void TickComponent( float DeltaTime, ELevelTick
  TickType, FActorComponentTickFunction* ThisTickFunction )
  override;
```

```
        UFUNCTION(BlueprintCallable, Category=Cookbook)
        void Spawn();

        UPROPERTY(EditAnywhere)
        TSubclassOf<AActor> ActorToSpawn;

};
ActorSpawnerComponent.cpp
#include "UE4Cookbook.h"
#include "ActorSpawnerComponent.h"

UActorSpawnerComponent::UActorSpawnerComponent()
{
  bWantsBeginPlay = true;
  PrimaryComponentTick.bCanEverTick = true;
}

void UActorSpawnerComponent::BeginPlay()
{
  Super::BeginPlay();
}

void UActorSpawnerComponent::TickComponent( float
DeltaTime, ELevelTick TickType,
FActorComponentTickFunction* ThisTickFunction )
{
  Super::TickComponent( DeltaTime, TickType,
  ThisTickFunction );
}

void UActorSpawnerComponent::Spawn()
{
  UWorld* TheWorld = GetWorld();
  if (TheWorld != nullptr)
  {
    FTransform ComponentTransform(this
    ->GetComponentTransform());
    TheWorld->SpawnActor(ActorToSpawn, &ComponentTransform);
  }
}
```

4. Compile and open your project. Drag an empty `Actor` into the scene and add your `ActorSpawnerComponent` to it. Select your new Component in the `Details` panel, and assign a value to `ActorToSpawn`. Now whenever `Spawn()` is called on an instance of your component, it will instantiate a copy of the `Actor` class specified in `ActorToSpawn`.

How it works...

1. We create the `Spawn UFUNCTION` and a variable called `ActorToSpawn`. The `ActorToSpawn UPROPERTY` is of type `TSubclassOf< >`, a template type that allows us to restrict a pointer to either a base class or subclasses thereof. This also means that within the editor, we will get a pre-filtered list of classes to pick from, preventing us from accidentally assigning an invalid value.

2. Inside the `Spawn` function's implementation, we get access to our world, and check it for validity.

3. `SpawnActor` wants an `FTransform*` to specify the location to spawn the new actor, so we create a new stack variable to contain a copy of the current component's transform.

4. If `TheWorld` is valid, we request it to spawn an instance of the `ActorToSpawn`-specified subclass, passing in the address of the `FTransform` we just created, and which now contains the desired location for the new actor.

▶ *Chapter 8, Integrating C++ and the Unreal Editor,* contains a much more detailed investigation into how you can make things Blueprint-accessible.

Creating a custom Primitive Component

`Primitive` components are the most complex type of `Actor` Component because they not only have a transform, but are also rendered on screen.

How to do it...

1. Create a custom C++ class based on `MeshComponent`. When Visual Studio loads, add the following to your class header file:

```
UCLASS(ClassGroup=Experimental, meta =
(BlueprintSpawnableComponent))
public:
virtual FPrimitiveSceneProxy* CreateSceneProxy() override;
TArray<int32> Indices;
TArray<FVector> Vertices;
UPROPERTY(EditAnywhere, BlueprintReadWrite, Category =
Materials)
UMaterial* TheMaterial;
```

2. We need to create an implementation for our overridden `CreateSceneProxy` function in our cpp file:

```
FPrimitiveSceneProxy* UMyMeshComponent::CreateSceneProxy()
{
  FPrimitiveSceneProxy* Proxy = NULL;
  Proxy = new FMySceneProxy(this);
  return Proxy;
}
```

3. This function returns an instance of `FMySceneProxy`, which we need to implement. Do so by adding the following code above the `CreateSceneProxy` function:

```
class FMySceneProxy : public FPrimitiveSceneProxy
{
  public:
  FMySceneProxy(UMyMeshComponent* Component)
  :FPrimitiveSceneProxy(Component),
  Indices(Component->Indices),
  TheMaterial(Component->TheMaterial)
  {
```

```
    VertexBuffer = FMyVertexBuffer();
    IndexBuffer = FMyIndexBuffer();
    for (FVector Vertex : Component->Vertices)
    {
      Vertices.Add(FDynamicMeshVertex(Vertex));
    }
};
UPROPERTY()
UMaterial* TheMaterial;
virtual FPrimitiveViewRelevance GetViewRelevance(const
FSceneView* View)  const override
{
  FPrimitiveViewRelevance Result;
  Result.bDynamicRelevance = true;
  Result.bDrawRelevance = true;
  Result.bNormalTranslucencyRelevance = true;
  return Result;
}
virtual void GetDynamicMeshElements(const TArray<const
FSceneView*>& Views, const FSceneViewFamily& ViewFamily,
uint32 VisibilityMap, FMeshElementCollector& Collector)
const override
{
  for (int32 ViewIndex = 0; ViewIndex < Views.Num();
  ViewIndex++)
  {
    FDynamicMeshBuilder MeshBuilder;
    if (Vertices.Num() == 0)
    {
      return;
    }
    MeshBuilder.AddVertices(Vertices);
    MeshBuilder.AddTriangles(Indices);
    MeshBuilder.GetMesh(FMatrix::Identity, new
    FColoredMaterialRenderProxy(TheMaterial
    ->GetRenderProxy(false), FLinearColor::Gray),
    GetDepthPriorityGroup(Views[ViewIndex]), true, true,
    ViewIndex, Collector);
  }
}
uint32 FMySceneProxy::GetMemoryFootprint(void) const
override
{
  return sizeof(*this);
}
```

```
        virtual ~FMySceneProxy() {};
        private:
        TArray<FDynamicMeshVertex> Vertices;
        TArray<int32> Indices;
        FMyVertexBuffer VertexBuffer;
        FMyIndexBuffer IndexBuffer;
    };
```

4. Our scene proxy requires a vertex buffer and an index buffer. The following subclasses should be placed above the Scene Proxy's implementation:

```
class FMyVertexBuffer : public FVertexBuffer
{
  public:
  TArray<FVector> Vertices;
  virtual void InitRHI() override
  {
    FRHIResourceCreateInfo CreateInfo;
    VertexBufferRHI = RHICreateVertexBuffer(Vertices.Num()
    * sizeof(FVector), BUF_Static, CreateInfo);
    void* VertexBufferData =
    RHILockVertexBuffer(VertexBufferRHI, 0, Vertices.Num()
    * sizeof(FVector), RLM_WriteOnly);
    FMemory::Memcpy(VertexBufferData, Vertices.GetData(),
    Vertices.Num() * sizeof(FVector));
    RHIUnlockVertexBuffer(VertexBufferRHI);
  }
};
class FMyIndexBuffer : public FIndexBuffer
{
  public:
  TArray<int32> Indices;
  virtual void InitRHI() override
  {
    FRHIResourceCreateInfo CreateInfo;
    IndexBufferRHI = RHICreateIndexBuffer(sizeof(int32),
    Indices.Num() * sizeof(int32), BUF_Static, CreateInfo);
    void* Buffer = RHILockIndexBuffer(IndexBufferRHI, 0,
    Indices.Num() * sizeof(int32), RLM_WriteOnly);
    FMemory::Memcpy(Buffer, Indices.GetData(),
    Indices.Num() * sizeof(int32));
    RHIUnlockIndexBuffer(IndexBufferRHI);
  }
};
```

5. Add the following constructor implementation:

```
UMyMeshComponent::UMyMeshComponent()
{
  static ConstructorHelpers::FObjectFinder<UMaterial>
  Material(TEXT
  ("Material'/Engine/BasicShapes/BasicShapeMaterial'"));
  if (Material.Object != NULL)
  {
    TheMaterial = (UMaterial*)Material.Object;
  }
  Vertices.Add(FVector(10, 0, 0));
  Vertices.Add(FVector(0, 10, 0));
  Vertices.Add(FVector(0, 0, 10));
  Indices.Add(0);
  Indices.Add(1);
  Indices.Add(2);
}
```

6. Verify that your code looks like the following:

```
#pragma once

#include "Components/MeshComponent.h"
#include "MyMeshComponent.generated.h"

UCLASS(ClassGroup = Experimental, meta =
(BlueprintSpawnableComponent))
class UE4COOKBOOK_API UMyMeshComponent : public
UMeshComponent
{
  GENERATED_BODY()
  public:
  virtual FPrimitiveSceneProxy* CreateSceneProxy()
  override;
  TArray<int32> Indices;
  TArray<FVector> Vertices;

  UPROPERTY(EditAnywhere, BlueprintReadWrite, Category =
  Materials)
  UMaterial* TheMaterial;
  UMyMeshComponent();
};

#include "UE4Cookbook.h"
#include "MyMeshComponent.h"
#include <VertexFactory.h>
```

```cpp
#include "DynamicMeshBuilder.h"

class FMyVertexBuffer : public FVertexBuffer
{
  public:
  TArray<FVector> Vertices;

  virtual void InitRHI() override
  {
    FRHIResourceCreateInfo CreateInfo;
    VertexBufferRHI = RHICreateVertexBuffer
    (Vertices.Num() *
    sizeof(FVector), BUF_Static, CreateInfo);

    void* VertexBufferData =
    RHILockVertexBuffer(VertexBufferRHI, 0, Vertices.Num()
    * sizeof(FVector), RLM_WriteOnly);
    FMemory::Memcpy(VertexBufferData, Vertices.GetData(),
    Vertices.Num() * sizeof(FVector));
    RHIUnlockVertexBuffer(VertexBufferRHI);
  }
};

class FMyIndexBuffer : public FIndexBuffer
{
  public:
  TArray<int32> Indices;

  virtual void InitRHI() override
  {
    FRHIResourceCreateInfo CreateInfo;
    IndexBufferRHI = RHICreateIndexBuffer(sizeof(int32),
    Indices.Num() * sizeof(int32), BUF_Static, CreateInfo);

    void* Buffer = RHILockIndexBuffer(IndexBufferRHI, 0,
    Indices.Num() * sizeof(int32), RLM_WriteOnly);
    FMemory::Memcpy(Buffer, Indices.GetData(),
    Indices.Num() * sizeof(int32));
    RHIUnlockIndexBuffer(IndexBufferRHI);
  }
};
class FMySceneProxy : public FPrimitiveSceneProxy
{
  public:
  FMySceneProxy(UMyMeshComponent* Component)
```

```
  :FPrimitiveSceneProxy(Component),
  Indices(Component->Indices),
  TheMaterial(Component->TheMaterial)
  {
    VertexBuffer = FMyVertexBuffer();
    IndexBuffer = FMyIndexBuffer();

    for (FVector Vertex : Component->Vertices)
    {
      Vertices.Add(FDynamicMeshVertex(Component
      ->GetComponentLocation() + Vertex));
    }
  };

UPROPERTY()
  UMaterial* TheMaterial;

  virtual FPrimitiveViewRelevance GetViewRelevance(const
  FSceneView* View)  const override
  {
    FPrimitiveViewRelevance Result;
    Result.bDynamicRelevance = true;
    Result.bDrawRelevance = true;
    Result.bNormalTranslucencyRelevance = true;
    return Result;
  }

  virtual void GetDynamicMeshElements(const TArray<const
  FSceneView*>& Views, const FSceneViewFamily& ViewFamily,
  uint32 VisibilityMap, FMeshElementCollector& Collector)
  const override
  {
    for (int32 ViewIndex = 0; ViewIndex < Views.Num();
    ViewIndex++)
    {
      FDynamicMeshBuilder MeshBuilder;
      if (Vertices.Num() == 0)
      {
        return;
      }
      MeshBuilder.AddVertices(Vertices);
      MeshBuilder.AddTriangles(Indices);
```

```
          MeshBuilder.GetMesh(FMatrix::Identity, new
          FColoredMaterialRenderProxy(TheMaterial
          ->GetRenderProxy(false), FLinearColor::Gray),
          GetDepthPriorityGroup(Views[ViewIndex]),
          true, true, ViewIndex, Collector);


      }
    }

    void FMySceneProxy::OnActorPositionChanged() override
    {
      VertexBuffer.ReleaseResource();
      IndexBuffer.ReleaseResource();
    }

    uint32 FMySceneProxy::GetMemoryFootprint(void) const
    override
    {
      return sizeof(*this);
    }
    virtual ~FMySceneProxy() {};
    private:
    TArray<FDynamicMeshVertex> Vertices;
    TArray<int32> Indices;
    FMyVertexBuffer VertexBuffer;
    FMyIndexBuffer IndexBuffer;
};

FPrimitiveSceneProxy* UMyMeshComponent::CreateSceneProxy()
{
  FPrimitiveSceneProxy* Proxy = NULL;
  Proxy = new FMySceneProxy(this);
  return Proxy;
}

UMyMeshComponent::UMyMeshComponent()
{
  static ConstructorHelpers::FObjectFinder<UMaterial>
  Material(TEXT
  ("Material'/Engine/BasicShapes/BasicShapeMaterial'"));

  if (Material.Object != NULL)
  {
    TheMaterial = (UMaterial*)Material.Object;
  }
```

```
        Vertices.Add(FVector(10, 0, 0));
        Vertices.Add(FVector(0, 10, 0));
        Vertices.Add(FVector(0, 0, 10));
        Indices.Add(0);
        Indices.Add(1);
        Indices.Add(2);
    }
```

7. Create an empty `Actor` in the editor and add the new mesh component to it to see that your triangle is rendered. Experiment by changing the values added with Vertices. Add and see how the geometry changes after a recompile.

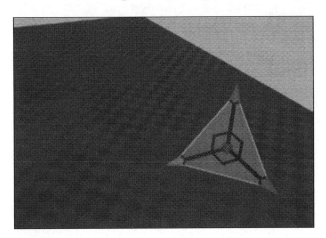

How it works...

1. In order for an `Actor` to be rendered, the data describing it needs to be made accessible to the rendering thread.

2. The easiest way to do this is with a Scene Proxy—a proxy object that is created on the render thread, and is designed to provide thread safety to the data transfer.

3. The `PrimitiveComponent` class defines a `CreateSceneProxy` function that returns `FPrimitiveSceneProxy*`. This function allows custom components like ours to return an object based on `FPrimitiveSceneProxy`, leveraging polymorphism.

4. We define the constructor of the `SceneProxy` object to take in an instance of our component so that each `SceneProxy` created knows about the component instance it is associated with.

5. That data is then cached in the Scene Proxy, and passed to the renderer using `GetDynamicMeshElements`.

6. We create an `IndexBuffer` and a `VertexBuffer`. Each of the buffer classes we create are helpers that assist the Scene Proxy with allocating platform-specific memory for the two buffers. They do so in the `InitRHI` (also known as Initialize Render Hardware Interface) function, wherein they use functions from the RHI API to create a vertex buffer, lock it, copy the required data, and then unlock it.

7. Inside the component's constructor, we look for a material asset that is built into the engine with the `ObjectFinder` template so that our mesh will have a material.

8. We then add some vertices and indexes to our buffers so that the mesh can be drawn when the renderer requests a Scene Proxy.

Creating an InventoryComponent for an RPG

An `InventoryComponent` enables its containing `Actor` to store `InventoryActors` in its inventory, and place them back into the game world.

Getting ready

Make sure you've followed the *Axis Mappings – keyboard, mouse and gamepad directional input for an FPS character* recipe in *Chapter 6, Input and Collision,* before continuing with this recipe, as it shows you how to create a simple character.

Also, the recipe *Instantiating an Actor using SpawnActor* in this chapter shows you how to create a custom `GameMode`.

How to do it...

1. Create an `ActorComponent` subclass using the engine called `InventoryComponent`, then add the following code to it:

```
UPROPERTY()
TArray<AInventoryActor*> CurrentInventory;
UFUNCTION()
int32 AddToInventory(AInventoryActor* ActorToAdd);

UFUNCTION()
void RemoveFromInventory(AInventoryActor* ActorToRemove);
```

2. Add the following function implementation to the source file:

```
int32 UInventoryComponent::AddToInventory(AInventoryActor*
ActorToAdd)
{
    return CurrentInventory.Add(ActorToAdd);
}
```

```
void
UInventoryComponent::RemoveFromInventory(AInventoryActor*
ActorToRemove)
{
    CurrentInventory.Remove(ActorToRemove);
}
```

3. Next, create a new `StaticMeshActor` subclass called `InventoryActor`. Add the following to its declaration:

```
virtual void PickUp();
virtual void PutDown(FTransform TargetLocation);
```

4. Implement the new functions in the implementation file:

```
void AInventoryActor::PickUp()
{
    SetActorTickEnabled(false);
    SetActorHiddenInGame(true);
    SetActorEnableCollision(false);
}

void AInventoryActor::PutDown(FTransform TargetLocation)
{
    SetActorTickEnabled(true);
    SetActorHiddenInGame(false);
    SetActorEnableCollision(true);
    SetActorLocation(TargetLocation.GetLocation());
}
```

5. Also, change the constructor to look like the following:

```
AInventoryActor::AInventoryActor()
:Super()
{
    PrimaryActorTick.bCanEverTick = true;
    auto MeshAsset =
    ConstructorHelpers::FObjectFinder<UStaticMesh>
    (TEXT("StaticMesh'/Engine/BasicShapes/Cube.Cube'"));
    if (MeshAsset.Object != nullptr)
    {
        GetStaticMeshComponent()
        ->SetStaticMesh(MeshAsset.Object);
        GetStaticMeshComponent()
        ->SetCollisionProfileName
        (UCollisionProfile::Pawn_ProfileName);
    }
```

```
GetStaticMeshComponent()
->SetMobility(EComponentMobility::Movable);
SetActorEnableCollision(true);
}
```

6. We need to add an `InventoryComponent` to our character so that we have an inventory that we can store items in. Create a new `SimpleCharacter` subclass using the editor, and add the following to its declaration:

```
UPROPERTY()
UInventoryComponent* MyInventory;

UFUNCTION()
virtual void SetupPlayerInputComponent(class
UInputComponent* InputComponent) override;

UFUNCTION()
void DropItem();
UFUNCTION()
void TakeItem(AInventoryActor* InventoryItem);

UFUNCTION()
virtual void NotifyHit(class UPrimitiveComponent* MyComp,
AActor* Other, class UPrimitiveComponent* OtherComp, bool
bSelfMoved, FVector HitLocation, FVector HitNormal, FVector
NormalImpulse, const FHitResult& Hit) override;
```

7. Add this line to the character's constructor implementation:

```
MyInventory =
CreateDefaultSubobject<UInventoryComponent>("MyInventory");
```

8. Add this code to the overriden `SetupPlayerInputComponent`:

```
void AInventoryCharacter::SetupPlayerInputComponent(class
UInputComponent* InputComponent)
{
   Super::SetupPlayerInputComponent(InputComponent);
   InputComponent->BindAction("DropItem",
   EInputEvent::IE_Pressed, this,
   &AInventoryCharacter::DropItem);
}
```

9. Finally, add the following function implementations:

```
void AInventoryCharacter::DropItem()
{
   if (MyInventory->CurrentInventory.Num() == 0)
   {
     return;
```

```
  }

  AInventoryActor* Item = MyInventory-
  >CurrentInventory.Last();
  MyInventory->RemoveFromInventory(Item);
  FVector ItemOrigin;
  FVector ItemBounds;
  Item->GetActorBounds(false, ItemOrigin, ItemBounds);
  FTransform PutDownLocation = GetTransform() +
  FTransform(RootComponent->GetForwardVector() *
  ItemBounds.GetMax());
  Item->PutDown(PutDownLocation);
}


void AInventoryCharacter::NotifyHit(class UPrimitiveComponent*
MyComp, AActor* Other, class UPrimitiveComponent* OtherComp, bool
bSelfMoved, FVector HitLocation, FVector HitNormal, FVector
NormalImpulse, const FHitResult& Hit)
{
  AInventoryActor* InventoryItem =
  Cast<AInventoryActor>(Other);
  if (InventoryItem != nullptr)
  {
    TakeItem(InventoryItem);
  }
}


void AInventoryCharacter::TakeItem(AInventoryActor*
InventoryItem)
{
  InventoryItem->PickUp();
  MyInventory->AddToInventory(InventoryItem);
}
```

10. Compile your code and test it in the Editor. Create a new level and drag a few instances of `InventoryActor` out into your scene.

11. Refer to the _Instantiating an Actor using SpawnActor_ recipe if you need a reminder of how to override the current game mode. Add the following line to the constructor of your Game Mode from that recipe, then set your level's `GameMode` to the one you created in that recipe:

```
DefaultPawnClass = AInventoryCharacter::StaticClass();
```

12. Verify your code against the listing here before compiling and launching your project.

```cpp
#pragma once

#include "GameFramework/Character.h"
#include "InventoryComponent.h"
#include "InventoryCharacter.generated.h"

UCLASS()
class UE4COOKBOOK_API AInventoryCharacter : public
ACharacter
{
  GENERATED_BODY()

  public:
  AInventoryCharacter();
  virtual void BeginPlay() override;
  virtual void Tick( float DeltaSeconds ) override;
  virtual void SetupPlayerInputComponent(class
  UInputComponent* InputComponent) override;

  UPROPERTY()
  UInventoryComponent* MyInventory;
  UPROPERTY()
  UCameraComponent* MainCamera;
  UFUNCTION()
  void TakeItem(AInventoryActor* InventoryItem);
  UFUNCTION()
  void DropItem();
  void MoveForward(float AxisValue);
  void MoveRight(float AxisValue);
  void PitchCamera(float AxisValue);
  void YawCamera(float AxisValue);

  UFUNCTION()
  virtual void NotifyHit(class UPrimitiveComponent* MyComp,
  AActor* Other, class UPrimitiveComponent* OtherComp, bool
  bSelfMoved, FVector HitLocation, FVector HitNormal,
  FVector NormalImpulse, const FHitResult& Hit) override;
  private:
  FVector MovementInput;
  FVector CameraInput;
};

#include "UE4Cookbook.h"
```

```cpp
#include "InventoryCharacter.h"

AInventoryCharacter::AInventoryCharacter()
:Super()
{
  PrimaryActorTick.bCanEverTick = true;
  MyInventory =
  CreateDefaultSubobject<UInventoryComponent>
  ("MyInventory");
  MainCamera = CreateDefaultSubobject<UCameraComponent>
  ("MainCamera");
  MainCamera->bUsePawnControlRotation = 0;
}

void AInventoryCharacter::BeginPlay()
{
  Super::BeginPlay();
  MainCamera->AttachTo(RootComponent);
}

void AInventoryCharacter::Tick( float DeltaTime )
{
  Super::Tick( DeltaTime );
  if (!MovementInput.IsZero())
  {
    MovementInput *= 100;
    FVector InputVector = FVector(0,0,0);
    InputVector += GetActorForwardVector()* MovementInput.X
    * DeltaTime;
    InputVector += GetActorRightVector()* MovementInput.Y *
    DeltaTime;
    GetCharacterMovement()->AddInputVector(InputVector);
    GEngine->AddOnScreenDebugMessage(-1, 1, FColor::Red,
    FString::Printf(TEXT("x- %f, y - %f, z -
    %f"),InputVector.X, InputVector.Y, InputVector.Z));
  }

  if (!CameraInput.IsNearlyZero())
  {
    FRotator NewRotation = GetActorRotation();
    NewRotation.Pitch += CameraInput.Y;
    NewRotation.Yaw += CameraInput.X;
    APlayerController* MyPlayerController
    =Cast<APlayerController>(GetController());
    if (MyPlayerController != nullptr)
```

```
      {
        MyPlayerController->AddYawInput(CameraInput.X);
        MyPlayerController->AddPitchInput(CameraInput.Y);
      }
      SetActorRotation(NewRotation);
  }
}
void AInventoryCharacter::SetupPlayerInputComponent(class
UInputComponent* InputComponent)
{
  Super::SetupPlayerInputComponent(InputComponent);
  InputComponent->BindAxis("MoveForward", this,
  &AInventoryCharacter::MoveForward);
  InputComponent->BindAxis("MoveRight", this,
  &AInventoryCharacter::MoveRight);
  InputComponent->BindAxis("CameraPitch", this,
  &AInventoryCharacter::PitchCamera);
  InputComponent->BindAxis("CameraYaw", this,
  &AInventoryCharacter::YawCamera);
  InputComponent->BindAction("DropItem",
  EInputEvent::IE_Pressed, this,
  &AInventoryCharacter::DropItem);
}
void AInventoryCharacter::DropItem()
{
  if (MyInventory->CurrentInventory.Num() == 0)
  {
    return;
  }
  AInventoryActor* Item = MyInventory
  ->CurrentInventory.Last();
  MyInventory->RemoveFromInventory(Item);
  FVector ItemOrigin;
  FVector ItemBounds;
  Item->GetActorBounds(false, ItemOrigin, ItemBounds);
  FTransform PutDownLocation = GetTransform() +
  FTransform(RootComponent->GetForwardVector() *
  ItemBounds.GetMax());
  Item->PutDown(PutDownLocation);
}


void AInventoryCharacter::MoveForward(float AxisValue)
{
  MovementInput.X = FMath::Clamp<float>(AxisValue, -1.0f,
  1.0f);
```

```cpp
}

void AInventoryCharacter::MoveRight(float AxisValue)
{
  MovementInput.Y = FMath::Clamp<float>(AxisValue, -1.0f,
  1.0f);
}

void AInventoryCharacter::PitchCamera(float AxisValue)
{
  CameraInput.Y = AxisValue;
}
void AInventoryCharacter::YawCamera(float AxisValue)
{
  CameraInput.X = AxisValue;
}
void AInventoryCharacter::NotifyHit(class
UPrimitiveComponent* MyComp, AActor* Other, class
UPrimitiveComponent* OtherComp, bool bSelfMoved, FVector
HitLocation, FVector HitNormal, FVector NormalImpulse,
const FHitResult& Hit)
{
  AInventoryActor* InventoryItem =
  Cast<AInventoryActor>(Other);
  if (InventoryItem != nullptr)
  {
    TakeItem(InventoryItem);
  }
}
void AInventoryCharacter::TakeItem(AInventoryActor*
InventoryItem)
{
  InventoryItem->PickUp();
  MyInventory->AddToInventory(InventoryItem);
}

#pragma once

#include "Components/ActorComponent.h"
#include "InventoryActor.h"
#include "InventoryComponent.generated.h"

UCLASS( ClassGroup=(Custom),
meta=(BlueprintSpawnableComponent))
```

```cpp
class UE4COOKBOOK_API UInventoryComponent : public
UActorComponent
{
  GENERATED_BODY()

  public:
  UInventoryComponent();
  virtual void TickComponent( float DeltaTime, ELevelTick
  TickType, FActorComponentTickFunction* ThisTickFunction )
  override;

  UPROPERTY()
  TArray<AInventoryActor*> CurrentInventory;
  UFUNCTION()
  int32 AddToInventory(AInventoryActor* ActorToAdd);

  UFUNCTION()
  void RemoveFromInventory(AInventoryActor* ActorToRemove);
};
#include "UE4Cookbook.h"
#include "InventoryComponent.h"

UInventoryComponent::UInventoryComponent()
{
  bWantsBeginPlay = true;
  PrimaryComponentTick.bCanEverTick = true;
}
void UInventoryComponent::TickComponent( float DeltaTime,
ELevelTick TickType, FActorComponentTickFunction*
ThisTickFunction )
{
  Super::TickComponent( DeltaTime, TickType,
  ThisTickFunction );
}

int32 UInventoryComponent::AddToInventory(AInventoryActor*
ActorToAdd)
{
  return CurrentInventory.Add(ActorToAdd);
}

void UInventoryComponent::RemoveFromInventory
(AInventoryActor* ActorToRemove)
{
  CurrentInventory.Remove(ActorToRemove);
}

#pragma once

#include "GameFramework/GameMode.h"
```

```
#include "UE4CookbookGameMode.generated.h"

UCLASS()
class UE4COOKBOOK_API AUE4CookbookGameMode : public
AGameMode
{
  GENERATED_BODY()

  public:
  AUE4CookbookGameMode();
  };

#include "UE4Cookbook.h"
#include "MyGameState.h"
#include "InventoryCharacter.h"
#include "UE4CookbookGameMode.h"

AUE4CookbookGameMode::AUE4CookbookGameMode()
{
  DefaultPawnClass = AInventoryCharacter::StaticClass();
  GameStateClass = AMyGameState::StaticClass();
}
```

13. Lastly, we need to add our InputAction to the bindings in the editor. To do this, bring up the **Project Settings...** window by selecting **Edit | Project Settings...**:

Then, select **Input** on the left-hand side. Select the plus symbol beside **Action Mappings,** and type `DropItem` into the text box that appears. Underneath it is a list of all the potential keys you can bind to this action. Select the one labelled `E`. Your settings should now look like the following:

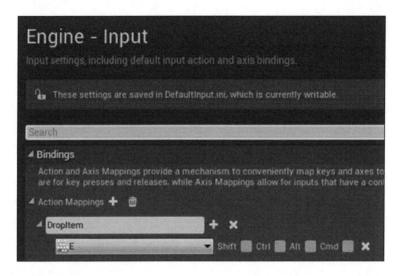

14. Then we can hit play, walk over to our inventory actor, and it will be picked up. Press *E* to place the actor in a new location! Test this with multiple inventory actors to see that they all get collected and placed correctly.

How it works...

1. Our new component contains an array of actors, storing them by pointer as well as declaring functions that add or remove items to the array. These functions are simple wrappers around the `TArray` add/remove functionality, but allow us to optionally do things such as checking if the array is within a specified size limit before going ahead with storing the item.

2. `InventoryActor` is a base class that can be used for all items that can be taken by a player.

3. In the `PickUp` function, we need to disable the actor when it is picked up. To do that, we have to do the following:

   - Disable actor ticking

   - Hide the actor

   - Disable collision

4. We do this with the functions `SetActorTickEnabled`, `SetActorHiddenInGame`, and `SetActorEnableCollision`.

5. The `PutDown` function is the reverse. We enable actor ticking, unhide the actor, and then turn its collision back on, and we transport the actor to the desired location.

6. We add an `InventoryComponent` to our new character as well as a function to take items.

7. In the constructor for our character, we create a default subobject for our `InventoryComponent`.

8. We also add a `NotifyHit` override so that we are notified when the character hits other Actors.

9. Inside this function, we cast the other actor to an `InventoryActor`. If the cast is successful, then we know our `Actor` was an `InventoryActor`, and so we can call the `TakeItem` function to take it.

10. In the `TakeItem` function, we notify the Inventory item actor that we want to pick it up, then we add it to our inventory.

11. The last piece of functionality in the `InventoryCharacter` is the `DropItem` function. This function checks if we have any items in our inventory. If it has any items, we remove it from our inventory, then we calculate a safe distance in front of our player character to drop the item using the Item Bounds to get its maximum bounding box dimension.

12. We then inform the item that we are placing it in the world at the desired location.

See also

▶ *Chapter 5, Handling Events and Delegates,* has a detailed explanation of how events and input handling work together within the Engine, as well as a recipe for the `SimpleCharacter` class mentioned in this recipe

▶ *Chapter 6, Input and Collision,* also has recipes concerning the binding of input actions and axes

Creating an OrbitingMovement Component

This component is similar to `RotatingMovementComponent` in that it is designed to make the components parented to it move in a particular way. In this instance, it will move any attached components in an orbit around a fixed point at a fixed distance.

This could be used, for example, for a shield that orbits around a character in an **Action RPG**.

How to do it...

1. Create a new `SceneComponent` subclass and add the following properties to the class declaration:

```
UPROPERTY()
bool RotateToFaceOutwards;
UPROPERTY()
float RotationSpeed;
UPROPERTY()
float OrbitDistance;
float CurrentValue;
```

2. Add the following to the constructor:

```
RotationSpeed = 5;
OrbitDistance = 100;
CurrentValue = 0;
RotateToFaceOutwards = true;
```

3. Add the following code to the `TickComponent` function:

```
float CurrentValueInRadians =
FMath::DegreesToRadians<float>(CurrentValue);
SetRelativeLocation(FVector(OrbitDistance *
FMath::Cos(CurrentValueInRadians), OrbitDistance *
FMath::Sin(CurrentValueInRadians), RelativeLocation.Z));
if (RotateToFaceOutwards)
{
  FVector LookDir = (RelativeLocation).GetSafeNormal();
  FRotator LookAtRot = LookDir.Rotation();
  SetRelativeRotation(LookAtRot);
}
CurrentValue = FMath::Fmod(CurrentValue + (RotationSpeed*
DeltaTime) ,360);
```

4. Verify your work against the following listing:

```
#pragma once
#include "Components/SceneComponent.h"
#include "OrbitingMovementComponent.generated.h"

UCLASS( ClassGroup=(Custom),
meta=(BlueprintSpawnableComponent) )
class UE4COOKBOOK_API UOrbitingMovementComponent : public
USceneComponent
{
  GENERATED_BODY()
  public:
```

```
  // Sets default values for this component's properties
  UOrbitingMovementComponent();

  // Called when the game starts
  virtual void BeginPlay() override;
  // Called every frame
  virtual void TickComponent( float DeltaTime, ELevelTick
  TickType, FActorComponentTickFunction* ThisTickFunction )
  override;

  UPROPERTY()
  bool RotateToFaceOutwards;
  UPROPERTY()
  float RotationSpeed;
  UPROPERTY()
  float OrbitDistance;
  float CurrentValue;
};
#include "UE4Cookbook.h"
#include "OrbitingMovementComponent.h"
// Sets default values for this component's properties
UOrbitingMovementComponent::UOrbitingMovementComponent()
{
  // Set this component to be initialized when the game
  starts, and to be ticked every frame. You can turn these
  features
  // off to improve performance if you don't need them.
  bWantsBeginPlay = true;
  PrimaryComponentTick.bCanEverTick = true;
  RotationSpeed = 5;
  OrbitDistance = 100;
  CurrentValue = 0;
  RotateToFaceOutwards = true;
  //...
}

// Called when the game starts
void UOrbitingMovementComponent::BeginPlay()
{
  Super::BeginPlay();
  //...
}
// Called every frame
```

```
void UOrbitingMovementComponent::TickComponent( float
DeltaTime, ELevelTick TickType,
FActorComponentTickFunction* ThisTickFunction )
{
  Super::TickComponent( DeltaTime, TickType,
  ThisTickFunction );
  float CurrentValueInRadians =
  FMath::DegreesToRadians<float>(CurrentValue);
  SetRelativeLocation(
  FVector(OrbitDistance * FMath::Cos
  (CurrentValueInRadians),
  OrbitDistance * FMath::Sin(CurrentValueInRadians),
  RelativeLocation.Z));
  if (RotateToFaceOutwards)
  {
    FVector LookDir = (RelativeLocation).GetSafeNormal();
    FRotator LookAtRot = LookDir.Rotation();
    SetRelativeRotation(LookAtRot);
  }
  CurrentValue = FMath::Fmod(CurrentValue + (RotationSpeed*
  DeltaTime) ,360);
  //...
}
```

5. You can test this component by creating a simple `Actor` Blueprint.

6. Add an `OrbitingMovement` Component to your `Actor`, then add a few meshes using the `Cube` component. Parent them to the `OrbitingMovement` component by dragging them on to it in the **Components** panel. The resulting hierarchy should look like the following:

7. Refer to the *Creating a custom Actor Component* recipe if you're unsure of the process.

8. Hit play to see the meshes moving around in a circular pattern around the center of the `Actor`.

How it works...

1. The properties that are added to the component are the basic parameters that we use to customize the circular motion of the component.

2. `RotateToFaceOutwards` specifies whether the component will orient to face away from the center of rotation on every update. `RotationSpeed` is the number of degrees the component rotates every second.

3. `OrbitDistance` indicates the distance that the components that rotate must be moved from the origin. `CurrentValue` is the current rotation position in degrees.

4. Inside our constructor, we establish some sane defaults for our new component.

5. In the `TickComponent` function, we calculate the location and rotation of our component.

6. The formula in the next step requires our angles to be expressed in radians rather than degrees. Radians describe an angle in terms of π. We first use the `DegreesToRadians` function to convert our current value in degrees to radians.

7. The `SetRelativeLocation` function uses the general equation for circular motion, that is—$Pos(\theta) = cos(\theta \text{ in radians}), sin(\theta \text{ in radians})$. We preserve the Z axis position of each object.

8. The next step is to rotate the object back towards the origin (or else, directly away from it). This is only calculated if `RotateToFaceOutwards` is `true`, and involves getting the relative offset of the component to its parent, and creating a rotator based on a vector pointing from the parent to the current relative offset. We then set the relative rotation to the resulting rotator.

9. Lastly, we increment the current value in degrees so that it moves `RotationSpeed` units per second, clamping the resulting value between 0 and 360 to allow the rotation to loop.

Creating a building that spawns units

For this recipe, we will create a building that spawns units at a fixed time interval at a particular location.

How to do it...

1. Create a new `Actor` subclass in the editor, as always, and then add the following implementation to the class:

```
UPROPERTY()
UStaticMeshComponent* BuildingMesh;
UPROPERTY()
UParticleSystemComponent* SpawnPoint;

UPROPERTY()
UClass* UnitToSpawn;

UPROPERTY()
float SpawnInterval;

UFUNCTION()
void SpawnUnit();

UFUNCTION()
void EndPlay(const EEndPlayReason::Type EndPlayReason)
override;

UPROPERTY()
FTimerHandle SpawnTimerHandle;
```

2. Add the following to the constructor:

```
BuildingMesh =
CreateDefaultSubobject<UStaticMeshComponent>("BuildingMesh"
);
SpawnPoint =
CreateDefaultSubobject<UParticleSystemComponent>("SpawnPoin
t");
SpawnInterval = 10;
auto MeshAsset =
ConstructorHelpers::FObjectFinder<UStaticMesh>(TEXT("Static
Mesh'/Engine/BasicShapes/Cube.Cube'"));
if (MeshAsset.Object != nullptr)
{
  BuildingMesh->SetStaticMesh(MeshAsset.Object);
  BuildingMesh->SetCollisionProfileName(UCollisionProfile
  ::Pawn_ProfileName);

}
auto ParticleSystem =
```

```
ConstructorHelpers::FObjectFinder<UParticleSystem>(TEXT("Pa
rticleSystem'/Engine/Tutorial/SubEditors/TutorialAssets/Tut
orialParticleSystem.TutorialParticleSystem'"));
if (ParticleSystem.Object != nullptr)
{
   SpawnPoint->SetTemplate(ParticleSystem.Object);
}
SpawnPoint->SetRelativeScale3D(FVector(0.5, 0.5, 0.5));
UnitToSpawn = ABarracksUnit::StaticClass();
```

3. Add the following to the `BeginPlay` function:

```
RootComponent = BuildingMesh;
SpawnPoint->AttachTo(RootComponent);
SpawnPoint->SetRelativeLocation(FVector(150, 0, 0));
GetWorld()->GetTimerManager().SetTimer(SpawnTimerHandle,
this, &ABarracks::SpawnUnit, SpawnInterval, true);
```

4. Create the implementation for the `SpawnUnit` function:

```
void ABarracks::SpawnUnit()
{
   FVector SpawnLocation = SpawnPoint
   ->GetComponentLocation();
   GetWorld()->SpawnActor(UnitToSpawn, &SpawnLocation);
}
```

5. Implement the overridden `EndPlay` function:

```
void ABarracks::EndPlay(const EEndPlayReason::Type
EndPlayReason)
{
   Super::EndPlay(EndPlayReason);
   GetWorld()
   ->GetTimerManager().ClearTimer(SpawnTimerHandle);
}
```

6. Next, create a new character subclass, and add one property:

```
UPROPERTY()
UParticleSystemComponent* VisualRepresentation;
```

7. Initialize the component in the constructor implementation:

```
VisualRepresentation =
CreateDefaultSubobject<UParticleSystemComponent>("SpawnPoin
t");
auto ParticleSystem =
ConstructorHelpers::FObjectFinder<UParticleSystem>(TEXT("Pa
rticleSystem'/Engine/Tutorial/SubEditors/TutorialAssets/Tut
orialParticleSystem.TutorialParticleSystem'"));
```

```
if (ParticleSystem.Object != nullptr)
{
  SpawnPoint->SetTemplate(ParticleSystem.Object);
}
SpawnPoint->SetRelativeScale3D(FVector(0.5, 0.5, 0.5));
SpawnCollisionHandlingMethod =
ESpawnActorCollisionHandlingMethod::AlwaysSpawn;
```

8. Attach the visual representation to the root component:

```
void ABarracksUnit::BeginPlay()
{
  Super::BeginPlay();
  SpawnPoint->AttachTo(RootComponent);
}
```

9. Lastly, add the following to the `Tick` function to get the spawned actor moving:

```
SetActorLocation(GetActorLocation() + FVector(10, 0, 0));
```

10. Verify against the following snippet, then compile your project. Place a copy of the barracks actor into the level. You can then observe it spawning the character at fixed intervals:

```
#pragma once
#include "GameFramework/Actor.h"
#include "Barracks.generated.h"
UCLASS()
class UE4COOKBOOK_API ABarracks : public AActor
{
  GENERATED_BODY()
  public:
  ABarracks();
  virtual void BeginPlay() override;
  virtual void Tick( float DeltaSeconds ) override;

  UPROPERTY()
  UStaticMeshComponent* BuildingMesh;
  UPROPERTY()
  UParticleSystemComponent* SpawnPoint;

  UPROPERTY()
  UClass* UnitToSpawn;

  UPROPERTY()
```

```cpp
  float SpawnInterval;

  UFUNCTION()
  void SpawnUnit();
  UFUNCTION()
  void EndPlay(const EEndPlayReason::Type EndPlayReason)
  override;

  UPROPERTY()
  FTimerHandle SpawnTimerHandle;
};

#include "UE4Cookbook.h"
#include "BarracksUnit.h"
#include "Barracks.h"

// Sets default values
ABarracks::ABarracks()
{
  // Set this actor to call Tick() every frame. You can
  turn this off to improve performance
  if you don't need it.
  PrimaryActorTick.bCanEverTick = true;
  BuildingMesh =
  CreateDefaultSubobject<UStaticMeshComponent>
  ("BuildingMesh");
  SpawnPoint =
  CreateDefaultSubobject<UParticleSystemComponent>
  ("SpawnPoint");
  SpawnInterval = 10;
  auto MeshAsset =
  ConstuctorHelpers::FObjectFinder<UStaticMesh>
  (TEXT("StaticMesh'/Engine/BasicShapes/Cube.Cube'"));
  if (MeshAsset.Object != nullptr)
  {
    BuildingMesh->SetStaticMesh(MeshAsset.Object);
    BuildingMesh->SetCollisionProfileName
    (UCollisionProfile::Pawn_ProfileName);

  }
  auto ParticleSystem =
  ConstuctorHelpers::FObjectFinder<UParticleSystem>
  (TEXT("ParticleSystem'/Engine/Tutorial
  /SubEditors/TutorialAssets
  /TutorialParticleSystem.TutorialParticleSystem'"));
  if (ParticleSystem.Object != nullptr)
```

```
    {
      SpawnPoint->SetTemplate(ParticleSystem.Object);
    }
    SpawnPoint->SetRelativeScale3D(FVector(0.5, 0.5, 0.5));
    UnitToSpawn = ABarracksUnit::StaticClass();
}
void ABarracks::BeginPlay()
{
  Super::BeginPlay();
  RootComponent = BuildingMesh;
  SpawnPoint->AttachTo(RootComponent);
  SpawnPoint->SetRelativeLocation(FVector(150, 0, 0));
  GetWorld()->GetTimerManager().SetTimer(SpawnTimerHandle,
  this, &ABarracks::SpawnUnit, SpawnInterval, true);
}

void ABarracks::Tick( float DeltaTime )
{
  Super::Tick( DeltaTime );
}
void ABarracks::SpawnUnit()
{
  FVector SpawnLocation = SpawnPoint
  ->GetComponentLocation();
  GetWorld()->SpawnActor(UnitToSpawn, &SpawnLocation);
}

void ABarracks::EndPlay(const EEndPlayReason::Type
EndPlayReason)
{
  Super::EndPlay(EndPlayReason);
  GetWorld()
  ->GetTimerManager().ClearTimer(SpawnTimerHandle);
}

#pragma once

#include "GameFramework/Character.h"
#include "BarracksUnit.generated.h"

UCLASS()
class UE4COOKBOOK_API ABarracksUnit : public ACharacter
{
  GENERATED_BODY()
```

```cpp
  public:
  ABarracksUnit();

  virtual void BeginPlay() override;
  virtual void Tick( float DeltaSeconds ) override;

  virtual void SetupPlayerInputComponent
  (class UInputComponent* InputComponent) override;

  UPROPERTY()
  UParticleSystemComponent* SpawnPoint;
};

#include "UE4Cookbook.h"
#include "BarracksUnit.h"

ABarracksUnit::ABarracksUnit()
{
  PrimaryActorTick.bCanEverTick = true;
  SpawnPoint =
  CreateDefaultSubobject<UParticleSystemComponent>
  ("SpawnPoint");
  auto ParticleSystem =
  ConstructorHelpers::FObjectFinder<UParticleSystem>
  (TEXT("ParticleSystem'/Engine/Tutorial
  /SubEditors/TutorialAssets/TutorialParticleSystem
  .TutorialParticleSystem'"));
  if (ParticleSystem.Object != nullptr)
  {
    SpawnPoint->SetTemplate(ParticleSystem.Object);
  }
  SpawnPoint->SetRelativeScale3D(FVector(0.5, 0.5, 0.5));
  SpawnCollisionHandlingMethod =
  ESpawnActorCollisionHandlingMethod::AlwaysSpawn;
}
void ABarracksUnit::BeginPlay()
{
  Super::BeginPlay();
  SpawnPoint->AttachTo(RootComponent);
}

void ABarracksUnit::Tick( float DeltaTime )
{
  Super::Tick( DeltaTime );
  SetActorLocation(GetActorLocation() + FVector(10, 0, 0));
```

```
}
void ABarracksUnit::SetupPlayerInputComponent(class
UInputComponent* InputComponent)
{
   Super::SetupPlayerInputComponent(InputComponent);
}
```

How it works...

1. Firstly, we create the barracks actor. We add a particle system component to indicate where the new units will be spawning, and a static mesh for the visual representation of the building.

2. In the constructor, we initialize the components, and then set their values using `FObjectFinder`. We also set the class to spawn using the `StaticClass` function to retrieve a `UClass*` instance from a class type.

3. In the `BeginPlay` function of the barracks, we create a timer that calls our `SpawnUnit` function at fixed intervals. We store the timer handle in a member variable in the class so that when our instance is being destroyed, we can halt the timer; otherwise, when the timer triggers again, we'll encounter a crash where the object pointer is dereferenced.

4. The `SpawnUnit` function gets the world space location of the `SpawnPoint` object, then asks the world to spawn an instance of our unit class at that location.

5. `BarracksUnit` has code in its `Tick()` function to move forward by 10 units every frame so that each spawned unit will move to make room for the next one.

6. The `EndPlay` function override calls the parent class implementation of the function, which is important if there are timers to cancel or deinitialization performed in the parent class. It then uses the timer handle stored in `BeginPlay` in order to cancel the timer.

5

Handling Events and Delegates

Unreal uses events for notifying classes about things that happen in the game world in an efficient manner. Events and delegates are useful to ensure that these notifications can be issued in a way which minimizes class coupling, and allows arbitrary classes to subscribe to be notified.

We will cover the following recipes in this chapter:

- Handling events implemented via virtual functions
- Creating a delegate that is bound to a UFUNCTION
- Unregistering a delegate
- Creating a delegate that takes input parameters
- Passing payload data with a delegate binding
- Creating a multicast delegate
- Creating a custom Event
- Creating a Time of Day handler
- Creating a respawning pickup for an First Person Shooter

Handling events implemented via virtual functions

Some `Actor` and `Component` classes provided with Unreal include event handlers in the form of virtual functions. This recipe will show you how to customize those handlers by overriding the virtual function in question.

How to do it...

1. Create an empty `Actor` in the Editor. Call it `MyTriggerVolume`.

2. Add the following code to the class header:

```
UPROPERTY()
UBoxComponent* TriggerZone;

UFUNCTION()
virtual void NotifyActorBeginOverlap(AActor* OtherActor)
override;
UFUNCTION()
virtual void NotifyActorEndOverlap(AActor* OtherActor)
override;
```

3. Add the implementation for the preceding functions to the cpp file:

```
void AMyTriggerVolume::NotifyActorBeginOverlap(AActor*
OtherActor)
{
  GEngine->AddOnScreenDebugMessage(-1, 1, FColor::Red,
  FString::Printf(TEXT("%s entered me"),
  *(OtherActor->GetName()))));
}

void AMyTriggerVolume::NotifyActorEndOverlap(AActor*
OtherActor)
{
  GEngine->AddOnScreenDebugMessage(-1, 1, FColor::Red,
  FString::Printf(TEXT("%s left me"), *(OtherActor-
  >GetName()))));
}
```

4. Compile your project, and place an instance of `MyTriggerActor` into the level. Verify that overlap/touch events are handled by walking into the volume, and seeing the output printed to the screen:

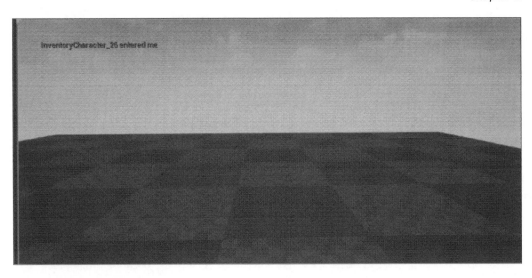

How it works...

1. As always, we first declare a UPROPERTY to hold a reference to our component subobject. We then create two UFUNCTION declarations. These are marked as virtual and override so that the compiler understands we want to replace the parent implementation, and that our function implementations can be replaced in turn.

2. In the implementation of the functions, we use FString::printf to create an FString from some preset text, and substitute some data parameters.

3. Note that the FString OtherActor->GetName() returns, and is dereferenced using the * operator before being passed into FString::Format. Not doing this results in an error.

4. This FString is then passed to a global engine function, AddOnScreenDebugMessage.

5. The first argument of -1 tells the engine that duplicate strings are allowed, the second parameter is the length of time the message should be displayed for in seconds, the third argument is the color, and the fourth is the actual string to print itself.

6. Now when a component of our actor overlaps something else, its UpdateOverlaps function will call NotifyActorBeginOverlap, and the virtual function dispatch will call our custom implementation.

Creating a delegate that is bound to a UFUNCTION

Delegates allow us to call a function without knowing which function is assigned. They are a safer version of a raw function pointer. This recipe shows you how to associate a UFUNCTION to a delegate so that it is called when the delegate is executed.

Getting ready

Ensure you've followed the previous recipe in order to create a `TriggerVolume` class.

How to do it...

1. Inside our `GameMode` header, declare the delegate with the following macro, just before the class declaration:

```
DECLARE_DELEGATE(FStandardDelegateSignature)
UCLASS()
class UE4COOKBOOK_API AUE4CookbookGameMode : public
AGameMode
```

2. Add a new member to our game mode:

```
FStandardDelegateSignature MyStandardDelegate;
```

3. Create a new `Actor` class called `DelegateListener`. Add the following to the declaration of that class:

```
UFUNCTION()
void EnableLight();

UPROPERTY()
UPointLightComponent* PointLight;
```

4. In the class implementation, add this to the constructor:

```
PointLight =
CreateDefaultSubobject<UPointLightComponent>("PointLight");
RootComponent = PointLight;
PointLight->SetVisibility(false);
```

5. In the `DelegateListener.cpp` file, add `#include "UE4CookbookGameMode.h"` between your project's `include` file and the `DelegateListener` header include. Inside the `DelegateListener::BeginPlay` implementation, add the following:

```
Super::BeginPlay();
if (TheWorld != nullptr)
{
  AGameMode* GameMode =
  UGameplayStatics::GetGameMode(TheWorld);
  AUE4CookbookGameMode * MyGameMode =
  Cast<AUE4CookbookGameMode>(GameMode);
  if (MyGameMode != nullptr)
  {
    MyGameMode->MyStandardDelegate.BindUObject(this,
    &ADelegateListener::EnableLight);
  }
}
```

6. Lastly, implement `EnableLight`:

```
void ADelegateListener::EnableLight()
{
  PointLight->SetVisibility(true);
}
```

7. Put the following code in our TriggerVolume's `NotifyActorBeginOverlap` function:

```
UWorld* TheWorld = GetWorld();
if (TheWorld != nullptr)
{
  AGameMode* GameMode =
  UGameplayStatics::GetGameMode(TheWorld);
  AUE4CookbookGameMode * MyGameMode =
  Cast<AUE4CookbookGameMode>(GameMode);
  MyGameMode->MyStandardDelegate.ExecuteIfBound();
}
```

8. Be sure to add `#include "UE4CookbookGameMode.h"` to your CPP file too so that the compiler knows about the class before we use it.

9. Compile your game. Make sure that your game mode is set in the current level (refer to the *Instantiating an Actor using SpawnActor* recipe in *Chapter 4, Actors and Components* if you don't know how), and drag a copy of your TriggerVolume out into the level. Also, drag a copy of `DelegateListener` out into the level, and place it about 100 units above a flat surface:

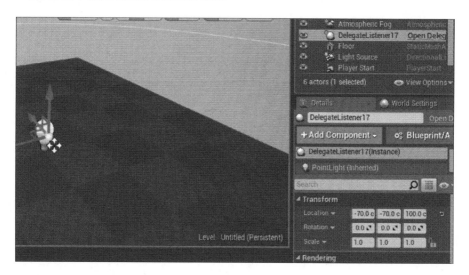

10. When you hit **Play**, and walk into the area covered by the Trigger volume, you should see the `PointLight` component, which we added to `DelegateListener`, turn on:

How it works...

1. Inside our GameMode header, we declare a type of delegate that doesn't take any parameters, called FTriggerHitSignature.

2. We then create an instance of the delegate as a member of our GameMode class.

3. We add a PointLight component inside DelegateListener so that we have a visual representation of the delegate being executed.

4. In the constructor, we initialize our PointLight, then disable it.

5. We override BeginPlay. We first call the parent class's implementation of BeginPlay(). Then we get the game world, retrieving the GameMode class using GetGameMode().

6. Casting the resulting AGameMode* to a pointer of our GameMode class requires the use of the Cast template function.

7. We can then access the delegate instance member of the GameMode, and bind our EnableLight function to the delegate, so it will be called when the delegate is executed.

8. In this case, we are binding to UFUNCTION(), so we use BindUObject. If we wanted to bind to a plain C++ class function, we would have used BindRaw. If we want to bind to a static function, we will use BindStatic().

9. When TriggerVolume overlaps the player, it retrieves GameMode, then calls ExecuteIfBound on the delegate.

10. ExecuteIfBound checks that there's a function bound to the delegate, and then invokes it for us.

11. The EnableLight function enables the PointLight component when invoked by the delegate object.

See also

▶ The next section, *Unregistering a delegate,* shows you how to safely unregister your delegate binding in the event of the Listener being destroyed before the delegate is called

Unregistering a delegate

Sometimes, it is necessary to remove a delegate binding. This is like setting a function pointer to nullptr so that it no longer references an object that has been deleted.

Getting ready

You'll need to follow the previous recipe in order for you to have a delegate to unregister.

How to do it...

1. In `DelegateListener`, add the following overridden function declaration:

```
UFUNCTION()
virtual void EndPlay(constEEndPlayReason::Type
EndPlayReason) override;
```

2. Implement the function like this:

```
void ADelegateListener::EndPlay(constEEndPlayReason::Type
EndPlayReason)
{
  Super::EndPlay(EndPlayReason);
  UWorld* TheWorld = GetWorld();
  if (TheWorld != nullptr)
  {
    AGameMode* GameMode =
    UGameplayStatics::GetGameMode(TheWorld);
    AUE4CookbookGameMode * MyGameMode =
    Cast<AUE4CookbookGameMode>(GameMode);
    if (MyGameMode != nullptr)
    {
      MyGameMode->MyStandardDelegate.Unbind();
    }
  }
}
```

How it works...

1. This recipe combines both of the previous recipes in this chapter so far. We override `EndPlay`, which is an event implemented as a virtual function, so that we can execute code when our `DelegateListener` leaves play.

2. In that overridden implementation, we call the `Unbind()` method on the delegate, which unlinks the member function from the `DelegateListener` instance.

3. Without this being done, the delegate dangles like a pointer, leaving it in an invalid state when the `DelegateListener` leaves the game.

Creating a delegate that takes input parameters

So far, the delegates that we've used haven't taken any input parameters. This recipe shows you how to change the signature of the delegate so that it accepts some input.

Getting ready

Be sure you've followed the recipe at the beginning of this chapter, which shows you how to create a `TriggerVolume` and the other infrastructure that we require for this recipe.

How to do it...

1. Add a new delegate declaration to `GameMode`:

```
DECLARE_DELEGATE_OneParam(FParamDelegateSignature,
FLinearColor)
```

2. Add a new member to `GameMode`:

```
FParamDelegateSignatureMyParameterDelegate;
```

3. Create a new `Actor` class called `ParamDelegateListener`. Add the following to the declaration:

```
UFUNCTION()
void SetLightColor(FLinearColorLightColor);
UPROPERTY()
UPointLightComponent* PointLight;
```

4. In the class implementation, add this to the constructor:

```
PointLight =
CreateDefaultSubobject<UPointLightComponent>("PointLight");
RootComponent = PointLight;
```

5. In the `ParamDelegateListener.cpp` file, add `#include "UE4CookbookGameMode.h"` between your project's `include` file and the `ParamDelegateListener` header include. Inside the `ParamDelegateListener::BeginPlay` implementation, add the following:

```
Super::BeginPlay();
UWorld* TheWorld = GetWorld();
if (TheWorld != nullptr)
{
  AGameMode* GameMode =
  UGameplayStatics::GetGameMode(TheWorld);
  AUE4CookbookGameMode * MyGameMode =
  Cast<AUE4CookbookGameMode>(GameMode);
  if (MyGameMode != nullptr)
  {
    MyGameMode->MyParameterDelegate.BindUObject(this,
    &AParamDelegateListener::SetLightColor);
  }
}
```

6. Lastly, implement `SetLightColor`:

```
void AParamDelegateListener::SetLightColor
(FLinearColorLightColor)
{
    PointLight->SetLightColor(LightColor);
}
```

7. Inside our `TriggerVolume`, in `NotifyActorBeginOverlap`, add the following line after the call to `MyStandardDelegate.ExecuteIfBound`:

```
MyGameMode
->MyParameterDelegate.ExecuteIfBound(FLinearColor(1, 0, 0,
1));
```

How it works...

1. Our new delegate signature uses a slightly different macro for declaration. Note the `_OneParam` suffix at the end of `DECLARE_DELEGATE_OneParam`. As you'd expect, we also need to specify what type our parameter will be.

2. Just like when we created a delegate without parameters, we need to create an instance of the delegate as a member of our `GameMode` class.

3. We now create a new type of `DelegateListener`, one that is expecting a parameter to be passed into the function that it binds to the delegate.

4. When we call the `ExecuteIfBound()` method for the delegate, we now need to pass in the value that will be inserted into the function parameter.

5. Inside the function that we have bound, we use the parameter to set the color of our light.

6. This means that `TriggerVolume` doesn't need to know anything about the `ParamDelegateListener` in order to call functions on it. The delegate has allowed us to minimize coupling between the two classes.

See also

▸ The *Unregistering a delegate* recipe shows you how to safely unregister your delegate binding in the event of the Listener being destroyed before the delegate is called

Passing payload data with a delegate binding

With only minimal changes, parameters can be passed through to a delegate at creation time. This recipe shows you how to specify data to be always passed as parameters to a delegate invocation. The data is calculated when the binding is created, and doesn't change from that point forward.

Getting ready

Be sure you've followed the previous recipe. We will be extending the functionality of the previous recipe to pass additional creation-time parameters to our bound delegate function.

How to do it...

1. Inside your `AParamDelegateListener::BeginPlay` function, change the call to `BindUObject` to the following:

```
MyGameMode->MyParameterDelegate.BindUObject(this,
&AParamDelegateListener::SetLightColor, false);
```

2. Change the declaration of `SetLightColor` to this:

```
void SetLightColor(FLinearColorLightColor, bool
EnableLight);
```

3. Alter the implementation of `SetLightColor` as follows:

```
void AParamDelegateListener::SetLightColor
(FLinearColorLightColor, bool EnableLight)
{
   PointLight->SetLightColor(LightColor);
   PointLight->SetVisibility(EnableLight);
}
```

4. Compile and run your project. Verify that when you walk into `TriggerVolume`, the light turns off because of the false payload parameter passed in when you bound the function.

How it works...

1. When we bind the function to the delegate, we specify some additional data (in this case, a Boolean of value `false`). You can pass up to four 'payload' variables in this fashion. They are applied to your function after any parameters declared in the `DECLARE_DELEGATE_*` macro that you used.

2. We change the function signature of our delegate so that it can accept the extra argument.

3. Inside the function, we use the extra argument to turn the light on or off depending on the value being true or false at compile time.

4. We don't need to change the call to `ExecuteIfBound`—the delegate system automatically applies the delegate parameters, passed in through `ExecuteIfBound`, first. It then applies any payload parameters, which are always specified after the function reference in a call to `BindUObject`.

See also

▸ The recipe *Unregistering a delegate* shows you how to safely unregister your delegate binding in the event of the Listener being destroyed before the delegate is called

Creating a multicast delegate

The standard delegates used so far in this chapter are essentially a function pointer—they allow you to call one particular function on one particular object instance. Multicast delegates are a collection of function pointers, each potentially on different objects, that will all be invoked when the delegate is **broadcast**.

Getting ready

This recipe assumes you have followed the initial recipe in the chapter, as it shows you how to create `TriggerVolume` that is used to broadcast the multicast delegate.

How to do it...

1. Add a new delegate declaration to the `GameMode` header:

   ```
   DECLARE_MULTICAST_DELEGATE(FMulticastDelegateSignature)
   ```

2. Create a new `Actor` class called `MulticastDelegateListener`. Add the following to the declaration:

   ```
   UFUNCTION()
   void ToggleLight();
   UFUNCTION()
   virtual void EndPlay(constEEndPlayReason::Type EndPlayReason)
   override;

   UPROPERTY()
   UPointLightComponent* PointLight;

   FDelegateHandleMyDelegateHandle;
   ```

3. In the class implementation, add this to the constructor:

   ```
   PointLight =
   CreateDefaultSubobject<UPointLightComponent>("PointLight");
   RootComponent = PointLight;
   ```

4. In the `MulticastDelegateListener.cpp` file, add `#include "UE4CookbookGameMode.h"` between your project's `include` file and the `MulticastDelegateListener` header include. Inside the `MulticastDelegateListener::BeginPlay` implementation, add the following:

```
Super::BeginPlay();
UWorld* TheWorld = GetWorld();
if (TheWorld != nullptr)
{
  AGameMode* GameMode =
  UGameplayStatics::GetGameMode(TheWorld);
  AUE4CookbookGameMode * MyGameMode =
  Cast<AUE4CookbookGameMode>(GameMode);
  if (MyGameMode != nullptr)
  {
    MyDelegateHandle  = MyGameMode-
    >MyMulticastDelegate.AddUObject(this,
    &AMulticastDelegateListener::ToggleLight);
  }
}
```

5. Implement `ToggleLight`:

```
void AMulticastDelegateListener::ToggleLight()
{
  PointLight->ToggleVisibility();
}
```

6. Implement our `EndPlay` overridden function:

```
void AMulticastDelegateListener::EndPlay
(constEEndPlayReason::Type EndPlayReason)
{
  Super::EndPlay(EndPlayReason);
  UWorld* TheWorld = GetWorld();
  if (TheWorld != nullptr)
  {
    AGameMode* GameMode =
    UGameplayStatics::GetGameMode(TheWorld);
    AUE4CookbookGameMode * MyGameMode =
    Cast<AUE4CookbookGameMode>(GameMode);
    if (MyGameMode != nullptr)
    {
      MyGameMode-
      >MyMulticastDelegate.Remove(MyDelegateHandle);
    }
  }
}
```

7. Add the following line to `TriggerVolume::NotifyActorBeginOverlap()`:

    `MyGameMode->MyMulticastDelegate.Broadcast();`

8. Compile and load your project. Set the `GameMode` in your level to be our cookbook game mode, then drag four or five instances of the `MulticastDelegateListener` into the scene.

9. Step into `TriggerVolume` to see all the `MulticastDelegateListener` toggle their light's visibility.

How it works...

1. As you might expect, the delegate type needs to be explicitly declared as a multicast delegate rather than a standard single-binding one.

2. Our new `Listener` class is very similar to our original `DelegateListener`. The primary difference is that we need to store a reference to our delegate instance in `FDelegateHandle`.

3. When the actor is destroyed, we safely remove ourselves from the list of functions bound to the delegate by using the stored `FDelegateHandle` as a parameter to `Remove()`.

4. The `Broadcast()` function is the multicast equivalent of `ExecuteIfBound()`. Unlike standard delegates, there is no need to check if the delegate is bound either in advance or with a call like `ExecuteIfBound`. `Broadcast()` is safe to run no matter how many functions are bound, or even if none are.

5. When we have multiple instances of our multicast listener in the scene, they each register themselves with the multicast delegate implemented in the `GameMode`.

6. Then, when the `TriggerVolume` overlaps a player, it broadcasts the delegate, and each Listener is notified causing them to toggle the visibility of their associated point light.

7. Multicast delegates can take parameters in exactly the same way that a standard delegate can.

Creating a custom Event

Custom delegates are quite useful, but one of their limitations is that they can be broadcast externally by some other third-party class, that is, their Execute/Broadcast methods are publically accessible.

At times, you may want a delegate that is externally assignable by other classes, but can only be broadcast by the class which contains them. This is the primary purpose of Events.

Getting ready

Make sure you've followed the initial recipe in this chapter so that you have the
`MyTriggerVolume` and `CookBookGameMode` implementations.

How to do it...

1. Add the following event declaration macro to the header of your `MyTriggerVolume`
    class:

    ```
    DECLARE_EVENT(AMyTriggerVolume, FPlayerEntered)
    ```

2. Add an instance of the declared event signature to the class:

    ```
    FPlayerEnteredOnPlayerEntered;
    ```

3. In `AMyTriggerVolume::NotifyActorBeginOverlap`, add this:

    ```
    OnPlayerEntered.Broadcast();
    ```

4. Create a new `Actor` class, called `TriggerVolEventListener`.

5. Add the following class members to its declaration:

    ```
    UPROPERTY()
    UPointLightComponent* PointLight;

    UPROPERTY(EditAnywhere)
    AMyTriggerVolume* TriggerEventSource;
    UFUNCTION()
    void OnTriggerEvent();
    ```

6. Initialize `PointLight` in the class constructor:

    ```
    PointLight =
    CreateDefaultSubobject<UPointLightComponent>("PointLight");
    RootComponent = PointLight;
    ```

7. Inside `BeginPlay`, add the following:

    ```
    if (TriggerEventSource != nullptr)
    {
      TriggerEventSource->OnPlayerEntered.AddUObject(this,
      &ATriggerVolEventListener::OnTriggerEvent);
    }
    ```

8. Lastly, implement `OnTriggerEvent()`:

    ```
    void ATriggerVolEventListener::OnTriggerEvent()
    {
      PointLight->SetLightColor(FLinearColor(0, 1, 0, 1));
    }
    ```

9. Compile your project, and launch the editor. Create a level with the game mode set to our `UE4CookbookGameMode`, then drag an instance of `ATriggerVolEventListener` and `AMyTriggerVolume` out into the level.

10. Select `TriggerVolEventListener`, and you'll see `TriggerVolEventListener` listed as a category in the **Details** panel, with the property **Trigger Event Source**:

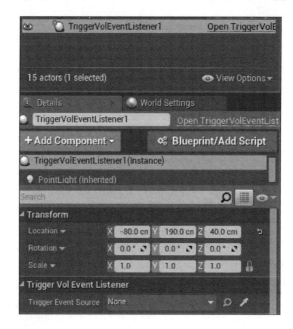

11. Use the drop-down menu to select your instance of `AMyTriggerVolume` so that the Listener knows which event to bind to:

12. Play your game, and enter the trigger volume's zone of effect. Verify that the color of your `EventListener` changes to green.

How it works...

1. As with all the other types of delegates, Events require their own special macro function.

2. The first parameter is the class that the event will be implemented into. This will be the only class able to call `Broadcast()`, so make sure it is the right one.

3. The second parameter is the type name for our new event function signature.

4. We add an instance of this type to our class. Unreal documentation suggests `On<x>` as a naming convention.

5. When something overlaps our `TriggerVolume`, we call broadcast on our own event instance.

6. Inside the new class, we create a point light as a visual representation of the event being triggered.

7. We also create a pointer to `TriggerVolume` to listen to events from. We mark the `UPROPERTY` as `EditAnywhere`, because this allows us to set it in the Editor rather than having to acquire the reference programmatically using `GetAllActorsOfClass` or something else.

8. Last is our event handler for when something enters the `TriggerVolume`.

9. We create and initialize our point light in the constructor as usual.

10. When the game starts, the Listener checks that our `TriggerVolume` reference is valid, then binds our `OnTriggerEvent` function to the `TriggerVolume` event.

11. Inside `OnTriggerEvent`, we change our light's color to green.

12. When something enters `TriggerVolume`, it causes `TriggerVolume` to call broadcast on its own event. Our `TriggerVolEventListener` then has its bound method invoked, changing our light's color.

Creating a Time of Day handler

This recipe shows you how to use the concepts introduced in the previous recipes to create an actor that informs other actors of the passage of time within your game.

How to do it...

1. Create a new `Actor` class called `TimeOfDayHandler`.

2. Add a multicast delegate declaration to the header:

```
DECLARE_MULTICAST_DELEGATE_TwoParams(FOnTimeChangedSignatur
e, int32, int32)
```

3. Add an instance of our delegate to the class declaration:

```
FOnTimeChangedSignatureOnTimeChanged;
```

4. Add the following properties to the class:

```
UPROPERTY()
int32 TimeScale;

UPROPERTY()
int32 Hours;
UPROPERTY()
int32 Minutes;

UPROPERTY()
float ElapsedSeconds;
```

5. Add the initialization of these properties to the constructor:

```
TimeScale = 60;
Hours = 0;
Minutes = 0;
ElapsedSeconds = 0;
```

6. Inside `Tick`, add the following code:

```
ElapsedSeconds += (DeltaTime * TimeScale);
if (ElapsedSeconds> 60)
{
  ElapsedSeconds -= 60;
  Minutes++;
  if (Minutes > 60)
  {
    Minutes -= 60;
    Hours++;
  }

  OnTimeChanged.Broadcast(Hours, Minutes);
}
```

7. Create a new `Actor` class called `Clock`.

8. Add the following properties to the class header:

```
UPROPERTY()
USceneComponent* RootSceneComponent;

UPROPERTY()
UStaticMeshComponent* ClockFace;
UPROPERTY()
USceneComponent* HourHandle;
UPROPERTY()
UStaticMeshComponent* HourHand;
```

```
UPROPERTY()
USceneComponent* MinuteHandle;
UPROPERTY()
UStaticMeshComponent* MinuteHand;

UFUNCTION()
void TimeChanged(int32 Hours, int32 Minutes);
FDelegateHandleMyDelegateHandle;
```

9. Initialize and transform the components in the constructor:

```
RootSceneComponent = CreateDefaultSubobject<USceneComponent>("Root
SceneComponent
");
ClockFace =
CreateDefaultSubobject<UStaticMeshComponent>("ClockFace");
HourHand =
CreateDefaultSubobject<UStaticMeshComponent>("HourHand");
MinuteHand =
CreateDefaultSubobject<UStaticMeshComponent>("MinuteHand");
HourHandle =
CreateDefaultSubobject<USceneComponent>("HourHandle");
MinuteHandle =
CreateDefaultSubobject<USceneComponent>("MinuteHandle");
auto MeshAsset =
ConstructorHelpers::FObjectFinder<UStaticMesh>(TEXT("Static
Mesh'/Engine/BasicShapes/Cylinder.Cylinder'"));
if (MeshAsset.Object != nullptr)
{
  ClockFace->SetStaticMesh(MeshAsset.Object);
  HourHand->SetStaticMesh(MeshAsset.Object);
  MinuteHand->SetStaticMesh(MeshAsset.Object);
}
RootComponent = RootSceneComponent;
HourHand->AttachTo(HourHandle);
MinuteHand->AttachTo(MinuteHandle);
HourHandle->AttachTo(RootSceneComponent);
MinuteHandle->AttachTo(RootSceneComponent);
ClockFace->AttachTo(RootSceneComponent);
ClockFace->SetRelativeTransform(FTransform(FRotator(90, 0,
0), FVector(10, 0, 0), FVector(2, 2, 0.1)));
HourHand->SetRelativeTransform(FTransform(FRotator(0, 0,
0), FVector(0, 0, 25), FVector(0.1, 0.1, 0.5)));
MinuteHand->SetRelativeTransform(FTransform(FRotator(0, 0,
0), FVector(0, 0, 50), FVector(0.1, 0.1, 1)));
```

10. Add the following to `BeginPlay`:

```
TArray<AActor*>TimeOfDayHandlers;
UGameplayStatics::GetAllActorsOfClass(GetWorld(),
ATimeOfDayHandler::StaticClass(), TimeOfDayHandlers);
if (TimeOfDayHandlers.Num() != 0)
{
  auto TimeOfDayHandler =
  Cast<ATimeOfDayHandler>(TimeOfDayHandlers[0]);
  MyDelegateHandle = TimeOfDayHandler-
  >OnTimeChanged.AddUObject(this, &AClock::TimeChanged);
}
```

11. Lastly, implement `TimeChanged` as your event handler.

```
void AClock::TimeChanged(int32 Hours, int32 Minutes)
{
  HourHandle->SetRelativeRotation(FRotator( 0, 0,30 *
  Hours));
  MinuteHandle->SetRelativeRotation(FRotator(0,0,6 *
  Minutes));
}
```

12. Place an instance of `TimeOfDayHandler` and the `AClock` into your level, and play to see that the hands on the clock are rotating:

How it works...

1. `TimeOfDayHandler` contains a delegate which takes two parameters, hence the use of the `TwoParams` variant of the macro.

2. Our class contains variables to store hours, minutes, and seconds, and the `TimeScale`, which is an acceleration factor used to speed up time for testing purposes.

3. Inside the handler's `Tick` function, we accumulate elapsed seconds based on the time elapsed since the last frame.

4. We check if the elapsed seconds have gone over 60. If so, we subtract 60, and increment `Minutes`.

5. Likewise with `Minutes`—if they go over 60, we subtract 60, and increment `Hours`.

6. If `Minutes` and `Hours` were updated, we broadcast our delegate to let any object that has subscribed to the delegate know that the time has changed.

7. The `Clock` actor uses a series of Scene components and Static meshes to build a mesh hierarchy that resembles a clock face.

8. In the `Clock` constructor, we parent the components in the hierarchy, and set their initial scale and rotations.

9. In `BeginPlay`, the clock uses `GetAllActorsOfClass()` to fetch all the time of day handlers in the level.

10. If there's at least one `TimeOfDayHandler` in the level, the `Clock` accesses the first one, and subscribes to its `TimeChanged` event.

11. When the `TimeChanged` event fires, the clock rotates the hour and minute hands based on how many hours and minutes the time currently has.

Creating a respawning pickup for an First Person Shooter

This recipe shows you how to create a placeable pickup that will respawn after a certain amount of time, suitable as an ammo or other pickup for an FPS.

How to do it...

1. Create a new `Actor` class called `Pickup`.

2. Declare the following delegate type in `Pickup.h`:

   ```
   DECLARE_DELEGATE(FPickedupEventSignature)
   ```

3. Add the following properties to the class header:

```
virtual void NotifyActorBeginOverlap(AActor* OtherActor) override;
UPROPERTY()
UStaticMeshComponent* MyMesh;

UPROPERTY()
URotatingMovementComponent* RotatingComponent;

FPickedupEventSignatureOnPickedUp;
```

4. Add the following code to the constructor:

```
MyMesh =
CreateDefaultSubobject<UStaticMeshComponent>("MyMesh");
RotatingComponent =
CreateDefaultSubobject<URotatingMovementComponent>("Rotatin
gComponent");
RootComponent = MyMesh;
auto MeshAsset =
ConstructorHelpers::FObjectFinder<UStaticMesh>(TEXT("Static
Mesh'/Engine/BasicShapes/Cube.Cube'"));
if (MeshAsset.Object != nullptr)
{
  MyMesh->SetStaticMesh(MeshAsset.Object);
}
MyMesh->SetCollisionProfileName(TEXT("OverlapAllDynamic"));
RotatingComponent->RotationRate = FRotator(10, 0, 10);
```

5. Implement the overridden `NotifyActorBeginOverlap`:

```
void APickup::NotifyActorBeginOverlap(AActor* OtherActor)
{
  OnPickedUp.ExecuteIfBound();
}
```

6. Create a second `Actor` class called `PickupSpawner`.

7. Add the following to the class header:

```
UPROPERTY()
USceneComponent* SpawnLocation;

UFUNCTION()
void PickupCollected();
UFUNCTION()
void SpawnPickup();
```

```
UPROPERTY()
APickup* CurrentPickup;
FTimerHandleMyTimer;
```

8. Add `Pickup.h` to the includes in the `PickupSpawner` implementation file.

9. Initialize our root component in the constructor:

```
SpawnLocation =
CreateDefaultSubobject<USceneComponent>("SpawnLocation");
```

10. Spawn a pickup when gameplay starts with the `SpawnPickup` function in `BeginPlay`:

```
SpawnPickup();
```

11. Implement `PickupCollected`:

```
void APickupSpawner::PickupCollected()
{
  GetWorld()->GetTimerManager().SetTimer(MyTimer, this,
  &APickupSpawner::SpawnPickup, 10, false);
  CurrentPickup->OnPickedUp.Unbind();
  CurrentPickup->Destroy();
}
```

12. Create the following code for `SpawnPickup`:

```
void APickupSpawner::SpawnPickup()
{
  UWorld* MyWorld = GetWorld();
  if (MyWorld != nullptr){
    CurrentPickup = MyWorld->
    SpawnActor<APickup>(APickup::StaticClass(),
    GetTransform());
    CurrentPickup->OnPickedUp.BindUObject(this,
    &APickupSpawner::PickupCollected);
  }
}
```

13. Compile and launch the editor, then drag an instance of `PickupSpawner` out into the level. Walk into the pickup represented by the spinning cube, and verify that it spawns again 10 seconds later:

How it works...

1. As usual, we need to create a delegate inside our `Pickup` that our Spawner can subscribe to so that it knows when the player collects the pickup.

2. The `Pickup` also contains a Static mesh as a visual representation, and a `RotatingMovementComponent` so that the mesh will spin in a way to attract the attention of the players.

3. Inside the `Pickup` constructor, we load one of the engine's inbuilt meshes as our visual representation.

4. We specify that the mesh will overlap with other objects, then set the rotation rate of our mesh at 10 units per second in the *X* and *Z* axes.

5. When the player overlaps the `Pickup`, it fires off its `PickedUp` delegate from the first step.

6. The `PickupSpawner` has a Scene component to specify where to spawn the pickup actor. It has a function for doing so, and a UPROPERTY-tagged reference to the currently spawned `Pickup`.

7. In the `PickupSpawner` constructor, we initialize our components as always.

8. When play begins, the Spawner runs its `SpawnPickup` function.

9. This function spawns an instance of our `Pickup`, then binds `APickupSpawner::PickupCollected` to the `OnPickedUp` function on the new instance. It also stores a reference to that current instance.

10. When `PickupCollected` runs after the player has overlapped the `Pickup`, a timer is created to respawn the pickup after 10 seconds.

11. The existing delegate binding to the collected pickup is removed, then the pickup is destroyed.

12. After 10 seconds, the timer fires, running `SpawnActor` again, which creates a new `Pickup`.

6
Input and Collision

This chapter covers recipes surrounding game control input (keyboard, mouse, and gamepad), and collisions with obstacles.

The following recipes will be covered in this chapter:

▶ Axis Mappings – keyboard, mouse, and gamepad directional input for an FPS character

▶ Axis Mappings – normalized input

▶ Action Mappings – one-button responses for an FPS character

▶ Adding Axis and Action Mappings from C++

▶ Mouse UI input handling

▶ UMG keyboard UI shortcut keys

▶ Collision – letting objects pass through one another using Ignore

▶ Collision – picking up objects using Overlap

▶ Collision – preventing interpenetration using Block

Introduction

Good input controls are extremely important in your game. Providing all of keyboard, mouse, and especially gamepad input is going to make your game much more palatable to users.

You can use Xbox 360 and PlayStation controllers on your Windows PC—they have USB input. Check your local electronics shops for USB game controllers in order to find some good ones. You can also use a wireless controller with a game controller wireless receiver adapter connected to your PC.

Axis Mappings – keyboard, mouse and gamepad directional input for an FPS character

There are two types of input mapping: **Axis mappings** and **Action mappings**. Axis mappings are inputs that you hold down for an extended period of time to get their effect (for example, holding the *W* key to move the player forward), while Action mappings are one-off inputs (such as pressing the *A* key on the gamepad to make the player jump). In this recipe, we'll cover how to set up keyboard, mouse, and gamepad axis-mapped input controls to move an FPS character.

Getting ready

You must have a UE4 project, which has a main character player in it, and a ground plane to walk on, ready for this recipe.

How to do it...

1. Create a C++ class, `Warrior`, deriving from `Character`:

```
UCLASS()
class CH6_API AWarrior : public ACharacter
{
  GENERATED_BODY()
};
```

2. Launch UE4, and derive a Blueprint, `BP_Warrior`, based on your `Warrior` class.

3. Create and select a new Blueprint for your `GameMode` class as follows:

    1. Go to **Settings | Project Settings | Maps & Modes**.

    2. Click on the **+** icon beside the default **GameMode** drop-down menu, which will create a new Blueprint of the `GameMode` class, and name of your choice (say, `BP_GameMode`).

    3. Double-click the new `BP_GameMode` Blueprint class that you have created to edit it.

4. Open your `BP_GameMode` blueprint, and select your Blueprinted `BP_Warrior` class as default `Pawn` Class.

5. To set up the keyboard's input driving the player, open **Settings | Project Settings | Input**. In the following steps, we will complete the process that drives the player forward in the game:

    1. Click on the **+** icon beside the **Axis Mappings** heading.

> **Axis Mappings** supports continuous (button-held) input, while **Action Mappings** supports one-off events.

    2. Give a name to the Axis mapping. This first example will show how to move the player forward, so name it something like **Forward**.

    3. Underneath **Forward**, select a keyboard key to assign to this Axis mapping, such as *W*.

    4. Click on the **+** icon beside **Forward**, and select a game controller input to map to moving the player Forward (such as gamepad Left Thumbstick Up).

    5. Complete **Axis Mappings** for Back, Left, and Right with keyboard, gamepad, and, optionally, mouse input bindings for each.

6. From your C++ code, override the `SetupPlayerInputComponent` function for the `AWarrior` class as follows:

```
void AWarrior::SetupPlayerInputComponent(UInputComponent* Input)
{
  check(Input);
  Input->BindAxis( "Forward", this, &AWarrior::Forward );
}
```

7. Provide a `Forward` function inside your `AWarrior` class as follows:

```
void AWarrior::Forward( float amount )
{
  if( Controller && amount )
  {
    // Moves the player forward by an amount in forward
    direction
    AddMovementInput(GetActorForwardVector(), amount );
  }
}
```

8. Write and complete functions for the rest of the input directions, `AWarrior::Back`, `AWarrior::Left`, and `AWarrior::Right`.

How it works...

The UE4 Engine allows wire-up input events directly to C++ function calls. The function called by an input event are member functions of some class. In the preceding example, we routed both the pressing of the *W* key and holding of the gamepad's Left Thumbstick Up to the `AWarrior::Forward` C++ function. The instance to call `AWarrior::Forward` on is the instance that routed the controller's input. That is controlled by the object set as the player's avatar in the `GameMode` class.

See also

> ▸ Instead of entering the `Forward` input axis binding in the UE4 editor, you can actually code it in from C++. We'll describe this in detail in a later recipe, *Adding Axis and Action Mappings from C++*.

Axis Mappings – normalized input

If you've noticed, inputs of 1.0 right and 1.0 forward will actually sum to a total of 2.0 units of speed. This means it is possible to move faster diagonally than it is to move in purely forward, backward, left, or right directions. What we really should do is clamp off any input value that results in speed in excess of 1.0 units while maintaining the direction of input indicated. We can do this by storing the previous input values, and overriding the `::Tick()` function.

Getting ready

Open a project, and set up a `Character` derivative class (let's call ours `Warrior`).

How to do it...

1. Override the `AWarrior::SetupPlayerInputComponent( UInputComponent* Input )` function as follows:

```
void AWarrior::SetupPlayerInputComponent( UInputComponent* Input )
{
  Input->BindAxis( "Forward", this, &AWarrior::Forward );
  Input->BindAxis( "Back", this, &AWarrior::Back );
  Input->BindAxis( "Right", this, &AWarrior::Right );
  Input->BindAxis( "Left", this, &AWarrior::Left );
}
```

2. Write the corresponding `::Forward`, `::Back`, `::Right` and `::Left` functions as follows:

```
void AWarrior::Forward( float amount ) {
  // We use a += of the amount added so that
  // when the other function modifying .Y
  // (::Back()) affects lastInput, it won't
  // overwrite with 0's
  lastInput.Y += amount;
}
void AWarrior::Back( float amount ) {
  lastInput.Y += -amount;
}
void AWarrior::Right( float amount ) {
  lastInput.X += amount;
}
void AWarrior::Left( float amount ) {
  lastInput.X += -amount;
}
```

3. In the `AWarrior::Tick()` function, modify the input values after normalizing any oversize in the input vector:

```
void AWarrior::Tick( float DeltaTime ) {
  Super::Tick( DeltaTime );
  if( Controller )
  {
    float len = lastInput.Size();
    if( len > 1.f )
      lastInput /= len;
    AddMovementInput(
    GetActorForwardVector(), lastInput.Y );
    AddMovementInput(GetActorRightVector(), lastInput.X);
    // Zero off last input values
    lastInput = FVector2D( 0.f, 0.f );
  }
}
```

How it works...

We normalize the input vector when it is over a magnitude of 1.0. This constricts the maximum input velocity to 1.0 units (rather than 2.0 units when full up and full right are pressed, for example).

Action Mappings – one button responses for an FPS character

An Action mapping is for handling single-button pushes (not buttons that are held down). For buttons that should be held down, be sure to use an Axis mapping instead.

Getting ready

Have a UE4 project ready with the actions that you need to complete, such as Jump or ShootGun.

How to do it...

1. Open **Settings | Project Settings | Input**.
2. Go to the **Action Mappings** heading, and click on the **+** icon beside it.
    1. Start to type in the actions that should be mapped to button pushes. For example, type in Jump for the first Action.
    2. Select a key to press for that action to occur, for example, **Space Bar**.
    3. If you would like the same action triggered by another key push, click on the **+** beside your **Action Mappings** name, and select another key to trigger the Action.
    4. If you want that the **Shift**, **Ctrl**, **Alt**, or **Cmd** keys should be held down for the Action to occur, be sure to indicate that in the checkboxes to the right of the key selection box.

3. To link your Action to a C++ code function, you need to override the SetupPlayerIn putComponent(UInputControl* control) function. Enter the following code inside that function:

```
voidAWarrior::SetupPlayerInputComponent(UInputComponent*
Input)
{
  check(Input );
  // Connect the Jump action to the C++ Jump function
```

```
    Input->BindAction("Jump", IE_Pressed, this,
    &AWarrior::Jump );
}
```

How it works...

Action Mappings are single-button-push events that fire off C++ code to run in response to them. You can define any number of actions that you wish in the UE4 Editor, but be sure to tie up **Action Mappings** to actual key pushes in C++.

See also

▶   You can list the Actions that you want mapped from C++ code. See the following recipe on *Adding Axis and Action Mappings from C++* for this.

Adding Axis and Action Mappings from C++

Axis Mappings and **Action Mappings** can be added to your game via the UE4 Editor, but we can also add them directly from C++ code. Since the wireup to C++ functions is from C++ code anyway, you may find it convenient to define your Axis and Action Mappings in C++ as well.

Getting ready

You need a UE4 project to which you'd like to add some Axis and Action mappings. You can delete the existing Axis and Action mappings listed in **Settings | Project Settings | Input** if you are adding them via C++ code. To add your custom axis and action mappings, there are two C++ functions that you need to know about: the UPlayerInput::AddAxisMapping and UPlayerInput:: AddActionMapping. These are member functions available on the UPlayerInput object. The UPlayerInput object is inside the PlayerController object, accessible via the following code:

```
GetWorld()->GetFirstPlayerController()->PlayerInput
```

You can also use the two static member functions of UPlayerInput to create your axis and action mappings if you'd prefer not to access player controllers individually:

```
UPlayerInput::AddEngineDefinedAxisMapping()
UPlayerInput::AddEngineDefinedActionMapping()
```

How to do it...

1. To begin with, we need to define our `FInputAxisKeyMapping` or `FInputActionKeyMapping` objects, depending on whether you are hooking up an Axis key mapping (for buttons that are held down for input) or an Action key mapping (for one-off events—buttons that are pressed once for input).

    1. For Axis key mappings, we define an `FInputAxisKeyMapping` object, as follows:

       ```
       FInputAxisKeyMapping backKey( "Back", EKeys::S, 1.f );
       ```

    2. This will include the string name for the action, the key to press (use the EKeys enum), and whether or not *Shift, Ctrl, Alt*, or *cmd* (Mac) should be held to trigger the event.

    3. For action key mappings, define `FInputActionKeyMapping`, as follows:

       ```
       FInputActionKeyMapping jump("Jump", EKeys::SpaceBar, 0, 0, 0, 0);
       ```

    4. This will include the string name for the action, the key to press, and whether or not *Shift, Ctrl, Alt*, or *cmd* (Mac) should be held to trigger the event.

2. In your player `Pawn` class `SetupPlayerInputComponent` function, register your axis and action key mappings to the following:

    1. The `PlayerInput` object connected to a specific controller:

       ```
       GetWorld()->GetFirstPlayerController()->PlayerInput
       ->AddAxisMapping( backKey ); // specific to a controller
       ```

    2. Or, alternatively, you could register to the static member functions of the `UPlayerInput` object directly:

       ```
       UPlayerInput::AddEngineDefinedActionMapping(jump );
       ```

> Be sure you're using the correct function for Axis versus Action mappings!

3. Register your Action and Axis mappings to C++ functions using C++ code just as shown in the preceding two recipes, for example:

   ```
   Input->BindAxis("Back", this, &AWarrior::Back);
   Input->BindAction("Jump", IE_Pressed, this, &AWarrior::Jump
   );
   ```

How it works...

The action and axis mapping registration functions allow you to set up your input mappings from C++ code directly. The C++ coded input mappings are essentially the same as entering the input mappings in the **Settings | Project Settings | Input** dialog.

Mouse UI input handling

When using the **Unreal Motion Graphics (UMG)** toolkit, you will find that mouse events are very easy to handle. We can register C++ functions to run after mouse clicks or other types of interactions with the UMG components.

Usually, event registration will be via Blueprints; but in this recipe, we will outline how to write and wire-up C++ functions to UMG events.

Getting ready

Create a UMG canvas in your UE4 project. From there, we'll register event handlers for the `OnClicked`, `OnPressed`, and `OnReleased` events.

How to do it...

1. Right-click in your **Content Browser** (or click on **Add New**), and select **User Interface | Widget Blueprint**, as shown in the following screenshot. This will add an editable widget blueprint to your project.

2. Double-click on your **Widget Blueprint** to edit it.
3. Add a button to the interface by dragging it from the palette on the left.
4. Scroll down the **Details** panel for your button until you find the **Events** subsection.

5. Click on the **+** icon beside any event that you'd like to handle.

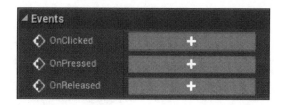

6. Connect the event that appears in Blueprints to any C++ UFUNCTION() that has the BlueprintCallable tag in the macro. For example, in your GameMode class derivative, you could include a function such as:

```
UFUNCTION(BlueprintCallable, Category = UIFuncs)
void ButtonClicked()
{
  UE_LOG(LogTemp, Warning, TEXT( "UI Button Clicked" ) );
}
```

7. Trigger the function call by routing to it in the Blueprints diagram under the event of your choice.

8. Construct and display your UI by calling **Create Widget**, followed by **Add to Viewport** in the **Begin Play** function of your GameMode (or any such main object).

How it works...

Your widget Blueprint's buttons events can be easily connected to Blueprints events, or C++ functions via the preceding method.

UMG keyboard UI shortcut keys

Every user interface needs shortcut keys associated with it. To program these into your UMG interface, you can simply wire-up certain key combinations to an Action mapping. When the Action triggers, just invoke the same Blueprints function that the UI button itself triggers.

Getting ready

You should have a UMG interface created already, as shown in the previous recipe.

How to do it...

1. In **Settings** | **Project Settings** | **Input**, define a new Action mapping for your hot key event, for example, `HotKey_UIButton_Spell`.

2. Wire up the event to your UI's function call either in Blueprints or in C++ code.

How it works...

Wiring up an Action Mapping with a short circuit to the function called by the UI will allow you to implement hot keys in your game program nicely.

Collision – letting objects pass through one another using Ignore

Collision settings are fairly easy to get hold of. There are three classes of intersection for collisions:

▸   `Ignore`: Collisions that pass through each other without any notification.

▸   `Overlap`: Collisions that trigger the `OnBeginOverlap` and `OnEndOverlap` events. Interpenetration of objects with an Overlap setting is allowed.

▸   `Block`: Collisions that prevent all interpenetration, and prevent objects from overlapping each other at all.

Objects are classed into one of many **Object Type**. The **Collision** settings for a particular Blueprint's Component allow you to class the object as an **Object Type** of your choice as well as to specify how that object collides with all other objects of all other types. This takes a tabular format in the **Details** | **Collision** section of the Blueprint Editor.

For example, the following screenshot shows the **Collision** settings for a character's `CapsuleComponent`:

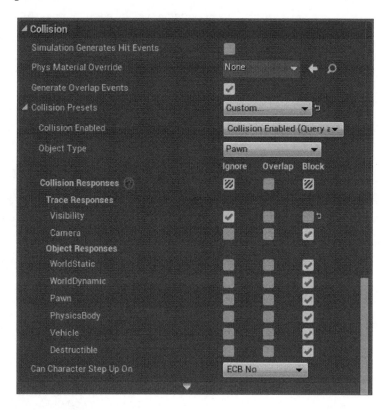

Getting ready

You should have a UE4 project with some objects that you'd like to program intersections for.

How to do it...

1. Open the Blueprint editor for the object that you'd like other objects to simply pass through and ignore. Under the **Components** listing, select the component that you'd like to program settings for.

2. With your component selected, see your **Details** tab (usually on the right). Under **Collision Presets**, select either the **NoCollision** or **Custom...** presets.

    1. If you select the **NoCollision** preset, you can just leave it at that, and all collisions will be ignored.

2. If you select the **Custom...** preset, then choose either of the following:

   1. **NoCollision** under the **Collision Enabled** drop-down menu.

   2. Select a collision mode under **Collision Enabled** involving Queries, and be sure to check the **Ignore** checkbox for each **Object Type** that you'd like it to ignore collisions with.

How it works...

Ignored collisions will not fire any events or prevent interpenetrations between objects marked as such.

Collision – picking up objects using Overlap

Item pickup is a pretty important thing to get down cleanly. In this recipe, we'll outline how to get item pickups working using **Overlap** events on Actor Component primitives.

Getting ready

The previous recipe, *Collisions: Letting Objects pass through each other using Ignore*, describes the basics of collisions. You should read it for background before beginning this recipe. What we'll do here is create a **New Object Channel...** to identify Item class objects so that they can be programmed for overlaps only with the player avatar's collision volume.

How to do it...

1. Start by creating a unique collision Channel for the Item object's collision primitive. Under **Project Settings | Collision**, create a new Object Channel by going to **New Object Channel...**

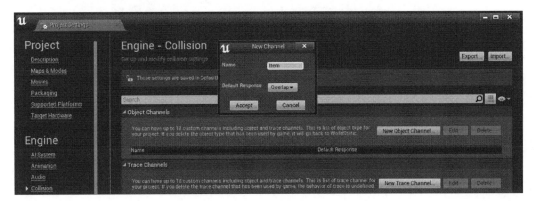

2. Name the new Object Channel as `Item`.

3. Take your `Item` actor and select the primitive component on it that is used to intersect for pickup with the player avatar. Make the **Object Type** of that primitive an `Item` class **Object Type**.

4. Check the **Overlap** checkbox against the `Pawn` class **Object Type** as shown in the following screenshot:

5. Ensure that the **Generate Overlap Events** checkbox is checked.

6. Take the player actor who will pick up the items, and select the component on him that feels for the items. Usually, this will be his `CapsuleComponent`. Check **Overlap** with the `Item` object.

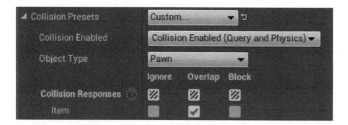

7. Now the Player overlaps the item, and the item overlaps the player pawn. We do have to signal overlaps it both ways (`Item` Overlaps `Pawn` and Pawn Overlaps `Item`) for it to work properly. Ensure that **Generate Overlap Events** is also checked for the `Pawn` intersecting component.

8. Next we have to complete the `OnComponentBeginOverlap` event for either the item or the Player's pickup volume, using either Blueprints or C++ code.

   1. If you prefer Blueprints, in the **Events** section of the **Details** pane of the Coin's intersectable Component, click on the **+** icon beside the **On Component Begin Overlap** event.

   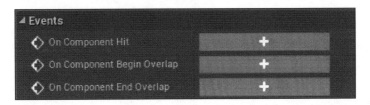

   2. Use the `OnComponentBeginOverlap` event that appears in your `Actor` Blueprint diagram to wire-in Blueprints code to run when an overlap with the Player's capsule volume occurs.

   3. If you prefer C++, you can write and attach a C++ function to the `CapsuleComponent`. Write a member function in your player's avatar class with a signature as follows:

   ```
   UFUNCTION(BlueprintNativeEvent, Category = Collision)
   void OnOverlapsBegin( UPrimitiveComponent* Comp, AActor*
   OtherActor,
   UPrimitiveComponent* OtherComp, int32 OtherBodyIndex,
   bool bFromSweep, const FHitResult& SweepResult );
   ```

In UE 4.13, the OnOverlapsBegin function's signature has changed to:
   ```
   OnOverlapsBegin( UPrimitiveComponent* Comp, AActor*
   OtherActor,UPrimitiveComponent* OtherComp, int32
   OtherBodyIndex, bool bFromSweep, const FHitREsult&
   SweepResult );
   ```

   4. Complete the implementation of the `OnOverlapsBegin()` function in your `.cpp` file, making sure to end the function name with `_Implementation`:

   ```
   void AWarrior::OnOverlapsBegin_Implementation( AActor*
   OtherActor, UPrimitiveComponent* OtherComp,
   int32 OtherBodyIndex,
   bool bFromSweep, const FHitResult& SweepResult )
   {
     UE_LOG(LogTemp, Warning, TEXT( "Overlaps began" ) );
   }
   ```

5. Then, provide a `PostInitializeComponents()` override to connect the `OnOverlapsBegin()` function with overlaps to the capsule in your avatar's class as follows:

```
void AWarrior::PostInitializeComponents()
{
  Super::PostInitializeComponents();
  if(RootComponent )
  {
    // Attach contact function to all bounding components.
    GetCapsuleComponent()
    ->OnComponentBeginOverlap.AddDynamic( this,
    &AWarrior::OnOverlapsBegin );
    GetCapsuleComponent()
    ->OnComponentEndOverlap.AddDynamic( this,
    &AWarrior::OnOverlapsEnd );
  }
}
```

How it works...

The **Overlap** event raised by the engine allows code to run when two UE4 `Actor` Components overlap, without preventing interpenetration of the objects.

Collision – preventing interpenetration using Block

Blocking means that the `Actor` components will be prevented from interpenetration in the engine, and any collision between two primitive shapes will be resolved, and not overlapping, after collisions are found.

Getting ready

Begin with a UE4 project that has some objects with Actors having collision primitives attached to them (`SphereComponents`, `CapsuleComponents`, or `BoxComponents`).

How to do it...

1. Open the Blueprint of an actor that you want to block another actor with. For example, we want the Player actor to block other Player actor instances.

2. Mark primitives inside the actor that you do not want interpenetrating with other components as Blocking those components in the **Details** pane.

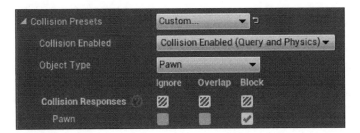

How it works...

When objects **Block** one another, they will not be allowed to interpenetrate. Any interpenetration will be automatically resolved, and the objects will be pushed off each other.

There's more...

You can override the `OnComponentHit` function to run code when two objects hit each other. This is distinct from the `OnComponentBeginOverlap` event.

7

Communication between Classes and Interfaces

This chapter shows you how to write your own UInterfaces, and demonstrates how to take advantage of them within C++ to minimize class coupling and help keep your code clean. The following recipes will be covered in this chapter:

- Creating a `UInterface`
- Implementing a `UInterface` on an object
- Checking if a class implements a `UInterface`
- Casting to a `UInterface` implemented in native code
- Calling native `UInterface` functions from C++
- Inheriting `UInterface` from one another
- Overriding `UInterface` functions in C++
- Exposing `UInterface` methods to Blueprint from a native base class
- Implementing `UInterface` functions in Blueprint
- Creating C++ `UInterface` function implementations that can be overridden in Blueprint
- Calling Blueprint-defined interface functions from C++
- Implementing a simple interaction system with UInterfaces

Introduction

In your game projects, you will sometimes require a series of potentially disparate objects to share a common functionality, but it would be inappropriate to use inheritance, because there is no "is-a" relationship between the different objects in question. Languages such as C++ tend to use multiple inheritance to solve this issue.

However, in Unreal, if you wanted functions from both the parent classes to be accessible to Blueprint, you would need to make both of them UCLASS. This is a problem for two reasons. Inheriting from UClass twice in the same object would break the concept that UObject should form a neatly traversable hierarchy. It also means that there are two instances of the UClass methods on the object, and they would have to be explicitly differentiated between within the code. The Unreal codebase solves this issue by borrowing a concept from C#—that of an explicit Interface type.

The reason for using this approach, instead of composition, is that Components are only available on Actors, not on UObjects in general. Interfaces can be applied to any UObject. Furthermore, it means that we are no longer modeling an "is-a" relationship between the object and the component; instead, it would only be able to represent "has-a" relationships.

Creating a UInterface

UInterfaces are a pair of classes that work together to enable classes to exhibit polymorphic behavior among multiple class hierarchies. This recipe shows you the basic steps involved in creating a UInterface purely in code.

How to do it...

1. UInterfaces don't show up inside the main class wizard within Unreal, so we'll need to add the class manually using Visual Studio.

2. Right click on your Source folder inside **Solution Explorer,** and select **Add | New Item**.

3. Select a .h file to start, and name it MyInterface.h.

4. Make sure you change the directory for the item to be placed in from Intermediate to Source/ProjectName.

5. Click on **OK** to create a new header file in your project folder.

6. Repeat the steps in order to create MyInterface.cpp as your implementation file.

7. Add the following code to the header file:

```
#include "MyInterface.generated.h"
/** */
UINTERFACE()
```

```
class UE4COOKBOOK_API UMyInterface: public UInterface
{
  GENERATED_BODY()
};

/** */
class UE4COOKBOOK_API IMyInterface
{
  GENERATED_BODY()

  public:
  virtualFStringGetTestName();
};
```

8. Implement the class with this code in the `.cpp` file:

```
#include "UE4Cookbook.h"
#include "MyInterface.h"

FString IMyInterface::GetTestName()
{
  unimplemented();
  return FString();
}
```

9. Compile your project to verify that the code was written without errors.

How it works...

1. UInterfaces are implemented as a pair of classes declared in the interface's header.

2. As always, because we are leveraging Unreal's reflection system, we need to include our generated header file. Refer to *Handling events implemented via virtual functions* in *Chapter 5, Handling Events and Delegates*, for more information.

3. As with classes that inherit from UObject, which uses UCLASS, we need to use the UINTERFACE macro to declare our new UInterface.

4. The class is tagged UE4COOKBOOK_API to help with the exporting of library symbols.

5. The base class for the UObject portion of the interface is UInterface.

6. Just like UCLASS types, we require a macro to be placed inside the body of our class so that the auto-generated code is inserted into it.

7. That macro is GENERATED_BODY() for UInterfaces. The macro must be placed at the very start of the class body.

8. The second class is also tagged UE4COOKBOOK_API, and is named in a specific way.

9. Note that the `UInterface`-derived class and the standard class have the same name but a different prefix. The `UInterface`-derived class has the prefix `U`, and the standard class has the prefix `I`.

10. This is important as this is how the Unreal Header Tool expects the classes to be named for the code it generates to work properly.

11. The plain native Interface class requires its own autogenerated content, which we include using the `GENERATED_BODY()` macro.

12. We declare functions that classes inheriting the interface should implement inside `IInterface`.

13. Within the implementation file, we implement the constructor for our `UInterface`, as it is declared by the Unreal Header Tool, and requires an implementation.

14. We also create a default implementation for our `GetTestName()` function. Without this, the linking phase of compilation will fail. This default implementation uses the `unimplemented()` macro, which will issue a debug assert when the line of code is executed.

See also

▶ Refer to *Passing payload data with a delegate binding* in *Chapter 5*, *Handling Events and Delegates*; the first recipe, in particular, explains some of the principles that we've applied here

Implementing a UInterface on an object

Ensure that you've followed the previous recipe in order to have a `UInterface` ready to be implemented.

How to do it...

1. Create a new `Actor` class using the Unreal Wizard, called `SingleInterfaceActor`.

2. Add `IInterface`—in this case, `IMyInterface`—to the public inheritance list for our new `Actor` class:

   ```
   class UE4COOKBOOK_API ASingleInterfaceActor : public
   AActor, public IMyInterface
   ```

3. Add an `override` declaration to the class for the `IInterface` function(s) that we wish to override:

   ```
   FStringGetTestName() override;
   ```

4. Implement the overridden function in the implementation file by adding the following code:

```
FStringASingleInterfaceActor::GetTestName()
{
    return IMyInterface::GetTestName();
}
```

How it works...

1. C++ uses multiple inheritance for the way it implements interfaces, so we leverage that mechanism here with the declaration of our `SingleInterfaceActor` class, where we add `public IMyInterface`.

2. We inherit from `IInterface` rather than `UInterface` to prevent `SingleInterfaceActor` from inheriting two copies of `UObject`.

3. Given that the interface declares a `virtual` function, we need to redeclare that function with the override specifier if we wish to implement it ourselves.

4. In our implementation file, we implement our overridden `virtual` function.

5. Inside our function override, for demonstration purposes, we call the base `IInterface` implementation of the function. Alternatively, we could write our own implementation, and avoid calling the base class one altogether.

6. We use `IInterface::` specifier rather than `Super`, because `Super` refers to the `UClass` that is the parent of our class, and IInterfaces aren't UClasses (hence, no `U` prefix).

7. You can implement a second, or multiple, IInterfaces on your object, as needed.

Checking if a class implements a UInterface

Follow the first two recipes so that you have a `UInterface` we can check for, and a class implementing the interface, which can be tested against.

How to do it...

1. Inside your Game Mode implementation, add the following code to the `BeginPlay` function:

```
FTransformSpawnLocation;
ASingleInterfaceActor* SpawnedActor = GetWorld()
->SpawnActor<ASingleInterfaceActor>
(ASingleInterfaceActor::StaticClass(), SpawnLocation);
if (SpawnedActor->GetClass()
->ImplementsInterface(UMyInterface::StaticClass()))
```

```
    {
      GEngine->AddOnScreenDebugMessage(-1, 1, FColor::Red,
      TEXT("Spawned actor implements interface!"));
    }
```

2. Given that we are referencing both `ASingleInterfaceActor` and `IMyInterface`, we need to `#include` both `MyInterface.h` and `SingleInterfaceActor.h` in our Source file.

How it works...

1. Inside `BeginPlay`, we create an empty `FTransform` function, which has the default value of `0` for all translation and rotation components, so we don't need to explicitly set any of them.

2. We then use the `SpawnActor` function from `UWorld` so that we can create an instance of our `SingleActorInterface`, storing the pointer to the instance into a temporary variable.

3. We then use `GetClass()` on our instance to get a reference to its associated `UClass`. We need a reference to `UClass`, because that object is the one which holds all of the reflection data for the object.

4. Reflection data includes the names and types of all `UPROPERTY` on the object, the inheritance hierarchy for the object, and a list of all the interfaces that it implements.

5. As a result, we can call `ImplementsInterface()` on `UClass`, and it will return `true` if the object implements the `UInterface` in question.

6. If the object implements the interface, and therefore, returns `true` from `ImplementsInterface`, we then print a message to the screen.

See also

▸ *Chapter 5, Handling Events and Delegates,* has a number of recipes relating to the spawning of actors

Casting to a UInterface implemented in native code

One advantage that UInterfaces provides you with as a developer is the ability to treat a collection of heterogeneous objects that implement a common interface as a collection of the same object, using `Cast< >` to handle the conversion.

[Please note that this won't work if your class implements the interface through a Blueprint.]

Getting ready

You should have a `UInterface`, and an `Actor` implementing the interface ready for this recipe.

Create a new game mode using the wizard within Unreal, or optionally, reuse a project and `GameMode` from a previous recipe.

How to do it...

1. Open your game mode's declaration, and add a new `UPROPERTY()` macro to it:

```
UPROPERTY()
TArray<IMyInterface*>MyInterfaceInstances;
```

2. Add `#include "MyInterface.h"` to the header's include section.

3. Add the following within the game mode's `BeginPlay` implementation:

```
for (TActorIterator<AActor> It(GetWorld(),
AActor::StaticClass()); It; ++It)
{
  AActor* Actor = *It;
  IMyInterface* MyInterfaceInstance =
Cast<IMyInterface>(Actor);
  if (MyInterfaceInstance)
  {
    MyInterfaceInstances.Add(MyInterfaceInstance);
  }
}
GEngine->AddOnScreenDebugMessage(-1, 1, FColor::Red,
FString::Printf(TEXT("%d actors implement the interface"),
MyInterfaceInstances.Num()));
```

4. Set the level's game mode override to your game mode, then drag a few instances of your custom Interface-implementing actor into the level.

5. When you play your level, a message should be printed on screen that indicates the number of instances of the interface that have been implemented in Actors in the level:

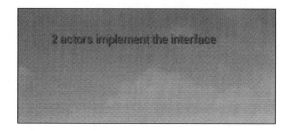

How it works...

1. We create an array of pointers to `MyInterface` implementations.

2. Inside `BeginPlay`, we use `TActorIterator<AActor>` to get all of the `Actor` instances in our level.

3. `TActorIterator` has the following constructor:

    ```
    explicitTActorIterator( UWorld* InWorld,
    TSubclassOf<ActorType>InClass = ActorType::StaticClass() )
    : Super(InWorld, InClass )
    ```

4. `TActorIterator` expects a world to act on as well as a `UClass` instance to specify what type of Actors we are interested in.

5. `ActorIterator` is an iterator like the STL iterator type. This means we can write a `for` loop of the following form:

    ```
    for (iterator-constructor;iterator;++iterator)
    ```

6. Inside the loop, we dereference the iterator to get an `Actor` pointer.

7. We then attempt to cast it to our interface; this will return a pointer to the interface if it does implement it, else it will return `nullptr`.

8. As a result, we can check if the interface pointer is `null`, and if not, we can add the interface pointer reference to our array.

9. Finally, once we've iterated through all the actors in `TActorIterator`, we can display a message on the screen, which displays the count of items that implemented the interface.

Calling native UInterface functions from C++

Follow the previous recipe to get an understanding of casting an `Actor` pointer to an Interface pointer.

 Note that as this recipe relies on the casting technique used in the previous recipe, it will only work with objects that implement the interface using C++ rather than Blueprint. This is because Blueprint classes are not available at compile time, and so, technically, don't inherit the interface.

How to do it...

1. Create a new `Actor` class using the editor wizard. Call it `AntiGravityVolume`.

2. Add `BoxComponent` to the new `Actor`.

```
UPROPERTY()
UBoxComponent* CollisionComponent;
```

3. Override the following `Actor virtual` functions in the header:

```
virtual void NotifyActorBeginOverlap(AActor* OtherActor) override;
virtual void NotifyActorEndOverlap(AActor* OtherActor) override;
```

4. Create an implementation within your source file, as follows:

```
voidAAntiGravityVolume::NotifyActorBeginOverlap(AActor*
OtherActor)
{
  IGravityObject* GravityObject =
Cast<IGravityObject>(OtherActor);
  if (GravityObject != nullptr)
  {
    GravityObject->DisableGravity();
  }
}

voidAAntiGravityVolume::NotifyActorEndOverlap(AActor*
OtherActor)
{
  IGravityObject* GravityObject =
Cast<IGravityObject>(OtherActor);
  if (GravityObject != nullptr)
  {
    GravityObject->EnableGravity();
  }
}
```

5. Initialize the `BoxComponent` in your constructor:

```
AAntiGravityVolume::AAntiGravityVolume()
{
  PrimaryActorTick.bCanEverTick = true;
  CollisionComponent =
  CreateDefaultSubobject<UBoxComponent>
  ("CollisionComponent");
  CollisionComponent->SetBoxExtent(FVector(200, 200, 400));
  RootComponent = CollisionComponent;


}
```

6. Create an interface called `GravityObject`.

7. Add the following `virtual` functions to `IGravityObject`:

```
virtual void EnableGravity();
virtual void DisableGravity();
```

8. Create the default implementation of the `virtual` functions inside the `IGravityObject` implementation file:

```
voidIGravityObject::EnableGravity()
{
  AActor* ThisAsActor = Cast<AActor>(this);
  if (ThisAsActor != nullptr)
  {
    TArray<UPrimitiveComponent*>PrimitiveComponents;
    ThisAsActor->GetComponents(PrimitiveComponents);
    for (UPrimitiveComponent* Component :
    PrimitiveComponents)
    {
      Component->SetEnableGravity(true);
    }
  }
}

voidIGravityObject::DisableGravity()
{
  AActor* ThisAsActor = Cast<AActor>(this);
  if (ThisAsActor != nullptr)
  {
```

```
TArray<UPrimitiveComponent*>PrimitiveComponents;
ThisAsActor->GetComponents(PrimitiveComponents);
for (UPrimitiveComponent* Component :
PrimitiveComponents)
{
  Component->SetEnableGravity(false);
}
}
}
```

9. Create a subclass of `Actor` called `PhysicsCube`.

10. Add a static mesh:

```
UPROPERTY()
UStaticMeshComponent* MyMesh;
```

11. Initialize the component in your constructor:

```
MyMesh =
CreateDefaultSubobject<UStaticMeshComponent>("MyMesh");
autoMeshAsset =
ConstructorHelpers::FObjectFinder<UStaticMesh>(TEXT("Static
Mesh'/Engine/BasicShapes/Cube.Cube'"));
if (MeshAsset.Object != nullptr)
{
  MyMesh->SetStaticMesh(MeshAsset.Object);
}
MyMesh->SetMobility(EComponentMobility::Movable);
MyMesh->SetSimulatePhysics(true);
SetActorEnableCollision(true);
```

12. To have `PhysicsCube` implement `GravityObject`, first `#include`
    `"GravityObject.h"` in the header file, then modify the class declaration:

```
class UE4COOKBOOK_API APhysicsCube : public AActor, public
IGravityObject
```

13. Compile your project.

14. Create a new level, and place an instance of our gravity volume in the scene.

15. Place an instance of `PhysicsCube` above the gravity volume, then rotate it slightly so that it has one corner lower than the others, as shown in the following image:

16. Verify that the gravity is turned off on the object when it enters the volume, then turns back on again.

 Note that the gravity volume doesn't need to know anything about your `PhysicsCube` actor, just the Gravity Object interface.

How it works...

1. We create a new `Actor` class, and add a box component to give the actor something that will collide with the character. Alternatively, you could subclass `AVolume` if you wanted to use the BSP functionality to define the volume's shape.

2. `NotifyActorBeginOverlap` and `NotifyActorEndOverlap` are overridden so that we can perform some operation when an object enters or leaves the `AntiGravityVolume` area.

3. Inside `NotifyActorBeginOverlap` implementation, we attempt to cast the object that overlapped us into an `IGravityObject` pointer.

4. This tests if the object in question implements the interface.

5. If the pointer is valid, then the object does implement the interface, so it is safe to use the interface pointer to call interface methods on the object.

6. Given that we are inside `NotifyActorBeginOverlap`, we want to disable the gravity on the object, so we call `DisableGravity()`.

7. Inside `NotifyActorEndOverlap`, we perform the same check, but we re-enable gravity on the object.

8. Within the default implementation of `DisableGravity`, we cast our own pointer (the `this` pointer) to `AActor`.

9. This allows us to confirm that the interface has been implemented only on the `Actor` subclasses as well as to call methods defined in `AActor`.

10. If the pointer is valid, we know we are an `Actor`, so we can use `GetComponents<class ComponentType>()` to get a `TArray` of all components of a specific type from ourselves.

11. `GetComponents` is a `template` function. It expects some template parameters:

```
template<class T, class AllocatorType>
voidGetComponents(TArray<T*, AllocatorType>&OutComponents)
const
```

12. Since the 2014 version of the standard, C++ supports compile-time deduction of template parameters. This means that we don't need to actually specify the template parameters when we call the function if the compiler can work them out from the normal function parameters that we provide.

13. The default implementation of `TArray` is `template<typename T, typename Allocator = FDefaultAllocator> class TArray;`

14. This means that we don't need to specify an allocator by default, so we just use `TArray<UPrimitiveComponent*>` when we declare the array.

15. When `TArray` is passed into the `GetComponents` function, the compiler knows it is actually `TArray<UPrimitiveComponent*, FDefaultAllocator>`, and it is able to fill in the template parameters `T` and `AllocatorType` with `UPrimitiveComponent` and `FDefaultAllocator`, so neither of those are required as template parameters for the function's invocation.

16. `GetComponents` iterates through the components that `Actor` has, and any components that inherit from `typename T` have pointers to them stored inside the `PrimitiveComponents` array.

17. Using a range-based `for` loop, another new feature of C++, we can iterate over the components that the function placed into our `TArray` without needing to use the traditional `for` loop structure.

18. Each of the components has `SetEnableGravity(false)` called on them, which disables gravity.

19. Likewise, the `EnableGravity` function iterates over all the primitive components contained in the actor, and enables gravity with `SetEnableGravity(true)`.

See also

▸ Look at *Chapter 4, Actors and Components,* for extensive discussions on Actors and Components. *Chapter 5, Handling Events and Delegates,* discusses events such as `NotifyActorOverlap`.

Inheriting UInterface from one another

Sometimes, you may need to create a `UInterface` that specializes on a more general `UInterface`.

This recipe shows you how to use inheritance with UInterfaces to specialize a **Killable** interface with an **Undead** interface that cannot be killed by normal means.

How to do it...

1. Create a `UINTERFACE`/`IInterface` called `UKillable`.

2. Add `UINTERFACE(meta=(CannotImplementInterfaceInBlueprint))` to the `UInterface` declaration.

3. Add the following functions to the header file:
   ```
   UFUNCTION(BlueprintCallable, Category=Killable)
   virtual bool IsDead();
   UFUNCTION(BlueprintCallable, Category = Killable)
   virtual void Die();
   ```

4. Provide default implementations for the interface inside the implementation file:
   ```
   boolIKillable::IsDead()
   {
     return false;
   }

   voidIKillable::Die()
   {
     GEngine->AddOnScreenDebugMessage(-1,1,
     FColor::Red,"Arrrgh");
     AActor* Me = Cast<AActor>(this);
     if (Me)
     {
       Me->Destroy();
     }

   }
   ```

5. Create a new `UINTERFACE`/`IInterface` called `Undead`. Modify them to inherit from `UKillable`/`IKillable`:
   ```
   UINTERFACE()
   class UE4COOKBOOK_API UUndead: public UKillable
   {
     GENERATED_BODY()
   ```

```
    };

    /**   */
    class UE4COOKBOOK_API IUndead: public IKillable
    {
        GENERATED_BODY()


    };
```

6. Ensure that you include the header defining the `Killable` interface.

7. Add some overrides and new method declarations to the new interface:

```
    virtual bool IsDead() override;
    virtual void Die() override;
    virtual void Turn();
    virtual void Banish();
```

8. Create implementations for the functions:

```
    bool IUndead::IsDead()
    {
        return true;
    }

    void IUndead::Die()
    {
        GEngine->AddOnScreenDebugMessage(-1,1, FColor::Red,"You
        can't kill what is already dead. Mwahaha");
    }

    void IUndead::Turn()
    {
        GEngine->AddOnScreenDebugMessage(-1,1, FColor::Red, "I'm
        fleeing!");

    }

    void IUndead::Banish()
    {
        AActor* Me = Cast<AActor>(this);
        if (Me)
        {
            Me->Destroy();
        }
    }
```

9. Create two new `Actor` classes in C++: one called `Snail`, and the other called `Zombie`.

10. Set the `Snail` class to implement the `IKillable` interface, and add the appropriate header file, #include.

11. Likewise, set the `Zombie` class to implement `IUndead`, and #include `"Undead.h"`.

12. Compile your project.

13. Launch the editor, and drag an instance of both `Zombie` and `Snail` into your level.

14. Add a reference to each of them in the **Level Blueprints**.

15. Call `Die` (Message) on each reference.

16. Connect the execution pins of the two message calls, then wire it up to `Event BeginPlay`.

    Run the game, and then verify that the `Zombie` is disdainful of your efforts to kill it, but the `Snail` groans and then dies (is removed from the world outliner).

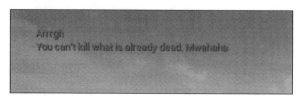

How it works...

1. To make it possible to test this recipe in the **Level Blueprints**, we need to make the interface functions callable via blueprint, so we need the `BlueprintCallable` specifier on our `UFUNCTION`.

2. However, in a `UInterface`, the compiler expects the interface to be implementable via both C++ and Blueprint by default. This conflicts with `BlueprintCallable`, which is merely saying that the function can be invoked from Blueprint, not that it can be overridden in it.

3. We can resolve the conflict by marking the interface as `CannotImplementInterfaceInBlueprint`.

4. This enables the use of `BlueprintCallable` as our `UFUNCTION` specifier rather than `BlueprintImplementableEvent` (which has extra overhead due to the extra code allowing for the function to be overridden via Blueprint).

5. We define `IsDead` and `Die` as `virtual` to enable them to be overridden in another C++ class which inherits this one.

6. In our default interface implementation, `IsDead` always returns `false`.

The default implementation of `Die` prints a death message to the screen, and then destroys the object implementing this interface if it is an `Actor`.

1. We can now create a second interface called `Undead`, which inherits from `Killable`.

2. We use the `public UKillable/public IKillable` in the class declarations to express this.

3. Of course, as a result, we need to include the header file that defines the `Killable` interface.

4. Our new interface overrides the two functions that `Killable` defines to provide more appropriate definitions of `IsDead/Die` for `Undead`.

5. Our overridden definitions have `Undead` already dead by returning `true` from `IsDead`.

6. When `Die` is called on `Undead`, we simply print a message with `Undead` laughing at our feeble attempt to kill it again, and do nothing.

7. We can also specify default implementations for our `Undead`-specific functions, namely `Turn()` and `Banish()`.

8. When `Undead` are Turned, they flee, and for demonstration purposes, we print a message to the screen.

9. If an `Undead` is Banished, however, they are annihilated and destroyed without a trace.

10. In order to test our implementation, we create two `Actors` that each inherit from one of the two interfaces.

11. After we add an instance of each actor to our level, we use **Level Blueprints** to access the level's `BeginPlay` event.

12. When the level begins play, we use a message call to try and call the `Die` function on our instances.

13. The messages that print out are different, and correspond to the two function implementations showing that the Zombie's implementation of `Die` is different, and has overridden the Snail's.

Overriding UInterface functions in C++

One side effect of UInterfaces allowing inheritance in C++ is that we can override default implementations in subclasses as well as in Blueprint. This recipe shows you how to do so.

Getting ready

Follow the recipe *Calling native UInterface functions from C++* in which a Physics Cube is created so that you have the class ready.

How to do it...

1. Create a new Interface called `Selectable`.

2. Define the following functions inside `ISelectable`:

```
virtual bool IsSelectable();

virtual bool TrySelect();

virtual void Deselect();
```

3. Provide a default implementation for functions like this:

```
boolISelectable::IsSelectable()
{
  GEngine->AddOnScreenDebugMessage(-1, 1, FColor::Red,
  "Selectable");
  return true;
}

boolISelectable::TrySelect()
{
  GEngine->AddOnScreenDebugMessage(-1, 1, FColor::Red,
  "Accepting Selection");
  return true;
}

voidISelectable::Deselect()
```

```
{
  unimplemented();
}
```

4. Create a class based on `APhysicsCube` called `SelectableCube`.

5. `#include "Selectable.h"` inside the `SelectableCube` class' header.

6. Modify the `ASelectableCube` declaration like this:

    ```
    class UE4COOKBOOK_API ASelectableCube : public
    APhysicsCube, public ISelectable
    ```

7. Add the following functions to the header:

    ```
    ASelectableCube();
    virtual void NotifyHit(class UPrimitiveComponent* MyComp,
    AActor* Other, class UPrimitiveComponent* OtherComp, bool
    bSelfMoved, FVectorHitLocation, FVectorHitNormal,
    FVectorNormalImpulse, constFHitResult& Hit) override;
    ```

8. Implement the functions:

    ```
    ASelectableCube::ASelectableCube()
    : Super()
    {
      MyMesh->SetNotifyRigidBodyCollision(true);
    }

    voidASelectableCube::NotifyHit(class UPrimitiveComponent*
    MyComp, AActor* Other, class UPrimitiveComponent*
    OtherComp, bool bSelfMoved, FVectorHitLocation,
    FVectorHitNormal, FVectorNormalImpulse, constFHitResult&
    Hit)
    {
      if (IsSelectable())
      {
        TrySelect();
      }
    }
    ```

9. Create a new class, called `NonSelectableCube`, which inherits from
    `SelectableCube`.

10. `NonSelectableCube` should override the functions from `SelectableInterface`:

    ```
    virtual bool IsSelectable() override;

    virtual bool TrySelect() override;

    virtual void Deselect() override;
    ```

11. The implementation file should be altered to include the following:

```
boolANonSelectableCube::IsSelectable()
{
  GEngine->AddOnScreenDebugMessage(-1, 1, FColor::Red, "Not
  Selectable");
  return false;
}

boolANonSelectableCube::TrySelect()
{
  GEngine->AddOnScreenDebugMessage(-1, 1, FColor::Red,
  "Refusing Selection");
  return false;
}

voidANonSelectableCube::Deselect()
{
  unimplemented();
}
```

12. Place an instance of `SelectableCube` into the level at a certain range above the ground, and play your game. You should get messages verifying that the actor is selectable, and that it has accepted the selection, when the cube hits the ground.

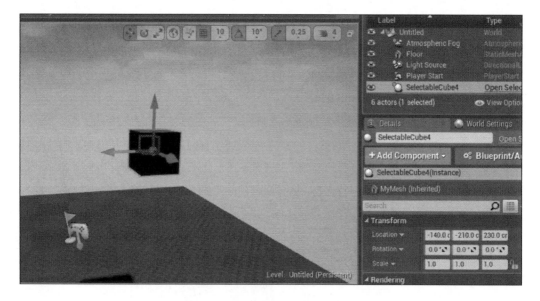

13. Remove `SelectableCube` and replace it with an instance of `NonSelectableCube` to see the alternative messages indicating that this actor isn't selectable, and has refused selection.

How it works...

1. We create three functions inside the `Selectable` interface.

2. `IsSelectable` returns a Boolean to indicate if the object is selectable. You could avoid this and simply use `TrySelect`, given that it returns a Boolean value to indicate success, but, for example, you might want to know if the object inside your UI is a valid selection without having to actually try it.

3. `TrySelect` actually attempts to select the object. There's no explicit contract forcing users to respect `IsSelectable` when trying to select the object, so `TrySelect` is named to communicate that the selection may not always succeed.

4. Lastly, `Deselect` is a function added to allow objects to handle losing the player selection. This could involve changing the UI elements, halting sounds or other visual effects, or simply removing a selection outline from around the unit.

5. The default implementations of the functions return `true` for `IsSelectable` (the default is for any object to be selectable), `true` for `TrySelect` (selection attempts always succeed), and issues a debug assert if `Deselect` is called without being implemented by the class.

6. You could also implement `Deselect` as a pure `virtual` function if you wish.

7. `SelectableCube` is a new class inheriting from `PhysicsCube`, but also implementing the `ISelectable` interface.

8. It also overrides `NotifyHit`, a `virtual` function defined in `AActor` that triggers when the actor undergoes a **RigidBody** collision.

9. We call the constructor from `PhysicsCube` with the `Super()` constructor call inside the implementation of `SelectableCube`. We then add our own implementation, which calls `SetNotifyRigidBodyCollision(true)` on our static mesh instance. This is necessary, because by default, RigidBodies (such as `PrimitiveComponents` with a collision) don't trigger `Hit` events as a performance optimization. As a result, our overridden `NotifyHit` function would never be called.

10. Within the implementation of `NotifyHit`, we call some of the `ISelectable` interface functions on ourselves. Given that we know we are an object that inherits from `ISelectable`, we don't need to cast to an `ISelectable*` in order to call them.

11. We check to see if the object is selectable with `IsSelectable`, and if so, we try to actually perform the selection using `TrySelect`.

12. `NonSelectableCube` inherits from `SelectableCube`, so we can force the object to never be selectable.

13. We accomplish this by overriding the `ISelectable` interface functions again.

14. Within `ANonSelectableCube::IsSelectable()`, we print a message to the screen so we can verify that the function is being called, and then return `false` to indicate that the object isn't selectable at all.

15. In case the user doesn't respect `IsSelectable()`, `ANonSelectableCube::TrySelect()` always returns `false` to indicate that the selection wasn't successful.

16. Given that it is impossible for `NonSelectableCube` to be selected, `Deselect()` calls `unimplemented()`, which throws an assert warning that the function was not implemented.

17. Now, when playing your scene, each time `SelectableCube/NonSelectableCube` hits another object, causing a RigidBody collision, the actor in question will attempt to select itself, and print messages to the screen.

See also

▶ Refer *Chapter 6, Input and Collision,* which shows you how to **Raycast** from the mouse cursor into the game world to determine what is being clicked on, and could be used to extend this recipe to allow the player to click on items to select them

Exposing UInterface methods to Blueprint from a native base class

Being able to define `UInterface` methods in C++ is great, but they should be accessible from Blueprint too. Otherwise, designers or others who are using Blueprint won't be able to interact with your `UInterface`. This recipe shows you how to make a function from an interface callable within the Blueprint system.

How to do it...

1. Create a `UInterface` called `UPostBeginPlay/IPostBeginPlay`.

2. Add the following `virtual` method to `IPostBeginPlay`:
```
UFUNCTION(BlueprintCallable, Category=Test)
virtual void OnPostBeginPlay();
```

3. Provide an implementation of the function:
```
voidIPostBeginPlay::OnPostBeginPlay()
{
  GEngine->AddOnScreenDebugMessage(-1, 1, FColor::Red,
  "PostBeginPlay called");
}
```

4. Create a new `Actor` class called `APostBeginPlayTest`.

5. Modify the class declaration so that it also inherits `IPostBeginPlay`:

    ```
    UCLASS()
    class UE4COOKBOOK_API APostBeginPlayTest : public AActor,
    public IPostBeginPlay
    ```

6. Compile your project. Inside the editor, drag an instance of `APostBeginPlayTest` into your level. With the instance selected, click on **Open Level Blueprint**:

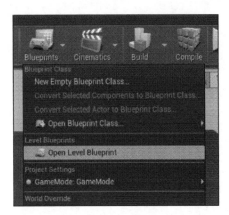

7. Inside the Level Blueprint, right-click and **Create a Reference to PostBeginPlayTest1**.

8. Drag away from the blue pin on the right-hand side of your actor reference, then search the context menu for `onpost` to see your new interface function available. Click on it to insert a call to your native `UInterface` implementation from Blueprint.

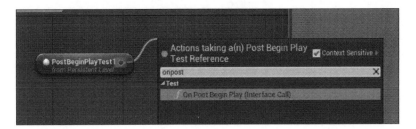

9. Finally, connect the execution pin (white arrow) from the `BeginPlay` node to the execution pin for `OnPostBeginPlay`.

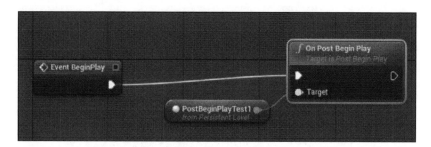

10. When you play your level, you should see the message **PostBeginPlay called** visible on screen for a short amount of time verifying that Blueprint has successfully accessed and called through to your native code implementation of the `UInterface`.

How it works...

1. The `UINTERFACE`/`IInterface` pair function as in other recipes, with the `UInterface` containing reflection information and other data, and the `IInterface` functioning as the actual interface class that can be inherited from.

2. The most significant element that allows the function inside `IInterface` to be exposed to Blueprint is the `UFUNCTION` specifier.

3. `BlueprintCallable` marks this function as one that can be called from the Blueprint system.

4. Any functions exposed to Blueprint in any way require a `Category` value also. This `Category` value specifies the heading under which the function will be listed in the context menu.

5. The function must also be marked `virtual`—this is so that a class that implements the interface via native code can override the implementations of the functions inside it. Without the `virtual` specifier, the Unreal Header Tool will give you an error indicating that you have to either add `virtual`, or `BlueprintImplementableEvent` as a `UFUNCTION` specifier.

6. The reason for this is that without either of those, the interface function wouldn't be overridable in C++ (due to the absence of `virtual`), or Blueprint (because `BlueprintImplementableEvent` was missing). An interface that can't be overridden, but only inherited, has limited utility, so Epic have chosen not to support it within UInterfaces.

7. We then provide a default implementation of the `OnPostBeginPlay` function, which uses the `GEngine` pointer to display a debug message confirming that the function was invoked.

See also

> ▸ *Refer to Chapter 8, Integrating C++ and the Unreal Editor,* for a number of recipes showing how you can integrate your C++ classes with Blueprint

Implementing UInterface functions in Blueprint

One of the key advantages of UInterface in Unreal is the ability for users to implement `UInterface` functions in the editor. This means the interface can be implemented strictly in Blueprint without needing any C++ code, which is helpful to designers.

How to do it...

1. Create a new `UInterface` called `AttackAvoider`.

2. Add the following function declaration to the header:

   ```
   UFUNCTION(BlueprintImplementableEvent, BlueprintCallable,
   Category = AttackAvoider)
   voidAttackIncoming(AActor* AttackActor);
   ```

3. Create a new **Blueprint Class** within the Editor:

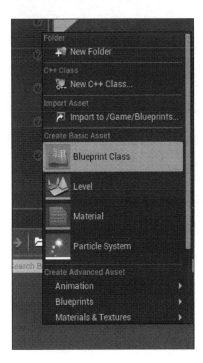

4. Base the class on **Actor**:

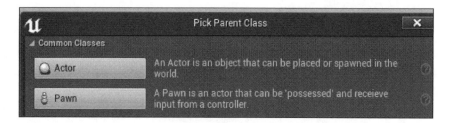

5. Open **Class Settings**:

6. Click on the drop-down menu for **Implement Interface**, and select **AttackAvoider**:

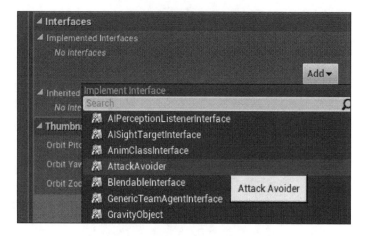

7. **Compile** your blueprint:

8. Right-click in the Event Graph, and type `event attack`. Within the **Context Sensitive** menu, you should see **Event Attack Incoming**. Select it to place an event node in your graph:

9. Drag out from the execution pin on the new node, and release. Type `print string` into the **Context Sensitive** menu to add a **Print String** node.

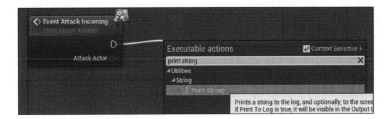

10. You have now implemented a `UInterface` function within Blueprint.

How it works...

1. The `UINTERFACE`/`IInterface` are created in exactly the same way that we see in other recipes in this chapter.

2. When we add a function to the interface, however, we use a new `UFUNCTION` specifier: `BlueprintImplementableEvent`.

3. `BlueprintImplementableEvent` tells the Unreal Header Tool to generate code that creates an empty stub function that can be implemented by Blueprint. We do not need to provide a default C++ implementation for the function.

4. We implement the interface inside Blueprint, which exposes the function for us in a way that allows us to define its implementation in Blueprint.

5. The autogenerated code created by the header tool forwards the calls to the `UInterface` function to our Blueprint implementation.

See also

▶ The following recipe shows you how to define a default implementation for your `UInterface` function in C++, then optionally override it in Blueprint if necessary

Creating C++ UInterface function implementations that can be overridden in Blueprint

Just as with the previous recipe, UInterfaces are useful, but that utility is severely limited without their functionality being usable by designers.

The previous recipe shows you how to call C++ `UInterface` functions from Blueprint; this recipe will show you how to replace the implementation of a `UInterface` function with your own custom Blueprint-only function.

How to do it...

1. Create a new interface called `Wearable` (`IWearable`, `UWearable`).

2. Add the following functions to the header:

```
UFUNCTION(BlueprintNativeEvent, BlueprintCallable, Category
= Wearable)
int32GetStrengthRequirement();
UFUNCTION(BlueprintNativeEvent, BlueprintCallable, Category
= Wearable)
boolCanEquip(APawn* Wearer);
UFUNCTION(BlueprintNativeEvent, BlueprintCallable, Category
= Wearable)
voidOnEquip(APawn* Wearer);
```

3. Add the following function implementations in the implementation file:

```
int32 IWearable::GetStrengthRequirement_Implementation()
{
  return 0;
}
```

```
Bool IWearable::CanEquip_Implementation(APawn* Wearer)
{
  return true;
}

Void IWearable::OnEquip_Implementation(APawn* Wearer)
{

}
```

4. Create a new `Actor` class called `Boots` inside the editor.

5. Add `#include "Wearable.h"` to the header file for `Boots`.

6. Modify the class declaration as follows:

```
UCLASS()
class UE4COOKBOOK_API ABoots : public AActor, public
IWearable
```

7. Add the following implementation of the pure `virtual` functions created by our Interface:

```
virtual void OnEquip_Implementation(APawn* Wearer) override
{
  IWearable::OnEquip_Implementation(Wearer);
}
virtual bool CanEquip_Implementation(APawn* Wearer) override
{
  return IWearable::CanEquip_Implementation(Wearer);
}
virtual int32 GetStrengthRequirement_Implementation() override
{
  return
  IWearable::GetStrengthRequirement_Implementation();
}
```

8. Create a new Blueprint class called `Gloves` based on `Actor`.

9. In the class settings, select `Wearable` as the interface that the `Gloves` actor will implement.

10. Within `Gloves`, override the `OnEquip` function like this:

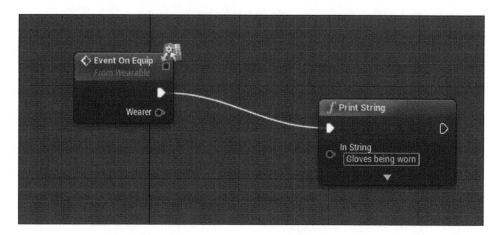

11. Drag a copy of both `Gloves` and `Boots` into your level for testing purposes.

12. Add the following blueprint code to your level:

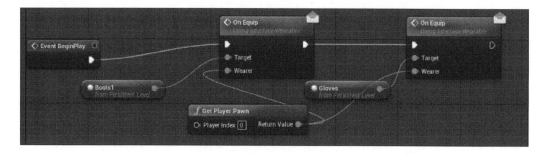

13. Verify that `Boots` performs the default behavior, but `Gloves` performs the blueprint-defined behavior.

How it works...

1. This recipe uses two `UFUNCTION` specifiers together: `BlueprintNativeEvent` and `BlueprintCallable`.

2. `BlueprintCallable` has been shown in previous recipes, and is a way of marking your `UFUNCTION` as visible and invokable in the Blueprint Editor.

3. `BlueprintNativeEvent` signifies a `UFUNCTION` that has a default C++ (native code) implementation, but is also overridable in Blueprint. It's the combination of a virtual function along with `BlueprintImplementableEvent`.

4. In order for this mechanism to work, the Unreal Header Tool generates the body of your functions so that the Blueprint version of the function is called if it exists; otherwise, it dispatches the method call through to the native implementation.

5. In order to separate your default implementation from the dispatch functionality though, UHT defines a new function that takes its name from your declared function, but appends `_Implementation` to the end.

6. This is why the header file declares `GetStrengthRequirement`, but has no implementation, because that is autogenerated.

7. It is also why your implementation file defines `GetStrengthRequirement_Implementation`, but there is no declaration for it, because it is also autogenerated.

8. The `Boots` class implements `IWearable`, but doesn't override the default functionality. However, because the `_Implementation` functions are defined as `virtual`, we still need to explicitly implement the interface functions, and then call the default implementation directly.

9. In contrast, `Gloves` also implements `IWearable`, but has an overridden implementation for `OnEquip` defined in Blueprint.

10. This can be verified when we use **Level Blueprints** to call `OnEquip` for the two actors.

Calling Blueprint-defined interface functions from C++

While the previous recipes have focused on C++ being usable in Blueprint, such as being able to call functions from C++ in Blueprint, and override C++ functions with Blueprint, this recipe shows you the reverse: calling a Blueprint-defined interface function from C++.

How to do it...

1. Create a new `UInterface` called `UTalker`/`ITalker`.

2. Add the following `UFUNCTION` implementation:

```
UFUNCTION(BlueprintNativeEvent, BlueprintCallable, Category
= Talk)
void StartTalking();
```

3. Provide a default empty implementation inside the .cpp file:

```
void ITalker::StartTalking_Implementation()
{


}
```

4. Create a new class based on StaticMeshActor.

5. Add #include and modify the class declaration to include the talker interface:

```
#include "Talker.h"
class UE4COOKBOOK_API ATalkingMesh : public
AStaticMeshActor, public ITalker
```

6. Also, add the following function to the class declaration:

```
void StartTalking_Implementation();
```

7. Within the implementation, add the following to the constructor:

```
ATalkingMesh::ATalkingMesh()
:Super()
{
  autoMeshAsset =
  ConstructorHelpers::FObjectFinder<UStaticMesh>
  (TEXT("StaticMesh'/Engine/BasicShapes/Cube.Cube'"));
  if (MeshAsset.Object != nullptr)
  {
    GetStaticMeshComponent()-
    >SetStaticMesh(MeshAsset.Object);
    //GetStaticMeshComponent()-
    >SetCollisionProfileName
    (UCollisionProfile::Pawn_ProfileName);
    GetStaticMeshComponent()->bGenerateOverlapEvents =
    true;
  }
  GetStaticMeshComponent()-
  >SetMobility(EComponentMobility::Movable);
  SetActorEnableCollision(true);
}
Implmement the default implementation of our StartTalking
function:
voidATalkingMesh::StartTalking_Implementation()
{
  GEngine->AddOnScreenDebugMessage(-1, 1, FColor::Red,
  TEXT("Hello there. What is your name?"));
}
```

8. Create a new class based on `DefaultPawn` to function as our player character.

9. Add some `UPROPERTY`/`UFUNCTION` to our class header:

```
UPROPERTY()
UBoxComponent* TalkCollider;
UFUNCTION()
voidOnTalkOverlap(AActor* OtherActor, UPrimitiveComponent*
OtherComp, int32 OtherBodyIndex, bool bFromSweep,
constFHitResult&SweepResult);
```

10. Modify the constructor:

```
ATalkingPawn::ATalkingPawn()
:Super()
{
  // Set this character to call Tick() every frame. You
  can turn this off to improve performance if you don't
  need it.
  PrimaryActorTick.bCanEverTick = true;
  TalkCollider =
  CreateDefaultSubobject<UBoxComponent>("TalkCollider");
  TalkCollider->SetBoxExtent(FVector(200, 200, 100));
  TalkCollider->OnComponentBeginOverlap.AddDynamic(this,
  &ATalkingPawn::OnTalkOverlap);
  TalkCollider->AttachTo(RootComponent);
}
```

11. Implement `OnTalkOverlap`:

```
voidATalkingPawn::OnTalkOverlap(AActor* OtherActor,
UPrimitiveComponent* OtherComp, int32 OtherBodyIndex, bool
bFromSweep, constFHitResult&SweepResult)
{
  if (OtherActor->GetClass()-
  >ImplementsInterface(UTalker::StaticClass()))
  {
    ITalker::Execute_StartTalking(OtherActor);
  }
}
```

12. Create a new `GameMode`, and set `TalkingPawn` as the default pawn class for the player.

13. Drag an instance of your `ATalkingMesh` class into the level.

14. Create a new Blueprint class based on `ATalkingMesh` by right-clicking on it, and selecting the appropriate option from the context menu:

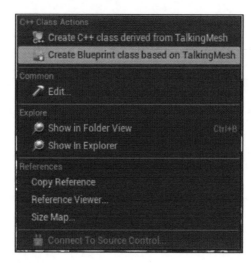

15. Name it `MyTalkingMesh`.

16. Inside the blueprint editor, create an implementation for `StartTalking` like this:

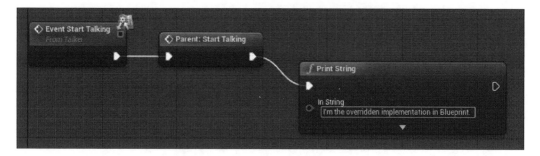

17. Drag a copy of your new Blueprint into the level beside your `ATalkingMesh` instance.

18. Walk up to the two actors, and verify that your custom Pawn is correctly invoking either the default C++ implementation or the Blueprint implementation, as appropriate.

How it works...

1. As always, we create a new interface, and then add some function definitions to the `IInterface` class.

2. We use the `BlueprintNativeEvent` specifier to indicate that we want to declare a default implementation in C++ that can then be overridden in Blueprint.

3. We create a new class (inheriting from `StaticMeshActor` for convenience), and implement the interface on it.

4. In the implementation of the new class constructor, we load a static mesh, and set our collision as usual.

5. We then add an implementation for our interface function, which simply prints a message to the screen.

6. If you were using this in a full-blown project, you could play animations, play audio, alter the user interface, and whatever else was necessary to start a conversation with your `Talker`.

7. At this point, though, we don't have anything to actually call `StartTalking` on our `Talker`.

8. The simplest way to implement this is to create a new `Pawn` subclass (again, inheriting from `DefaultPawn` for convenience) that can start talking to any `Talker` actors that it collides with.

9. In order for this to work, we create a new `BoxComponent` to establish the radius at which we will trigger a conversation.

10. As always, it is a UPROPERTY, so it won't get garbage collected.

11. We also create the definition for a function that will get triggered when the new `BoxComponent` overlaps another `Actor` in the scene.

12. The constructor for our `TalkingPawn` initializes the new `BoxComponent`, and sets its extents appropriately.

13. The constructor also binds the `OnTalkOverlap` function as an event handler to handle collisions with our `BoxComponent`.

14. It also attaches the box component to our `RootComponent` so that it moves with the rest of the player character as the player moves around the level.

15. Inside `OnTalkOverlap`, we need to check if the other actor, which is overlapping our box, implements the `Talker` interface.

16. The most reliable way to do this is with the `ImplementsInterface` function in `UClass`. This function uses the class information generated by the Unreal Header Tool during compilation, and correctly handles both C++ and Blueprint-implemented interfaces.

17. If the function returns `true`, we can use a special autogenerated function contained in our `IInterface` to invoke the interface method of our choice on our instance.

18. This is a static method of the form `<IInterface>::Execute_<FunctionName>`. In our instance, our `IInterface` is `ITalker`, and the function is `StartTalking`, so the function we want to invoke is `ITalker::Execute_StartTalking()`.

19. The reason we need this function is that when an interface is implemented in Blueprint, the relationship isn't actually established at compile time. C++ is, therefore, not aware of the fact that the interface is implemented, and so we can't cast the Blueprint class to `IInterface` to call functions directly.

20. The `Execute_` functions take a pointer to the object that implements the interface, and call a number of internal methods to invoke the desired function's Blueprint implementation.

21. When you play the level, and walk around, the custom `Pawn` is constantly receiving notifications when it's `BoxComponent` overlaps other objects.

22. If they implement the `UTalker`/`ITalker` interface, the pawn then tries to invoke `StartTalking` on the `Actor` instance in question, which then prints the appropriate message on screen.

Implementing a simple interaction system with UInterfaces

This recipe will show you how to combine a number of other recipes in this chapter to demonstrate a simple interaction system, and a door with an interactable doorbell to cause the door to open.

How to do it...

1. Create a new interface, `Interactable`.

2. Add the following functions to the `IInteractable` class declaration:
```
UFUNCTION(BlueprintNativeEvent, BlueprintCallable,
Category=Interactable)
boolCanInteract();
UFUNCTION(BlueprintNativeEvent, BlueprintCallable, Category
= Interactable)
voidPerformInteract();
```

3. Create default implementations for both functions in the implementation file:
```
boolIInteractable::CanInteract_Implementation()
{
  return true;
}
```

```
voidIInteractable::PerformInteract_Implementation()
{

}
```

4. Create a second interface, `Openable`.

5. Add this function to its declaration:
```
UFUNCTION(BlueprintNativeEvent, BlueprintCallable,
Category=Openable)
void Open();
```

6. As with `Interactable`, create a default implementation for the `Open` function:
```
voidIOpenable::Open_Implementation()
{
}
```

7. Create a new class, based on `StaticMeshActor`, called `DoorBell`.

8. `#include "Interactable.h"` in `DoorBell.h`, and add the following functions to the class declaration:
```
virtual bool CanInteract_Implementation() override;
virtual void PerformInteract_Implementation() override;
UPROPERTY(BlueprintReadWrite, EditAnywhere)
AActor* DoorToOpen;
private:
boolHasBeenPushed;
```

9. In the `.cpp` file for `DoorBell`, `#include "Openable.h"`.

10. Load a static mesh for our `DoorBell` in the constructor:
```
HasBeenPushed = false;
autoMeshAsset =
ConstructorHelpers::FObjectFinder<UStaticMesh>(TEXT("Static
Mesh'/Engine/BasicShapes/Cube.Cube'"));
if (MeshAsset.Object != nullptr)
{
  GetStaticMeshComponent()-
  >SetStaticMesh(MeshAsset.Object);
  //GetStaticMeshComponent()-
  >SetCollisionProfileName(UCollisionProfile
  ::Pawn_ProfileName);
  GetStaticMeshComponent()->bGenerateOverlapEvents = true;
}
```

```
GetStaticMeshComponent()-
>SetMobility(EComponentMobility::Movable);
GetStaticMeshComponent()-> SetWorldScale3D(FVector(0.5,
0.5, 0.5));
SetActorEnableCollision(true);

DoorToOpen = nullptr;
```

11. Add the following function implementations to implement the
    `Interactable` interface on our `DoorBell`:

```
boolADoorBell::CanInteract_Implementation()
{
   return !HasBeenPushed;
}


voidADoorBell::PerformInteract_Implementation()
{
   HasBeenPushed = true;
   if (DoorToOpen->GetClass()-
   >ImplementsInterface(UOpenable::StaticClass()))
   {
      IOpenable::Execute_Open(DoorToOpen);
   }
}
```

12. Now create a new `StaticMeshActor`-based class called `Door`.

13. `#include` the Openable and Interactable interfaces into the class header, then
    modify Door's declaration:

```
class UE4COOKBOOK_API ADoor : public AStaticMeshActor,
public IInteractable, public IOpenable
```

14. Add the interface functions to `Door`:

```
UFUNCTION()
virtual bool CanInteract_Implementation() override { return
IInteractable::CanInteract_Implementation(); };
UFUNCTION()
virtual void PerformInteract_Implementation() override;

UFUNCTION()
virtual void Open_Implementation() override;
```

15. As with `DoorBell`, in the `Door` constructor, initialize our mesh component, and load a model in:

```
autoMeshAsset =
ConstructorHelpers::FObjectFinder<UStaticMesh>(TEXT("Static
Mesh'/Engine/BasicShapes/Cube.Cube'"));
if (MeshAsset.Object != nullptr)
{
  GetStaticMeshComponent()-
  >SetStaticMesh(MeshAsset.Object);
  //GetStaticMeshComponent()-
  >SetCollisionProfileName(UCollisionProfile
  ::Pawn_ProfileName);
  GetStaticMeshComponent()->bGenerateOverlapEvents = true;
}
GetStaticMeshComponent()-
>SetMobility(EComponentMobility::Movable);
GetStaticMeshComponent()->SetWorldScale3D(FVector(0.3, 2,
3));
SetActorEnableCollision(true);
```

16. Implement the interface functions:

```
voidADoor::PerformInteract_Implementation()
{
  GEngine->AddOnScreenDebugMessage(-1, 5, FColor::Red,
  TEXT("The door refuses to budge. Perhaps there is a
  hidden switch nearby?"));
}

voidADoor::Open_Implementation()
{
  AddActorLocalOffset(FVector(0, 0, 200));
}
```

17. Create a new `DefaultPawn`-based class called `AInteractingPawn`.

18. Add the following functions to the `Pawn` class header:

```
voidTryInteract();

private:
virtual void SetupPlayerInputComponent(UInputComponent*
InInputComponent) override;
```

19. Inside the implementation file for the `Pawn`, `#include "Interactable.h"`, and then provide implementations for both functions from the header:

```
voidAInteractingPawn::TryInteract()
{
  APlayerController* MyController =
  Cast<APlayerController>(Controller);
  if (MyController)
  {
    APlayerCameraManager* MyCameraManager = MyController-
    >PlayerCameraManager;
    autoStartLocation = MyCameraManager-
    >GetCameraLocation();
    autoEndLocation = MyCameraManager->GetCameraLocation()
    + (MyCameraManager->GetActorForwardVector() * 100);
    FHitResultHitResult;
    GetWorld()->SweepSingleByObjectType(HitResult,
    StartLocation, EndLocation, FQuat::Identity,
    FCollisionObjectQueryParams
    (FCollisionObjectQueryParams::AllObjects),
    FCollisionShape::MakeSphere(25),
    FCollisionQueryParams(FName("Interaction"),true,this));
    if (HitResult.Actor != nullptr)
    {
      if (HitResult.Actor->GetClass()-
      >ImplementsInterface(UInteractable::StaticClass()))
      {
        if
        (IInteractable::Execute_CanInteract
        (HitResult.Actor.Get()))
        {
          IInteractable::Execute_PerformInteract
          (HitResult.Actor.Get());
        }
      }
    }
  }
}
voidAInteractingPawn::SetupPlayerInputComponent(UInputCompo
nent* InInputComponent)
{
  Super::SetupPlayerInputComponent(InInputComponent);
  InInputComponent->BindAction("Interact", IE_Released,
  this, &AInteractingPawn::TryInteract);
}
```

20. Now, either create a new `GameMode` in C++ or Blueprint, and set `InteractingPawn` as our default `Pawn` class.

21. Drag a copy of both `Door` and `Doorbell` into the level:

22. Use the eyedropper beside doorbell's **Door to Open**, as shown in the following screenshot, then click on the door actor instance in your level:

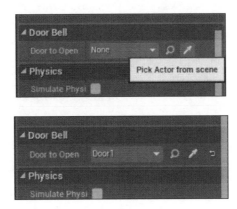

23. Create a new Action binding in the editor called `Interact`, and bind it to a key of your choice:

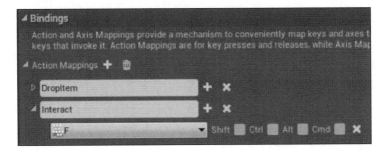

24. Play your level, and walk up to the doorbell. Look at it, and press whatever key you bound `Interact` with. Verify that the door moves once.

25. You can also interact with the door directly to receive some information about it.

How it works...

1. As in previous recipes, we mark `UFUNCTION` as `BlueprintNativeEvent` and `BlueprintCallable` in order to allow the `UInterface` to be implemented in either native code or Blueprint, and allow the functions to be called with either method.

2. We create `DoorBell` based on `StaticMeshActor` for convenience, and have `DoorBell` implement the `Interactable` interface.

3. Inside the constructor for `DoorBell`, we initialize `HasBeenPushed` and `DoorToOpen` to the default safe values.

4. Within the implementation for `CanInteract`, we return the inverse of `HasBeenPushed` so that once the button has been pushed it, can't be interacted with.

5. Inside `PerformInteract`, we check if we have a reference to a door object to open.

6. If we have a valid reference, we verify that the door actor implements `Openable`, then we invoke the `Open` function on our door.

7. Within `Door`, we implement both `Interactable` and `Openable`, and override the functions from each.

8. We define the `Door` implementation of `CanInteract` to be the same as the default.

9. Within `PerformInteract`, we display a message to the user.

10. Inside `Open`, we use `AddActorLocalOffset` to move the door a certain distance away. With Timeline in Blueprint or a linear interpolation, we could make this transition smooth rather than a teleport.

11. Lastly, we create a new `Pawn` so that the player can actually interact with objects.

12. We create a `TryInteract` function, which we bind to the `Interact` input action in the overridden `SetupPlayerInputComponent` function.

13. This means that when the player performs the input that is bound to `Interact`, our `TryInteract` function will run.

14. `TryInteract` gets a reference to `PlayerController`, casting the generic controller reference that all Pawns have.

15. `PlayerCameraManager` is retrieved through `PlayerController`, so we can access the current location and rotation of the player camera.

16. We create start and end points using the camera's location, then 100 units in the forward direction away from the camera's location, and pass those into `GetWorld::SweepSingleByObjectType`.

17. This function takes in a number of parameters. `HitResult` is a variable that allows the function to return information about any object hit by the trace. `CollisionObjectQueryParams` allows us to specify if we are interested in dynamic, static items, or both.

18. We accomplish a sphere trace by passing the shape in using the `MakeSphere` function.

19. Sphere traces allow for slightly more human error by defining a cylinder to check for objects rather than a straight line. Given that the players might not look exactly at your object, you can tweak the sphere's radius as appropriate.

20. The final parameter, `SweepSingleByObjectType`, is a struct that gives the trace a name, lets us specify if we are colliding against complex collision geometry, and most importantly, allows us to specify that we want to ignore the object which is initiating the trace.

21. If `HitResult` contains an actor after the trace is done, we check if the actor implements our interface, then attempt to call `CanInteract` on it.

22. If the actor indicates yes, it can be interacted with, so we then tell it to actually perform the interaction.

8
Integrating C++ and the Unreal Editor

In this chapter, we will cover following recipes:

- ▶ Using a class or `struct` as a blueprint variable
- ▶ Creating classes or structs that can be subclassed in Blueprint
- ▶ Creating functions that can be called in Blueprint
- ▶ Creating events that can be implemented in Blueprint
- ▶ Exposing multi-cast delegates to Blueprint
- ▶ Creating C++ enums that can be used in Blueprint
- ▶ Editing class properties in different places in the editor
- ▶ Making properties accessible in the Blueprint editor graph
- ▶ Responding to property – changed events from the editor
- ▶ Implementing a native code Construction Script
- ▶ Creating a new editor module
- ▶ Creating new toolbar buttons
- ▶ Creating new menu entries
- ▶ Creating a new editor window
- ▶ Creating a new Asset type
- ▶ Creating custom context menu entries for Assets
- ▶ Creating new console commands
- ▶ Creating a new graph pin visualizer for Blueprint
- ▶ Inspecting types with custom **Details** panels

Introduction

One of Unreal's primary strengths is that it provides programmers with the ability to create Actors and other objects that can be customized or used by designers in the editor. This chapter shows how. Following that, we will try to customize the editor by creating custom Blueprint and Animation nodes from scratch. We will also implement custom editor windows and custom **Details** panels for inspecting the types created by users.

Using a class or struct as a blueprint variable

Types that you declare in C++ do not automatically get incorporated into Blueprint for use as variables. This recipe shows you how to make them accessible so that you can use custom native code types as Blueprint function parameters.

How to do it...

1. Create a new class using the editor. Unlike previous chapters, we are going to create an Object-based class. Object isn't visible in the default list of common classes, so we need to tick the **Show all classes** button in the editor UI, then select **Object**. Call your new **Object** subclass `TileType`.

2. Add the following properties to the `TileType` definition:
    ```
    UPROPERTY()
    int32 MovementCost;
    UPROPERTY()
    bool CanBeBuiltOn;

    UPROPERTY()
    FString TileName;
    ```

3. Compile your code.

4. Inside the editor, create a new Blueprint class based on `Actor`. Call it `Tile`.

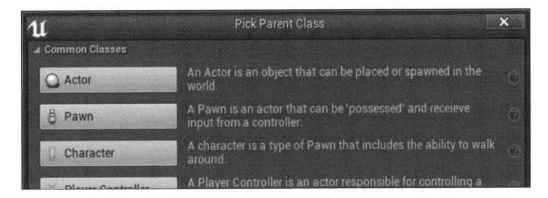

5. Within the blueprint editor for `Tile`, add a new variable to the Blueprint. Check the list of types that you can create as variables, and verify that `TileType` is not there.

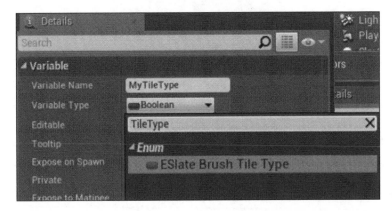

6. Add `BlueprintType` to the `UCLASS` macro as follows:

```
UCLASS(BlueprintType)
class UE4COOKBOOK_API UTileType : public UObject
{
}
```

7. Recompile the project, then return to the `Tile` blueprint editor.

8. Now when you add a new variable to your actor, you can select `TileType` as the type for your new variable.

9. We've now established a "has-a" relationship between `Tile` and `TileType`.

10. Now `TileType` is a Blueprint type that can be used as a function parameter. Create a new function on your `Tile` blueprint called `SetTileType`.

11. Add a new input:

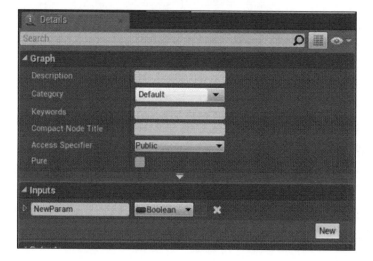

12. Set the input parameter's type to `TileType`.

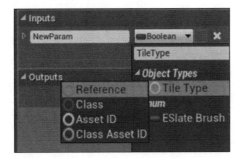

13. You can drag our `Type` variable into the viewport, and select **Set**.

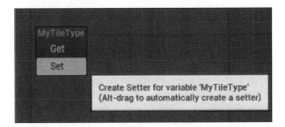

14. Assign the **Exec** pin and input parameter from `SetTileType` to the **Set** node.

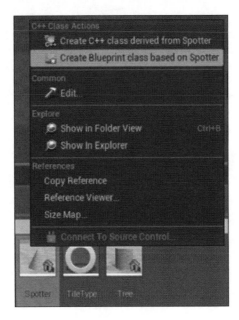

How it works...

1. For performance reasons, Unreal assumes that classes do not require the extra reflection code that is needed to make the type available to Blueprint.

2. We can override this default by specifying `BlueprintType` in our `UCLASS` macro.

3. With the specifier included, the type is now made available as a parameter or variable in Blueprint.

There's more...

This recipe shows that you can use a type as a function parameter in Blueprint if its native code declaration includes `BlueprintType`.

However, at the moment, none of the properties that we defined in C++ are accessible to Blueprint.

Other recipes in this chapter deal with making those properties accessible so that we can actually do something meaningful with our custom objects.

Creating classes or structs that can be subclassed in Blueprint

While this book focuses on C++, when developing with Unreal, a more standard workflow is to implement core gameplay functionality as well as performance-critical code in C++, and expose those features to Blueprint to allow designers to prototype gameplay, which can then be refactored by programmers with additional Blueprint features, or pushed back down to the C++ layer.

One of the most common tasks, then, is to **mark up** our classes and structs in such a way that they are visible to the Blueprint system.

How to do it...

1. Create a new `Actor` class using the editor wizard; call it `BaseEnemy`.

2. Add the following `UPROPERTY` to the class:
   ```
   UPROPERTY()
   FString WeaponName;
   UPROPERTY()
   int32 MaximumHealth;
   ```

3. Add the following class specifier to the UCLASS macro:

```
UCLASS(Blueprintable)
class UE4COOKBOOK_API ABaseEnemy : public AActor
```

4. Open the editor and create a new blueprint class. Expand the list to show all classes and select our BaseEnemyclass as the parent.

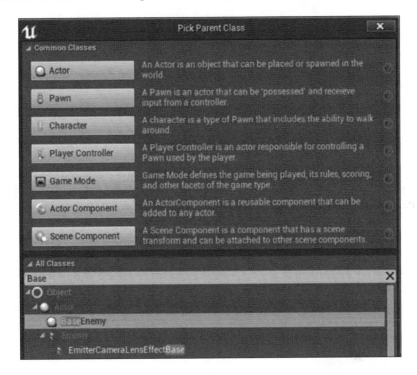

5. Name the new Blueprint EnemyGoblin and open it in the Blueprint editor.

6. Note that the UPROPERTY macro we created earlier still aren't there because we haven't yet included the appropriate markup for them to be visible to Blueprint.

How it works...

1. The previous recipe demonstrated the use of BlueprintType as a class specifier. BlueprintType allows the type to be used as a type within the Blueprint editor (that is, it can be a variable or a function input/return value).

2. However, we may want to create blueprints based on our type (using inheritance) rather than composition (placing an instance of our type inside an Actor, for example).

3. This is why Epic provided `Blueprintable` as a class specifier. `Blueprintable` means a developer can mark a class as inheritable by the Blueprint classes.

4. We have both `BlueprintType` and `Blueprintable` instead of a single combined specifier, because sometimes, you may only want partial functionality. For example, certain classes should be usable as variables, but performance reasons forbid creating them in Blueprint. In that instance, you would use `BlueprintType` rather than both specifiers.

5. On the other hand, perhaps we want to use the Blueprint editor to create new subclasses, but we don't want to pass object instances around inside the `Actor` blueprints. It is recommended to use `Blueprintable`, but omit `BlueprintType` in this case.

6. As before, neither `Blueprintable` or `BlueprintType` specifies anything about the member functions or member variables contained inside our class. We'll make those available in later recipes.

Creating functions that can be called in Blueprint

While marking classes as `BlueprintType` or `Blueprintable` allows us to pass instances of the class around in Blueprint, or to subclass the type with a Blueprint class, those specifiers don't actually say anything about member functions or variables, and if they should be exposed to Blueprint.

This recipe shows you how to mark a function so that it can be called within Blueprint graphs.

How to do it...

1. Create a new `Actor` class using the editor. Call the actor `SlidingDoor`.

2. Add the following UPROPERTY to the new class:

```
UFUNCTION(BlueprintCallable, Category = Door)
void Open();
UPROPERTY()
bool IsOpen;

UPROPERTY()
FVector TargetLocation;
```

3. Create the class implementation by adding the following to the `.cpp` file:

```
ASlidingDoor::ASlidingDoor()
:Super()
{
  auto MeshAsset =
  ConstructorHelpers::FObjectFinder<UStaticMesh>
  (TEXT("StaticMesh'/Engine/BasicShapes/Cube.Cube'"));
  if (MeshAsset.Object != nullptr)
  {
    GetStaticMeshComponent()
    ->SetStaticMesh(MeshAsset.Object);
    GetStaticMeshComponent()->bGenerateOverlapEvents =
    true;
  }
  GetStaticMeshComponent()
  ->SetMobility(EComponentMobility::Movable);
  GetStaticMeshComponent()->SetWorldScale3D(FVector(0.3, 2,
  3));
  SetActorEnableCollision(true);
  IsOpen = false;
  PrimaryActorTick.bStartWithTickEnabled = true;
  PrimaryActorTick.bCanEverTick = true;
}
void ASlidingDoor::Open()
{
  TargetLocation =
  ActorToWorld().TransformPositionNoScale(FVector(0, 0,
  200));
  IsOpen = true;
}

void ASlidingDoor::Tick(float DeltaSeconds)
{
  if (IsOpen)
  {
    SetActorLocation(FMath::Lerp(GetActorLocation(),
    TargetLocation, 0.05));
  }
}
```

4. Compile your code and launch the editor.

5. Drag a copy of your door out into the level.

6. Make sure you have your `SlidingDoor` instance selected, then open the Level blueprint. Right-click on the empty canvas, and expand **Call function on Sliding Door 1**.

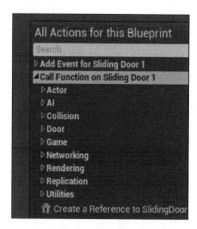

7. Expand the **Door** section, then select the `Open` function.

8. Link the execution pin (white arrow) from `BeginPlay` to the white arrow on the `Open` node, as seen in the following screenshot:

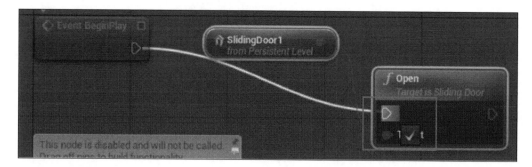

9. Play your level, and verify that the door moves up as expected when `Open` is invoked on your door instance.

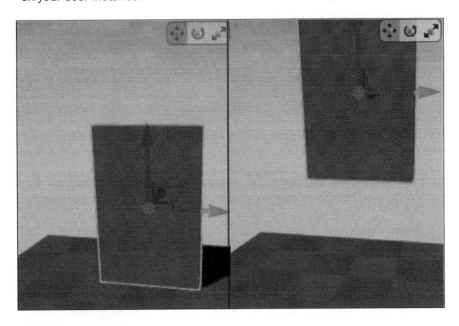

How it works...

1. Within the declaration of the door, we create a new function for opening the door, a Boolean to track if the door has been told to open, and a vector allowing us to precompute the target location of the door.

2. We also override the `Tick` actor function so that we can perform some behavior on every frame.

3. Within the constructor, we load in the cube mesh and scale it to represent our door.

4. We also set `IsOpen` to a known good value of `false` and enable actor ticking by using `bCanEverTick` and `bStartWithTickEnabled`.

5. These two Booleans control if ticking can be enabled for this actor and if ticking starts in an enabled state respectively.

6. Inside the `Open` function, we calculate the target location relative to the door's starting position.

7. We also change the `IsOpen` Boolean from `false` to `true`.

8. Now that the `IsOpen` Boolean is `true`, inside the `Tick` function, the door tries to move itself towards the target location using `SetActorLocation` and `Lerp` to interpolate between the current location and the destination.

▶ Chapter 5, *Handling Events and Delegates,* has a number of recipes relating to the spawning of actors

Creating events that can be implemented in Blueprint

Another way that C++ can be more tightly integrated with Blueprint is the creation of functions that can have Blueprint implementations in native code. This allows for a programmer to specify an event, and invoke it, without needing to know anything about the implementation. The class can then be subclassed in Blueprint, and another member of the production team can implement a handler for the event without ever having to go near a line of C++.

How to do it...

1. Create a new `StaticMeshActor` class called `Spotter`.

2. Make sure the following functions are defined and overridden in the class header:

```
virtual void Tick( float DeltaSeconds ) override;
UFUNCTION(BlueprintImplementableEvent)
void OnPlayerSpotted(APawn* Player);
```

3. Add this code to the constructor:

```
PrimaryActorTick.bCanEverTick = true;
auto MeshAsset =
ConstructorHelpers::FObjectFinder<UStaticMesh>
(TEXT("StaticMesh'/Engine/BasicShapes/Cone.Cone'"));
if (MeshAsset.Object != nullptr)
{
  GetStaticMeshComponent()
  ->SetStaticMesh(MeshAsset.Object);
  GetStaticMeshComponent()->bGenerateOverlapEvents = true;
}
GetStaticMeshComponent()
->SetMobility(EComponentMobility::Movable);
GetStaticMeshComponent()->SetRelativeRotation(FRotator(90,
0, 0));
```

4. Add this to the `Tick` function:

```
Super::Tick( DeltaTime );

auto EndLocation = GetActorLocation() +
ActorToWorld().TransformVector(FVector(0,0,-200));
FHitResult HitResult;
GetWorld()->SweepSingleByChannel(HitResult,
GetActorLocation(), EndLocation, FQuat::Identity,
ECC_Camera, FCollisionShape::MakeSphere(25),
FCollisionQueryParams("Spot", true, this));
APawn* SpottedPlayer = Cast<APawn>(HitResult.Actor.Get());

if (SpottedPlayer!= nullptr)
{
  OnPlayerSpotted(SpottedPlayer);
}
DrawDebugLine(GetWorld(), GetActorLocation(), EndLocation,
FColor::Red);
```

5. Compile and start the editor. Find your `Spotter` class in **Content Browser**, then left-click and drag a copy out into the game world.

6. When you play the level, you'll see the red line showing the trace that the `Actor` is performing. However, nothing will happen, because we haven't implemented our `OnPlayerSpotted` event.

7. In order to implement this event, we need to create a blueprint subclass of our `Spotter`.

8. Right-click on `Spotter` in **Content Browser**, and select **Create Blueprint class based on Spotter**. Name the class `BPSpotter`.

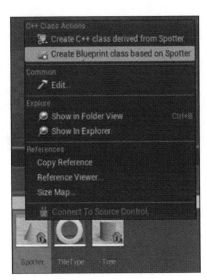

9. Inside the Blueprint editor, click on the **Override** button in the **Functions** section of the **My Blueprint** panel:

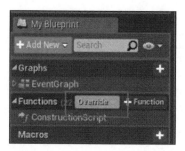

10. Select **On Player Spotted**:

11. Left-click and drag from the white execution pin on our event. In the context menu that appears, select and add a `Print String` node so that it is linked to the event.

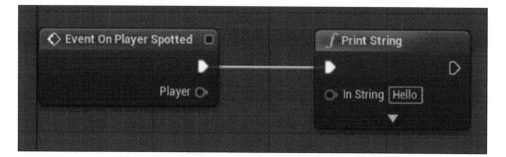

12. Play the level again, and verify that walking in front of the trace that the `Spotter` is using now prints a string to the screen.

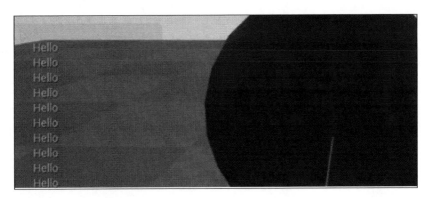

How it works...

1. In the constructor for our `Spotter` object, we load one of the basic primitives, a cone, into our Static Mesh Component as a visual representation.

2. We then rotate the cone so that it resembles a spotlight pointing to the X axis of the actor.

3. During the `Tick` function, we get the actor's location, and then find a point 200 units away from the actor along its local X axis. We call the parent class implementation of `Tick` using `Super::` to ensure that any other tick functionality is preserved despite our override.

4. We convert a local position into a world space position by first acquiring the Actor-to-World transform for the `Actor`, then using that to transform a vector specifying the position.

5. The transform is based on the orientation of the root component, which is the static mesh component that we rotated during the constructor.

6. As a result of that existing rotation, we need to rotate the vector we want to transform. Given that we want the vector to point out of what was the bottom of the cone, we want a distance along the negative up axis, that is, we want a vector of the form (0,0,-d), where *d* is the actual distance away.

7. Having calculated our end location for our trace, we actually perform the trace with the `SweepSingleByChannel` function.

8. Once the sweep is performed, we try to cast the resulting hit `Actor` into a pawn.

9. If the cast was successful, we invoke our Implementable Event of `OnPlayerSpotted`, and the user-defined Blueprint code executes.

Exposing multi-cast delegates to Blueprint

Multi-cast delegates are a great way to broadcast an event to multiple objects who **listen** or **subscribe** to the event in question. They are particularly invaluable if you have a C++ module that generates events that potentially arbitrary Actors might want to be notified about. This recipe shows you how to create a multi-cast delegate in C++ that can notify a group of other Actors during runtime.

How to do it...

1. Create a new `StaticMeshActor` class called `King`. Add the following to the class header:

```
DECLARE_DYNAMIC_MULTICAST_DELEGATE_OneParam(FOnKing
DeathSignature, AKing*, DeadKing);
```

2. Add a new `UFUNCTION` to the class:

```
UFUNCTION(BlueprintCallable, Category = King)
void Die();
```

3. Add an instance of our multicast delegate to the class:

```
UPROPERTY(BlueprintAssignable)
FOnKingDeathSignature OnKingDeath;
```

4. Add our mesh initialization to the constructor:

```
auto MeshAsset =
ConstructorHelpers::FObjectFinder<UStaticMesh>(TEXT("Static
Mesh'/Engine/BasicShapes/Cone.Cone'"));
if (MeshAsset.Object != nullptr)
{
  GetStaticMeshComponent()
  ->SetStaticMesh(MeshAsset.Object);
  GetStaticMeshComponent()->bGenerateOverlapEvents = true;
}
GetStaticMeshComponent()
->SetMobility(EComponentMobility::Movable);
```

5. Implement the `Die` function:

```
void AKing::Die()
{
  OnKingDeath.Broadcast(this);
}
```

6. Create a new class called `Peasant`, also based on `StaticMeshActor`.

7. Declare a default constructor in the class:

```
APeasant();
```

8. Declare the following function:

```
UFUNCTION(BlueprintCallable, category = Peasant)
void Flee(AKing* DeadKing);
```

9. Implement the constructor:

```
auto MeshAsset =
ConstructorHelpers::FObjectFinder<UStaticMesh>(TEXT("Static
Mesh'/Engine/BasicShapes/Cube.Cube'"));
if (MeshAsset.Object != nullptr)
{
  GetStaticMeshComponent()
  ->SetStaticMesh(MeshAsset.Object);
  GetStaticMeshComponent()->bGenerateOverlapEvents = true;
}
GetStaticMeshComponent()
->SetMobility(EComponentMobility::Movable);
```

10. Implement the function in the `.cpp` file:

```
void APeasant::Flee(AKing* DeadKing)
{
  GEngine->AddOnScreenDebugMessage(-1, 2, FColor::Red,
  TEXT("Waily Waily!"));
  FVector FleeVector = GetActorLocation() - DeadKing
  ->GetActorLocation();
  FleeVector.Normalize();
  FleeVector *= 500;
  SetActorLocation(GetActorLocation() + FleeVector);
}
```

11. Open Blueprint and create a Blueprint class based on `APeasant` called `BPPeasant`.

12. Within the blueprint, click and drag away from the white (execution) pin of your `BeginPlay` node. Type `get all`, and you should see **Get All Actors Of Class**. Select the node to place it in your graph.

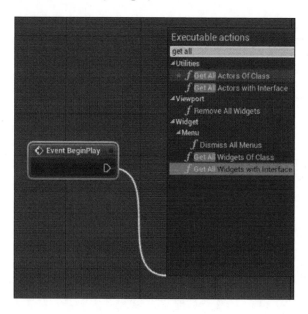

13. Set the value of the purple (class) node to `King`. You can type `king` in the search bar to make locating the class in the list easier.

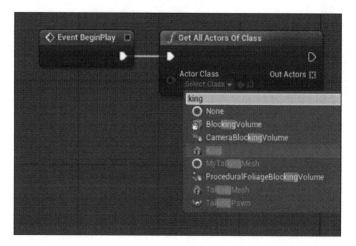

14. Drag from the blue grid (object array) node out into empty space and place a get node.

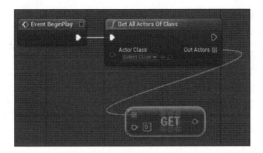

15. Drag away from the blue output pin of the get node, and place a Not Equal (object) node.

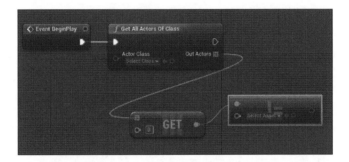

16. Connect the red (bool) pin of the Not Equal node to a `Branch` node, and wire the execution pin of `Branch` to our `Get All Actors Of Class` node.

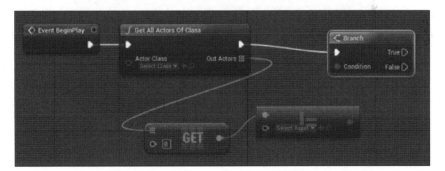

17. Connect the **True** pin of the branch to the **Bind Event to OnKing Death** node.

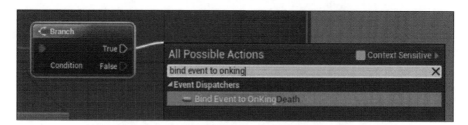

 Note that you will probably have to untick **Context Sensitive** in the context menu for the **Bind Event** node to be visible.

18. Drag out the red pin on the **Bind Event** node, and select **Add Custom Event...** in the context menu which appears after you release your left mouse button.

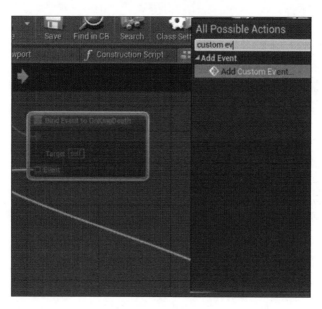

19. Give your event a name, then connect the white execution pin to a new node named `Flee`.

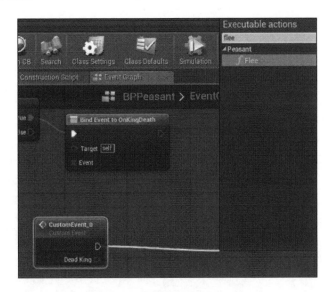

20. Verify that your Blueprint looks like the following figure:

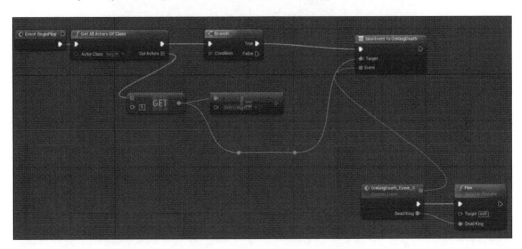

21. Drag a copy of your `King` class into the level, then add a few `BPPeasant` instances around it in a circle.

22. Open the level Blueprint. Inside it, drag away from `BeginPlay`, and add a `Delay` node. Set the delay to **5** seconds.

23. With your `King` instance selected in the level, right-click in the graph editor for the Level Blueprint.

24. Select **Call function on King 1**, and look in the `King` category for a function called `Die`.

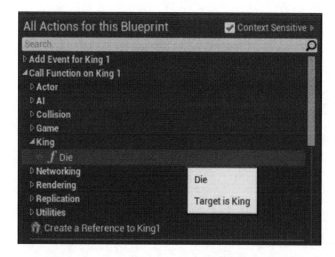

25. Select `Die`, then connect its execution pin to the output execution pin from the delay.

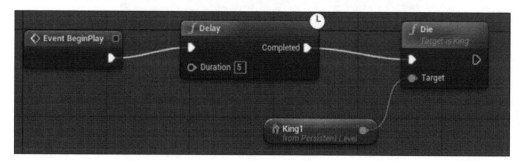

26. When you play your level, you should see that the king dies after 5 seconds, and the peasants all wail and flee directly away from the king.

How it works...

1. We create a new actor (based on `StaticMeshActor` for convenience, as it saves us having to declare or create a Static Mesh component for the `Actor` visual representation).

2. We declare a dynamic multicast delegate using the `DECLARE_DYNAMIC_MULTICAST_DELEGATE_OneParam` macro. Dynamic multicast delegates allow an arbitrary number of objects to subscribe (listen) and unsubscribe (stop listening) so that they will be notified when the delegate is broadcast.

3. The macro takes a number of arguments—the type name of the new delegate signature being created, the type of the signature's parameter, then the name of the signature's parameter.

4. We also add a function to `King` that will allow us to tell it to die. Because we want to expose the function to Blueprints for prototyping, we mark it as `BlueprintCallable`.

5. The `DECLARE_DYNAMIC_MULTICAST_DELEGATE` macro that we used earlier only declared a type; it didn't declare an instance of the delegate, so we do that now, referencing the type name that we provided earlier when invoking the macro.

6. Dynamic multicast delegates can be marked `BlueprintAssignable` in their `UPROPERTY` declaration. This indicates to Unreal that the Blueprint system can dynamically assign events to the delegate that will be called when the delegate's `Broadcast` function is called.

7. As always, we assign a simple mesh to our `King` so that it has a visual representation in the game scene.

8. Within the `Die` function, we call `Broadcast` on our own delegate. We specified that the delegate would have a parameter that is a pointer to the king which died, so we pass this pointer as a parameter to the broadcast function.

> If you want the king to be destroyed, rather than play an animation or other effect when it dies, you would need to change the delegate's declaration and pass in a different type. For example, you could use `FVector`, and simply pass in the location of the dead king directly so that the peasants could still flee appropriately.
>
> Without this, you potentially could have a situation where the `King` pointer is valid when `Broadcast` is called, but the call to `Actor::Destroy()` invalidates it before your bound functions are executed.

9. Within our next `StaticMeshActor` subclass, called `Peasant`, we initialize the static mesh component as usual using, a different shape to the one that we used for the `King`.

10. Inside the implementation of the peasant's `Flee` function, we simulate the peasants playing sound by printing a message on the screen.

11. We then calculate a vector to make the peasants flee by first finding a vector from the dead king to this peasant's location.

12. We normalize the vector to retrieve a unit vector (with a length of 1) pointing in the same direction.

13. Scaling the normalized vector and adding it to our current location calculates a position at a fixed distance, in the exact direction for the peasant to be fleeing directly away from the dead king.

14. `SetActorLocation` is then used to actually teleport the peasants to that location.

> If you used a Character with an AI controller, you could have the `Peasant` pathfind to the target location rather than teleporting. Alternatively, you could use a `Lerp` function invoked during the peasant's `Tick` to make them slide smoothly rather than jump directly to the location.

See also

▶ Look at *Chapter 4, Actors and Components,* for more extended discussions about Actors and Components. *Chapter 5, Handling Events and Delegates,* discusses events such as `NotifyActorOverlap`.

Creating C++ enums that can be used in Blueprint

Enums are commonly used in C++ as flags or inputs to switch statements. However, what if you want to pass an `enum` value to or from C++ from a Blueprint? Alternatively, if you want to use a `switch` statement in Blueprint that uses an `enum` from C++, how do you let the Blueprint editor know that your `enum` should be accessible within the editor? This recipe shows you how to make enums visible in Blueprint.

How to do it...

1. Create a new `StaticMeshActor` class called `Tree` using the editor.

2. Insert the following code above the class declaration:

```
UENUM(BlueprintType)
enum TreeType
{
  Tree_Poplar,
  Tree_Spruce,
  Tree_Eucalyptus,
  Tree_Redwood
};
```

3. Add the following UPROPERTY in the `Tree` class:

```
UPROPERTY(BlueprintReadWrite)
TEnumAsByte<TreeType> Type;
```

4. Add the following to the `Tree` constructor:

```
auto MeshAsset =
ConstructorHelpers::FObjectFinder<UStaticMesh>(TEXT("Static
Mesh'/Engine/BasicShapes/Cylinder.Cylinder'"));
if (MeshAsset.Object != nullptr)
{
  GetStaticMeshComponent()
  ->SetStaticMesh(MeshAsset.Object);
  GetStaticMeshComponent()->bGenerateOverlapEvents = true;
}
GetStaticMeshComponent()
->SetMobility(EComponentMobility::Movable);
```

5. Create a new Blueprint class, called `MyTree`, based on `Tree`.

6. Inside the blueprint editor for `MyTree`, click on the **Construction Script** tab.

7. Right-click in the empty window, and type `treetype`. There is a **Get number of entries in TreeType** node.

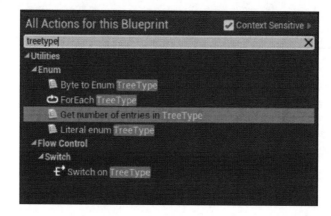

8. Place it, and then connect its output pin to a **Random Integer** node.

9. Connect the output of the random integer to a `ToByte` node.

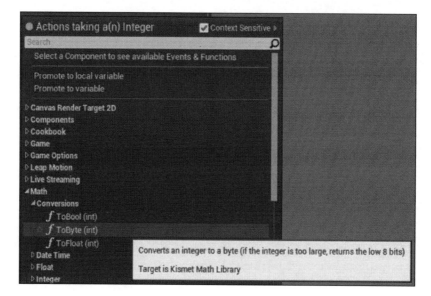

10. In the **Variables** section of the Blueprint panel, expand **Tree** and select **Type**.

11. Drag this into the graph, and select **Set** when you see a small context menu appear.

12. Connect the output of the ToByte node to the input of the **SET Type** node. You'll see an extra conversion node automatically appear.

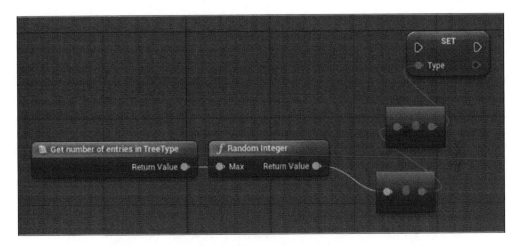

13. Lastly, connect the execution pin of **Construction Script** to the **SET Type** node's execution pin.

14. Your Blueprint should look like the following:

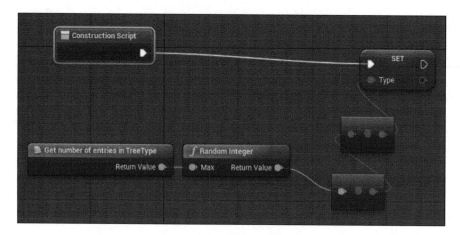

15. To verify that the blueprint is correctly functioning and randomly assigning a type to our tree, we are going to add some nodes to the Event Graph.

16. Place a `Print String` node after the **Event BeginPlay** event node.

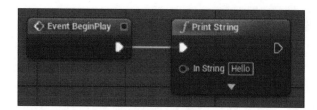

17. Place a `Format Text` node, and connect its output to the input of the `Print String` node. A conversion node will be added for you.

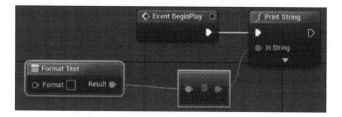

18. Inside the `Format Text` node, add My Type is {0}! to the textbox.

19. Drag `Type` from the variables section of the Blueprint into the graph selecting **Get** from the menu.

20. Add an **Enum to Name** node to `Type` output pin.

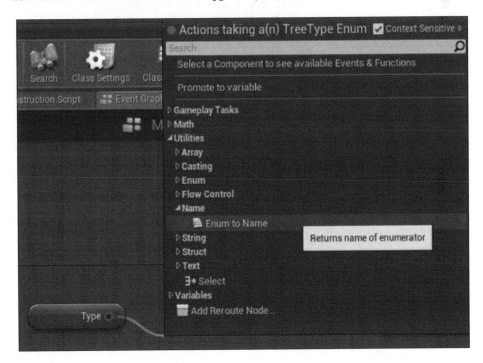

21. Connect the Name output to the input pin on `Format Text` labelled 0.

22. Your Event Graph should now look like the following:

23. Drag a few copies of your Blueprint into the level and hit **Play**. You should see a number of trees printing information regarding their type, verifying that types are being randomly assigned by the Blueprint code that we created.

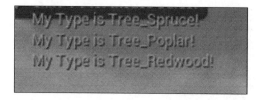

How it works...

1. As usual, we use `StaticMeshActor` as the base class for our `Actor` so that we can easily give it a visual representation in the level.

2. Enumerated types are exposed to the reflection system using the `UENUM` macro.

3. We mark the `enum` as Blueprint-available using the `BlueprintType` specifier.

4. The `enum` declaration is just the same as we would use in any other context.

5. Our `Tree` requires a `TreeType`. Because *tree has tree-type* is the relationship we want to embody, we include an instance of `TreeType` in our `Tree` class.

6. As usual, we need to use `UPROPERTY()` to make the member variable accessible to the reflection system.

7. We use the `BlueprintReadWrite` specifier to mark the property as having both get and set support within Blueprint.

8. Enumerated types require being wrapped in the `TEnumAsByte` template when used in `UPROPERTY`, so we declare an instance of `TEnumAsByte<TreeType>` as the Tree's `Type` variable.

9. The constructor changes for `Tree` are simply the standard load and initialize our static mesh component preamble used in other recipes.

10. We create a Blueprint that inherits from our `Tree` class so that we can demonstrate the Blueprint-accessibility of the `TreeType` enum.

11. In order to have the Blueprint assign a type to the tree at random when we create an instance, we need to use the Blueprint **Construction Script**.

12. Within the **Construction Script**, we calculate the number of entries in the `TreeType` enum.

13. We generate a random number, and use that as an index in the `TreeType` enum type to retrieve a value to store as our `Type`.

14. The Random number node, however, returns integers. Enumerated types are treated as bytes in Blueprint, so we need to use a `ToByte` node, which can then be implicitly converted by Blueprint into an `enum` value.

15. Now that we have **Construction Script** assigning a type to our tree instances as they are created, we need to display the tree's type at runtime.

16. We do so with the graph attached to the `BeginPlay` event within the Event Graph tab.

17. To display text on screen, we use a `Print String` node.

18. To perform string substitution and print our type out as a human-readable string, we use the `Format Text` node.

19. The `Format Text` node takes terms enclosed in curly braces, and allows you to substitute other values for those terms returning the final string.

20. To substitute our `Type` into the `Format Text` node, we need to convert our variable stores from the `enum` value into the actual name of the value.

21. We can do so by accessing our `Type` variable, then using the `Enum to Name` node.

22. `Name`, or `FNames` in native code, are a type of variable that can be converted to strings by Blueprint, so we can connect our `Name` to the input on the `Format Text` node.

23. When we hit play, the graph executes retrieving the type of tree instances placed in the level, and printing the names to the screen.

Editing class properties in different places in the editor

When developing with Unreal, it is common for programmers to implement properties on Actors or other objects in C++, and make them visible to the editor for designer use. However, sometimes it makes sense to view a property, or to make it editable, but only on the object's default state. Sometimes the property should only be modifiable at runtime with the default specified in C++. Fortunately, there are some specifiers that can help us restrict when a property is available.

How to do it...

1. Create a new `Actor` class in the editor called `PropertySpecifierActor`.

2. Add the following property definitions to the class:

```
UPROPERTY(EditDefaultsOnly)
bool EditDefaultsOnly;
UPROPERTY(EditInstanceOnly)
bool EditInstanceOnly;
UPROPERTY(EditAnywhere)
bool EditAnywhere;
UPROPERTY(VisibleDefaultsOnly)
bool VisibleDefaultsOnly;
UPROPERTY(VisibleInstanceOnly)
bool VisibleInstanceOnly;
UPROPERTY(VisibleAnywhere)
bool VisibleAnywhere;
```

3. Compile your code and launch the editor.

4. Create a new blueprint based on the class.

5. Open the blueprint, and look at the **Class Defaults** section.

6. Note which properties are editable and visible.

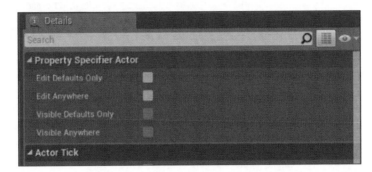

7. Place instances in the level, and view their **Details** panels.

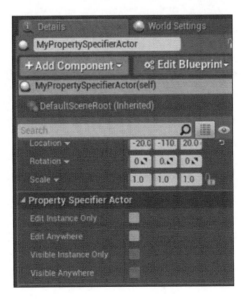

8. Note that a different set of properties are editable.

How it works...

1. When specifying UPROPERTY, we can indicate where we want that value to be available inside the Unreal editor.

2. Visible* prefixes indicate that the value is viewable in the **Details** panel for the indicated object. The value won't be editable, however.

3. This doesn't mean that the variable is a const qualifier; however, native code can change the value, for instance.

4. Edit* prefixes indicate that the property can be altered within the **Details** panels inside the editor.

5. InstanceOnly as a suffix indicates that the property will only be displayed in the **Details** panels for instances of your class that have been placed into the game. They won't be visible in the **Class Defaults** section of the Blueprint editor, for example.

6. DefaultsOnly is the inverse of InstanceOnly— UPROPERTY will only display in the **Class Defaults section**, and can't be viewed on individual instances within the level.

7. The suffix Anywhere is the combination of the two previous suffixes—the UPROPERTY will be visible in all **Details** panels that inspect either the object's defaults or a particular instance in the level.

See also

▸ This recipe makes the property in question visible in the inspector, but doesn't allow the property to be referenced in the actual Blueprint Event Graph. See the next recipe for a description of how to make that possible.

Making properties accessible in the Blueprint editor graph

The specifiers mentioned in the previous recipe are all well and good, but they only control the visibility of UPROPERTY in the **Details** panel. By default, even with those specifiers used appropriately, UPROPERTY won't be viewable or accessible in the actual editor graph for use at runtime.

Other specifiers, which can optionally be used in conjunction with the ones in the previous recipe, can be used to allow interacting with properties in the Event Graph.

How to do it...

1. Create a new `Actor` class called `BlueprintPropertyActor` using the editor wizard.

2. Add the following `UPROPERTY` to the actor using Visual Studio:

```
UPROPERTY(BlueprintReadWrite, Category = Cookbook)
bool ReadWriteProperty;
UPROPERTY(BlueprintReadOnly, Category = Cookbook)
bool ReadOnlyProperty;
```

3. Compile your project, and start the editor.

4. Create a Blueprint class based on your `BlueprintPropertyActor`, and open its graph.

5. Verify that the properties are visible under the category **Cookbook** in the **Variables** section of the **My Blueprint** panel.

6. Left-click and drag the ReadWrite property into the event graph, and select `Get`.

7. Repeat the previous step selecting `Set`.

8. Drag the `ReadOnly` property into the graph, and note that the `Set` node is disabled.

How it works...

1. `BlueprintReadWrite` as a UPROPERTY specifier indicates to the Unreal Header Tool that the property should have both `Get` and `Set` operations exposed for use in Blueprints.

2. `BlueprintReadOnly` is, as the name implies, a specifier that only allows Blueprint to retrieve the value of the property; never set it.

3. `BlueprintReadOnly` can be useful when a property is set by native code, but should be accessible within Blueprint.

4. It should be noted that `BlueprintReadWrite` and `BlueprintReadOnly` don't specify anything about the property being accessible in the **Details** panels or the **My Blueprint** section of the editor—these specifiers only control the generation of the getter/setter nodes for use in Blueprint graphs.

Responding to property – changed events from the editor

When a designer changes the properties of an `Actor` placed in the level, it is often important to show any visual results of that change immediately rather than just when the level is simulated or played.

When changes are made using the **Details** panels, there's a special event that the editor emits called `PostEditChangeProperty`, which gives the class instance a chance to respond to the property being edited.

This recipe shows you how to handle `PostEditChangeProperty` for immediate in-editor feedback.

How to do it...

1. Create a new `Actor` called `APostEditChangePropertyActor` based on `StaticMeshActor`.

2. Add the following `UPROPERTY` to the class:

   ```
   UPROPERTY(EditAnywhere)
   bool ShowStaticMesh;
   ```

3. Add the following function definition:

   ```
   virtual void PostEditChangeProperty(FPropertyChangedEvent&
   PropertyChangedEvent) override;
   ```

4. Add the following to the class constructor:

   ```
   auto MeshAsset =
   ConstructorHelpers::FObjectFinder<UStaticMesh>(TEXT("Static
   Mesh'/Engine/BasicShapes/Cone.Cone'"));
   if (MeshAsset.Object != nullptr)
   {
     GetStaticMeshComponent()
     ->SetStaticMesh(MeshAsset.Object);
     GetStaticMeshComponent()->bGenerateOverlapEvents = true;
   }
   GetStaticMeshComponent()
   ->SetMobility(EComponentMobility::Movable);
   ShowStaticMesh = true;
   ```

5. Implement `PostEditChangeProperty`:

   ```
   void
   APostEditChangePropertyActor::PostEditChangeProperty(FPrope
   rtyChangedEvent& PropertyChangedEvent)
   {
     if (PropertyChangedEvent.Property != nullptr)
     {
       const FName PropertyName(PropertyChangedEvent.Property
       ->GetFName());
       if (PropertyName ==
       GET_MEMBER_NAME_CHECKED(APostEditChangePropertyActor,
       ShowStaticMesh))
       {
         if (GetStaticMeshComponent() != nullptr)
         {
           GetStaticMeshComponent()
           ->SetVisibility(ShowStaticMesh);
   ```

```
            }
          }
        }
      Super::PostEditChangeProperty(PropertyChangedEvent);
    }
```

6. Compile your code, and launch the editor.

7. Drag an instance of your class into the game world, and verify that toggling the boolean value for `ShowStaticMesh` toggles the visibility of the mesh in the editor viewport.

How it works...

1. We create a new `Actor` based on `StaticMeshActor` for easy access to a visual representation via the Static Mesh.

2. `UPROPERTY` is added to give us a property to change, to cause `PostEditChangeProperty` events to be triggered.

3. `PostEditChangeProperty` is a virtual function defined in `Actor`.

4. As a result, we override the function in our class.

5. Within our class constructor, we initialize our mesh as usual, and set the default state of our `bool` property to match the visibility of the component it controls.

6. Inside `PostEditChangeProperty`, we first check that the property is valid.

7. Assuming it is, we retrieve the name of the property using `GetFName()`.

8. `FNames` are stored internally by the engine as a table of unique values.

9. Next we need to use the `GET_MEMBER_NAME_CHECKED` macro. The macro takes a number of parameters.

10. The first one is the name of the class to check.

11. The second parameter is the property to check the class for.

12. The macro will, at compile-time, verify that the class contains the member specified by name.

13. We compare the class member name that the macro returns against the name that our property contains.

14. If they are the same, then we verify that our `StaticMeshComponent` is initialized correctly.

15. If it is, we set its visibility to match the value of our `ShowStaticMesh` Boolean.

Implementing a native code Construction Script

Within Blueprint, **Construction Script** is an event graph that runs any time a property is changed on the object it is attached to—whether from being dragged in the editor viewport or changed via direct entry in a **Details** panel.

Construction scripts allow the object in question to 'rebuild' itself based on its new location, for instance, or to change the components it contains based on user-selected options.

When coding in C++ with Unreal Engine, the equivalent concept is the `OnConstruction` function.

How to do it...

1. Create a new `Actor` called `AOnConstructionActor` based on `StaticMeshActor`.

2. Add the following `UPROPERTY` to the class:

```
UPROPERTY(EditAnywhere)
bool ShowStaticMesh;
```

3. Add the following function definition:

```
virtual void OnConstruction(const FTransform& Transform)
override;
```

4. Add the following to the class constructor:

```
auto MeshAsset =
ConstructorHelpers::FObjectFinder<UStaticMesh>(TEXT("Static
Mesh'/Engine/BasicShapes/Cone.Cone'"));
if (MeshAsset.Object != nullptr)
{
  GetStaticMeshComponent()
  ->SetStaticMesh(MeshAsset.Object);
  GetStaticMeshComponent()->bGenerateOverlapEvents = true;
}
GetStaticMeshComponent()
->SetMobility(EComponentMobility::Movable);
ShowStaticMesh = true;
```

5. Implement `OnConstruction`:

```
void AOnConstructionActor::OnConstruction(const FTransform&
Transform)
{
  GetStaticMeshComponent()->SetVisibility(ShowStaticMesh);
}
```

6. Compile your code, and launch the editor.

7. Drag an instance of your class into the game world, and verify that toggling the Boolean value for `ShowStaticMesh` toggles the visibility of the mesh in the editor viewport.

8. `OnConstruction` does not currently run for C++ actors placed in a level if they are moved.

9. To test this, place a breakpoint in your `OnConstruction` function, then move your actor around the level.

To place a breakpoint, place your cursor on the desired line, and hit *F9* in Visual Studio.

10. You'll notice that the function doesn't get called, but if you toggle the `ShowStaticMesh` Boolean, it does, causing your breakpoint to trigger.

In order to see why, take a look at `AActor::PostEditMove`:

```
UBlueprint* Blueprint = Cast<UBlueprint>(GetClass()
->ClassGeneratedBy);
if(Blueprint && (Blueprint-
>bRunConstructionScriptOnDrag || bFinished)
&& !FLevelUtils::IsMovingLevel() )
{
  FNavigationLockContext NavLock(GetWorld(),
  ENavigationLockReason::AllowUnregister);
  RerunConstructionScripts();
}
```

The top line here casts `UClass` for the current object to `UBlueprint`, and will only run the construction scripts and `OnConstruction` again if the class is a Blueprint.

How it works...

1. We create a new Actor based on `StaticMeshActor` for easy access to a visual representation via the Static Mesh.

2. `UPROPERTY` is added to give us a property to change—to cause `PostEditChangeProperty` events to be triggered.

3. `OnConstruction` is a virtual function defined in Actor.

4. As a result, we override the function in our class.

5. Within our class constructor, we initialize our mesh as usual, and set the default state of our `bool` property to match the visibility of the component that it controls.

6. Inside `OnConstruction`, the actor rebuilds itself using any properties that are required for doing so.

7. For this simple example, we set the visibility of the mesh to match the value of our `ShowStaticMesh` property.

8. This could also be extended to changing other values based on the value of the `ShowStaticMesh` variable.

9. You'll note that we don't explicitly filter on a particular property being changed like the previous recipe does with `PostEditChangeProperty`.

10. The `OnConstruction` script runs in its entirety for every property that gets changed on the object.

11. It has no way of testing which property was just edited, so you need to be judicious about placing computationally intensive code within it.

Creating a new editor module

The following recipes all interact with editor mode-specific code and engine modules. As a result, it is considered good practice to create a new module that will only be loaded when the engine is running in editor mode so that we can place all our editor-only code inside it.

How to do it...

1. Open your project's `.uproject` file in a text editor such as Notepad or Notepad++.

2. Add the bolded section of the following to the file:

```
{
  "FileVersion": 3,
  "EngineAssociation": "4.11",
  "Category": "",
  "Description": "",
  "Modules": [
    {
      "Name": "UE4Cookbook",
      "Type": "Runtime",
      "LoadingPhase": "Default",
      "AdditionalDependencies": [
        "Engine",
        "CoreUObject"
      ]
    },
    {
      "Name": "UE4CookbookEditor",
      "Type": "Editor",
      "LoadingPhase": "PostEngineInit",
      "AdditionalDependencies": [
        "Engine",
        "CoreUObject"
      ]
    }
  ]
}
```

3. Note the comma after the first module before the second set of curly braces.

4. In your source folder, create a new folder using the same name as you specified in your `uproject` file (in this instance, `"UE4CookbookEditor"`).

5. Inside this new folder, create a file called `UE4CookbookEditor.Build.cs`.

6. Insert the following into the file:

```
using UnrealBuildTool;

public class UE4CookbookEditor : ModuleRules
{
  public UE4CookbookEditor(TargetInfo Target)
  {
    PublicDependencyModuleNames.AddRange(new string[] {
    "Core", "CoreUObject", "Engine", "InputCore", "RHI",
    "RenderCore", "ShaderCore" });
    PublicDependencyModuleNames.Add("UE4Cookbook");
    PrivateDependencyModuleNames.AddRange(new string[] {
    "UnrealEd" });
  }
}
```

7. Create a new file called `UE4CookbookEditor.h` and add the following:

```
#pragma once
#include "Engine.h"
#include "ModuleManager.h"
#include "UnrealEd.h"


class FUE4CookbookEditorModule: public IModuleInterface
{
};
```

8. Lastly, create a new source file called `UE4CookbookEditor.cpp`.

9. Add the following code:

```
#include "UE4CookbookEditor.h"
IMPLEMENT_GAME_MODULE(FUE4CookbookEditorModule,
UE4CookbookEditor)
```

10. Finally, close Visual Studio if you have it open, then right-click on the `.uproject` file, and select **Generate Visual Studio Project files**.

11. You should see a small window launch, display a progress bar, and then close.

12. You can now launch Visual Studio, verify that your new module is visible in the IDE, and compile your project successfully.

13. The module is now ready for the next set of recipes.

 Code changes made in this editor module won't support hot-reloading in the same way that code in runtime modules does. If you get a compilation error that mentions changes to generated header files, simply close the editor, and rebuild from within your IDE instead.

How it works...

1. Unreal projects use the .uproject file format to specify a number of different pieces of information about the project.

2. This information is used to inform the Header and Build tools about the modules that comprise this project, and is used for code generation and makefile creation.

3. The file uses JSON-style formatting.

4. These include the following:

   - The engine version that the project should be opened in
   - A list of modules that are used in the project
   - A list of module declarations

5. Each of these module declarations contain the following:

   - The name of the module.
   - The type of the module—is it an editor module (only runs in editor builds, has access to editor-only classes) or a Runtime module (runs in both editor and Shipping builds).
   - The loading phase of the module—modules can be loaded at different points during program startup. This value specifies the point at which the module should be loaded, for example, if there are dependencies in other modules that should be loaded first.
   - A list of dependencies for the module. These are essential modules that contain exported functions or classes that the module relies on.

6. We ad a new module to the `uproject file`. The module's name is `UE4CookbookEditor` (conventionally, `Editor` should be appended to the main game module for an editor module).

7. This module is marked as an editor module, and is set to load after the baseline engine so that it can use the classes declared in Engine code.

8. Our module's dependencies are left at the default values for now.

9. With the `uproject` file altered to contain our new module, we need a build script for it.

10. Build scripts are written in C#, and take the name `<ModuleName>.Build.cs`.

11. C#, unlike C++, doesn't use a separate header file and implementation—it's all there in the one `.cs` file.

12. We want to access the classes declared in the `UnrealBuildTool` module, so we include a `using` statement to indicate that we want to access that namespace.

13. We create a `public` class with the same name as our module, and which inherits from `ModuleRules`.

14. Inside our constructor, we add a number of modules to the dependencies of this module.

15. There are both private dependencies and public dependencies. According to the code of the `ModuleRules` class, Public dependencies are modules that your module's public header files depend on. Private dependencies are modules that the private code depends on. Anything used in both public headers and private code should go into the `PublicDependencyModuleNames` array.

16. You'll note that our `PublicDependencyModuleNames` array contains our main game module. This is because some recipes in this chapter will extend the editor to better support the classes defined within our main game module.

17. Now that we've told the build system that we have a new module to build through the project file, and we've specified how to build the module with the build script, we need to create the C++ class that is our actual module.

18. We create a header file that includes the Engine header, the `ModuleManager` header, and the `UnrealEd` header.

19. We include `ModuleManager` because it defines `IModuleInterface`, the class that our module will inherit from.

20. We also include `UnrealEd` because we're writing an editor module that will need to access the editor functionality.

21. The class we declare inherits from `IModuleInterface`, and takes its name from the usual prefix, `F`, followed by the module name.

22. Inside the `.cpp` file, we include our module's header, and then use the `IMPLEMENT_GAME_MODULE` macro.

23. IMPLEMENT_GAME_MODULE declares an exported C function, InitializeModule(), which returns an instance of our new module class.

24. This means that Unreal can simply call InitializeModule() on any library that exports it to retrieve a reference to the actual module implementation without needing to know what class it is.

25. Having added our new module, we now need to rebuild our Visual Studio solution, so we close Visual Studio and then regenerate the project files using the context menu.

26. With the project rebuilt, the new module will be visible in Visual Studio, and we can add code to it as usual.

Creating new toolbar buttons

If you have created a custom tool or window for display within the editor, you probably need some way to let the user make it appear. The easiest way to do this is to create a toolbar customization that adds a new toolbar button, and have it display your window when clicked.

Create a new engine module by following the previous recipe, as we'll need it to initialize our toolbar customization.

How to do it...

1. Create a new header file, and insert the following class declaration:

```
#pragma once
#include "Commands.h"
#include "EditorStyleSet.h"
/**
 *
 */
class FCookbookCommands : public
TCommands<FCookbookCommands>
{
  public:
  FCookbookCommands()
  :TCommands<FCookbookCommands>
  (FName(TEXT("UE4_Cookbook")),
  FText::FromString("Cookbook Commands"), NAME_None,
  FEditorStyle::GetStyleSetName())
  {
  };
  virtual void RegisterCommands() override;

  TSharedPtr<FUICommandInfo> MyButton;
};
```

2. Implement the new class by placing the following in the `.cpp` file:

```
#include "UE4CookbookEditor.h"
#include "Commands.h"
#include "CookbookCommands.h"

void FCookbookCommands::RegisterCommands()
{
  #define LOCTEXT_NAMESPACE ""
  UI_COMMAND(MyButton, "Cookbook", "Demo Cookbook Toolbar
  Command", EUserInterfaceActionType::Button,
  FInputGesture());
  #undef LOCTEXT_NAMESPACE
}
```

3. Add the following within your module class:

```
virtual void StartupModule() override;
virtual void ShutdownModule() override;
TSharedPtr<FExtender> ToolbarExtender;
TSharedPtr<const FExtensionBase> Extension;
void MyButton_Clicked()
{
  TSharedRef<SWindow> CookbookWindow = SNew(SWindow)
  .Title(FText::FromString(TEXT("Cookbook Window")))
  .ClientSize(FVector2D(800, 400))
  .SupportsMaximize(false)
  .SupportsMinimize(false);

  IMainFrameModule& MainFrameModule =
  FModuleManager::LoadModuleChecked<IMainFrameModule>
  (TEXT("MainFrame"));

  if (MainFrameModule.GetParentWindow().IsValid())
  {
    FSlateApplication::Get().AddWindowAsNativeChild
    (CookbookWindow,MainFrameModule.GetParentWindow()
    .ToSharedRef());
  }
  else
  {
    FSlateApplication::Get().AddWindow(CookbookWindow);
  }
};
void AddToolbarExtension(FToolBarBuilder &builder)
{
```

```
    FSlateIcon IconBrush =
    FSlateIcon(FEditorStyle::GetStyleSetName(),
    "LevelEditor.ViewOptions",
    "LevelEditor.ViewOptions.Small");

    builder.AddToolBarButton(FCookbookCommands::Get()
    .MyButton, NAME_None, FText::FromString("My Button"),
    FText::FromString("Click me to display a message"),
    IconBrush, NAME_None);
};
```

4. Be sure to #include the header file for your command class as well.

5. We now need to implement StartupModule and ShutdownModule:

```
void FUE4CookbookEditorModule::StartupModule()
{
    FCookbookCommands::Register();
    TSharedPtr<FUICommandList> CommandList =
    MakeShareable(new FUICommandList());
    CommandList->MapAction(FCookbookCommands::Get().MyButton,
    FExecuteAction::CreateRaw(this,
    &FUE4CookbookEditorModule::MyButton_Clicked),
    FCanExecuteAction());
    ToolbarExtender = MakeShareable(new FExtender());
    Extension = ToolbarExtender
    ->AddToolBarExtension("Compile", EExtensionHook::Before,
    CommandList, FToolBarExtensionDelegate::CreateRaw(this,
    &FUE4CookbookEditorModule::AddToolbarExtension));

    FLevelEditorModule& LevelEditorModule =
    FModuleManager::LoadModuleChecked<FLevelEditorModule>
    ("LevelEditor");
    LevelEditorModule.GetToolBarExtensibilityManager()
    ->AddExtender(ToolbarExtender);
}

void FUE4CookbookEditorModule::ShutdownModule()
{
    ToolbarExtender
    ->RemoveExtension(Extension.ToSharedRef());
    Extension.Reset();
    ToolbarExtender.Reset();
}
```

6. Add the following includes:

```
#include "LevelEditor.h"
#include "SlateBasics.h"
#include "MultiBoxExtender.h"
#include "Chapter8/CookbookCommands.h"
```

7. Compile your project, and start the editor.

8. Verify that there's a new button on the toolbar in the main level editor, which can be clicked on to open a new window:

How it works...

1. Unreal's editor UI is based on the concept of commands. Commands are a design pattern that allows looser coupling between the UI and the actions that it needs to perform.

2. In order to create a class that contains a set of commands, it is necessary to inherit from `TCommands`.

3. `TCommands` is a template class that leverages the **Curiously Recurring Template Pattern** (**CRTP**). The CRTP is used commonly throughout **Slate** UI code as a means of creating compile-time polymorphism.

4. In the initializer list for `FCookbookCommands` constructor, we invoke the parent class constructor, passing in a number of parameters.

5. The first parameter is the name of the command set, and is a simple `FName`.

6. The second parameter is a tooltip/human readable string, and as such, uses `FText` so it can support localization if necessary.

7. If there's a parent group of commands, the third parameter contains the name of the group. Otherwise, it contains `NAME_None`.

8. The final parameter for the constructor is the Slate Style set that contains any command icons that the command set will be using.

9. The `RegisterCommands()` function allows `TCommands`-derived classes to create any command objects that they require. The resulting `FUICommandInfo` instances returned from that function are stored inside the `Commands` class as members so that UI elements or functions can be bound to the commands.

10. This is why we have the member variable `TSharedPtr<FUICommandInfo>` `MyButton`.

11. In the implementation for the class, we simply need to create our commands in `RegisterCommands`.

12. The `UI_COMMAND` macro used to create an instance of `FUICommandInfo` expects a localization namespace to be defined even if it is just an empty default namespace.

13. As a result, we need to enclose our `UI_COMMAND` calls with `#defines` to set a valid value for `LOCTEXT_NAMESPACE` even if we don't intend to use localization.

14. The actual `UI_COMMAND` macro takes a number of parameters.

15. The first parameter is the variable to store the `FUICommandInfo` in.

16. The second parameter is a human-readable name for the command.

17. The third parameter is a description for the command.

18. The fourth parameter is `EUserInterfaceActionType`. This enumeration essentially specifies what sort of button is being created. It supports `Button`, `ToggleButton`, `RadioButton`, and `Check` as valid types.

19. Buttons are simple generic buttons. A toggle button stores on and off states. The radio button is similar to a toggle, but is grouped with other radio buttons, and only one can be enabled at a time. Lastly, the checkbox displays a read-only checkbox adjacent to the button.

20. The last parameter for `UI_COMMAND` is the input chord, or the combination of keys required to activate the command.

21. This parameter is primarily useful for defining key combinations for hotkeys linked to the command in question rather than buttons. As a result, we use an empty `InputGesture`.

22. So we now have a set of commands, but we haven't told the engine we want to add the set to the commands that show on the toolbar. We also haven't set up what actually happens when the button is clicked. In order to do this, we need to perform some initialization when our module begins, so we place some code into the `StartupModule/ShutdownModule` functions.

23. Inside `StartupModule`, we call the static `Register` function on the commands class that we defined earlier.

24. We then create a shared pointer to a list of commands using the `MakeShareable` function.

25. In the command list, we use `MapAction` to create a mapping, or association, between the `UICommandInfo` object, which we set as a member of the `FCookbookCommands`, and the actual function we want to execute when the command is invoked.

26. You'll note that we don't explicitly set anything regarding what could be used to invoke the command here.

27. To perform this mapping, we call the `MapAction` function. The first parameter to `MapAction` is a `FUICommandInfo` object, which we can retrieve from `FCookbookCommands` by using its static `Get()` method to retrieve the instance.

28. `FCookbookCommands` is implemented as a singleton—a class with a single instance that exists throughout the application. You'll see the pattern in most places—there's a static `Get()` method available in the engine.

29. The second parameter of the `MapAction` function is a delegate bound to the function to be invoked when the command is executed.

30. Because `UE4CookbookEditorModule` is a raw C++ class rather than a `UObject`, and we want to invoke a member function rather than a `static` function, we use `CreateRaw` to create a new delegate bound to a raw C++ member function.

31. `CreateRaw` expects a pointer to the object instance, and a function reference to the function to invoke on that pointer.

32. The third parameter for `MapAction` is a delegate to call to test if the action can be executed. Because we want the command to be executable all the time, we can use a simple pre-defined delegate that always returns `true`.

33. With an association created between our command and the action it should call, we now need to actually tell the extension system that we want to add new commands to the toolbar.

34. We can do this via the `FExtender` class, which can be used to extend menus, context menus, or toolbars.

35. We initially create an instance of `FExtender` as a shared pointer so that our extensions are uninitialized when the module is shut down.

36. We then call `AddToolBarExtension` on our new extender, storing the results in a shared pointer so that we can remove it on module uninitialization.

37. `AddToolBarExtension`'s first argument is the name of the extension point where we want to add our extension.

38. To find where we want to place our extension, we first need to turn on the display of extension points within the editor UI.

39. To do so, open **Editor Preferences** in the **Edit** menu within the editor:

40. Open **General** | **Miscellaneous**, and select **Display UIExtension Points**:

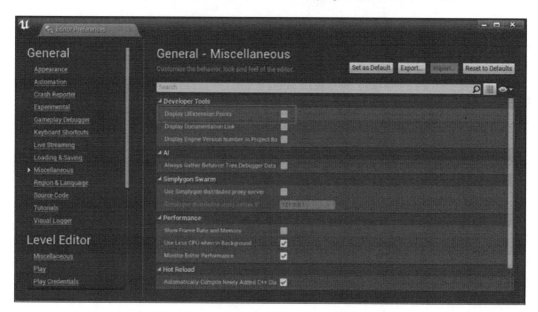

41. Restart the editor, and you should see green text overlaid on the editor UI, as in the following screenshot:

42. The green text indicates `UIExtensionPoint`, and the text's value is the string we should provide to the `AddToolBarExtension` function.

43. We're going to add our extension to the **Compile** extension point in this recipe, but of course, you could use any other extension point you wish.

44. It's important to note that adding a toolbar extension to a menu extension point will fail silently, and vice versa.

45. The second parameter to `AddToolBarExtension` is a location anchor relative to the extension point specified. We've selected `FExtensionHook::Before`, so our icon will be displayed before the compile point.

46. The next parameter is our command list containing mapped actions.

47. Finally, the last parameter is a delegate that is responsible for actually adding UI controls to the toolbar at the extension point and the anchor that we specified earlier.

48. The delegate is bound to a function that has the form void (`*func`) (`FToolBarBuilder` and `builder`). In this instance, it is a function called `AddToolbarExtension` defined in our module class.

49. When the function is invoked, calling commands on the `builder` that add UI elements will apply those elements to the location in the UI we specified.

50. Lastly, we need to load the level editor module within this function so that we can add our extender to the main toolbar within the level editor.

51. As usual, we can use `ModuleManager` to load a module and return a reference to it.

52. With that reference in hand, we can get the Toolbar Extensibility Manager for the module, and tell it to add our Extender.

53. While this may seem cumbersome at first, the intention is to allow you to apply the same toolbar extension to multiple toolbars in different modules if you would like to create a consistent UI layout between different editor windows.

54. The counterpart to initializing our extension, of course, is removing it when our module is unloaded. To do that, we remove our extension from the extender, then null the shared pointers for both Extender and extension reclaiming their memory allocation.

55. The `AddToolBarExtension` function within the editor module is the one which is responsible for actually adding UI elements to the toolbar that can invoke our commands.

56. It does this by calling functions on the `FToolBarBuilder` instance passed in as a function parameter.

57. Firstly, we retrieve an appropriate icon for our new toolbar button using the `FSlateIcon` constructor.

58. With the icon loaded, we invoke `AddToolBarButton` on the `builder` instance.

59. `AddToolbarButton` has a number of parameters.

60. The first parameter is the command to bind to—you'll notice it's the same `MyButton` member that we accessed earlier when binding the action to the command.

61. The second parameter is an override for the extension hook we specified earlier, but we don't want to override that so we can use `NAME_None`.

62. The third parameter is a label override for the new button that we create.

63. Parameter four is a tooltip for the new button.

64. The second-last parameter is the button's icon, and the last parameter is a name used to refer to this button element for highlighting support if you wish to use the in-editor tutorial framework.

Creating new menu entries

The workflow for creating new menu entries is almost identical to that for creating new toolbar buttons, so this recipe will build on the previous one, and show you how to add the command created therein to a menu rather than a toolbar.

How to do it...

1. Create a new function in your `module` class:

```
void AddMenuExtension(FMenuBuilder &builder)
{
  FSlateIcon IconBrush =
  FSlateIcon(FEditorStyle::GetStyleSetName(),
  "LevelEditor.ViewOptions",
  "LevelEditor.ViewOptions.Small");

  builder.AddMenuEntry(FCookbookCommands::Get().MyButton);
};
```

2. Find the following code within the `StartupModule` function:

```
Extension = ToolbarExtender->AddToolBarExtension("Compile",
EExtensionHook::Before, CommandList,
FToolBarExtensionDelegate::CreateRaw(this,
&FUE4CookbookEditorModule::AddToolbarExtension));
LevelEditorModule.GetToolBarExtensibilityManager()-
>AddExtender(ToolbarExtender);
```

3. Replace the preceding code with the following:

```
Extension = ToolbarExtender
->AddMenuExtension("LevelEditor", EExtensionHook::Before,
CommandList, FMenuExtensionDelegate::CreateRaw(this,
&FUE4CookbookEditorModule::AddMenuExtension));
LevelEditorModule.GetMenuExtensibilityManager()
->AddExtender(ToolbarExtender);
```

4. Compile your code, and launch the editor.

5. Verify that you now have a menu entry under the **Window** menu that displays the **Cookbook** window when clicked. If you followed the preceding recipe, you'll also see the green text listing the UI extension points, including the one we used in this recipe (**LevelEditor**).

How it works...

1. You'll note that `ToolbarExtender` is of type `FExtender` rather than `FToolbarExtender` or `FMenuExtender`.

2. By using a generic `FExtender` class rather than a specific subclass, the framework allows you to create a series of command-function mappings that can be used on either menus or toolbars. The delegate that actually adds the UI controls (in this instance, `AddMenuExtension`) can link those controls to a subset of commands from your `FExtender`.

3. This way, you don't need to have different `TCommands` classes for different types of extensions, and you can place the commands into a single central class regardless of where those commands are invoked from the UI.

4. As a result, the only changes that are required are as follows:

   1. Swapping calls to `AddToolBarExtension` with `AddMenuExtension`.
   2. Creating a function that can be bound to `FMenuExtensionDelegate` rather than `FToolbarExtensionDelegate`.
   3. Adding the extender to a Menu Extensibility Manager rather than a Toolbar Extensibility Manager.

Creating a new editor window

Custom editor windows are useful when you have a new tool with user-configurable settings, or want to display some information to people using your customized editor.

Be sure to have an editor module by following the recipe earlier in this chapter before you start.

Read through either the *Creating new menu entries* or *Creating new toolbar buttons* recipes so that you can create a button within the editor that will launch our new window.

How to do it...

1. Inside your command's bound function, add the following code:

```
TSharedRef<SWindow> CookbookWindow = SNew(SWindow)
.Title(FText::FromString(TEXT("Cookbook Window")))
.ClientSize(FVector2D(800, 400))
.SupportsMaximize(false)
.SupportsMinimize(false)
[
    SNew(SVerticalBox)
    +SVerticalBox::Slot()
    .HAlign(HAlign_Center)
    .VAlign(VAlign_Center)
    [
        SNew(STextBlock)
        .Text(FText::FromString(TEXT("Hello from Slate")))
    ]
];
IMainFrameModule& MainFrameModule =
FModuleManager::LoadModuleChecked<IMainFrameModule>(TEXT
("MainFrame"));

if (MainFrameModule.GetParentWindow().IsValid())
{
```

```
    FSlateApplication::Get().AddWindowAsNativeChild
    (CookbookWindow, MainFrameModule.GetParentWindow()
    .ToSharedRef());
}
else
{
    FSlateApplication::Get().AddWindow(CookbookWindow);
}
```

2. Compile your code, and launch the editor.

3. When you activate the command you created, either by selecting the custom menu option or the toolbar option that you added, you should see that the window has been displayed with some centered text in the middle:

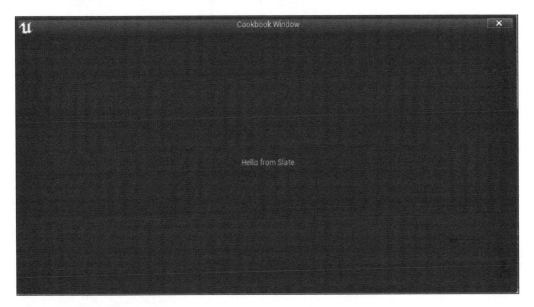

How it works...

1. As should be self-explanatory, your new editor window won't display itself, and so, at the start of this recipe, it is mentioned that you should have implemented a custom menu or toolbar button or a console command that we can use to trigger the display of our new window.

2. All of Slate's widgets are usually interacted with in the form of TSharedRef< > or TSharedPtr< >.

3. The SNew() function returns a TSharedRef templated on the requested widget class.

4. As has been mentioned elsewhere in this chapter, Slate widgets have a number of functions that they implement, which all return the object that the function was invoked on. This allows for method chaining to be used to configure the object at creation time.

5. This is what allows for the Slate syntax of `<Widget>.Property(Value).Property(Value)`.

6. The properties that are set on the widget in this recipe are the window title, the window size, and whether the window can be maximized and minimized.

7. Once all the requisite properties on a widget have been set, the bracket operators (`[]`) can be used to specify the content to be placed inside the widget, for example, a picture or label inside a button.

8. `SWindow` is a top-level widget with only one slot for child widgets, so we don't need to add a slot for it ourselves. We place content into that slot by creating it inside the pair of brackets.

9. The content we create is `SVerticalBox`, which is a widget that can have an arbitrary number of slots for child widgets that are displayed in a vertical list.

10. For each widget we want to place into the vertical list, we need to create a **slot**.

11. The easiest way to do this is to use the overloaded + operator and the `SVerticalBox::Slot()` function.

12. `Slot()` returns a widget like any other, so we can set properties on it like we did on our `SWindow`.

13. This recipe centers the Slot's content on both horizontal and vertical axes using `HAlign` and `VAlign`.

14. A `Slot` has a single child widget, and it's created inside the `[]` operators just as for `SWindow`.

15. Inside the `Slot` content, we create a text block with some custom text.

16. Our new `SWindow` now has its child widgets added, but it isn't being displayed yet, because it isn't added to the window hierarchy.

17. The main frame module is used to check if we have a top-level editor window, and if it exists, our new window is added as a child.

18. If there's no top-level window to be added as a child to, then we use the Slate Application singleton to add our window without a parent.

19. If you would like to see the hierarchy of the window we've created, you can use the Slate Widget Reflector, which can be accessed via **Window | Developer Tools | Widget Reflector**.

20. If you select **Pick Live Widget**, and hover your cursor over the text in the center of our custom window, you will be able to see the **SWindow** with our custom widgets added to its hierarchy.

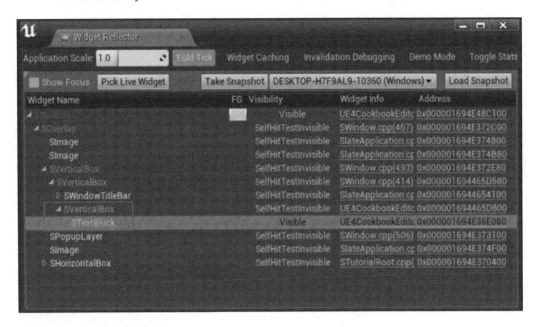

See also

▶ *Chapter 9, User Interfaces – UI and UMG*, is all about UI, and will show you how to add additional elements to your new custom window

Creating a new Asset type

At some point in your project, you might need to create a new custom Asset class, for example, an Asset to store conversation data in an RPG.

In order to properly integrate these with **Content Browser**, you'll need to create a new Asset type.

How to do it...

1. Create a custom Asset based on `UObject`:

```cpp
#pragma once

#include "Object.h"
#include "MyCustomAsset.generated.h"

/**
 *
 */
UCLASS()
class UE4COOKBOOK_API UMyCustomAsset : public UObject
{
  GENERATED_BODY()
  public:
  UPROPERTY(EditAnywhere, Category = "Custom Asset")
  FString Name;
};
```

2. Create a class called `UCustomAssetFactory` based on `UFactory`, overriding `FactoryCreateNew`:

```cpp
#pragma once

#include "Factories/Factory.h"
#include "CustomAssetFactory.generated.h"

/**
 *
 */
UCLASS()
class UE4COOKBOOK_API UCustomAssetFactory : public UFactory
{
  GENERATED_BODY()

  public:
  UCustomAssetFactory();

  virtual UObject* FactoryCreateNew(UClass* InClass,
  UObject* InParent, FName InName, EObjectFlags Flags,
  UObject* Context, FFeedbackContext* Warn, FName
  CallingContext) override;
};
```

3. Implement the class:

```cpp
#include "UE4Cookbook.h"
#include "MyCustomAsset.h"
#include "CustomAssetFactory.h"
```

```
UCustomAssetFactory::UCustomAssetFactory()
:Super()
{
  bCreateNew = true;
  bEditAfterNew = true;
  SupportedClass = UMyCustomAsset::StaticClass();
}

UObject* UCustomAssetFactory::FactoryCreateNew(UClass*
InClass, UObject* InParent, FName InName, EObjectFlags
Flags, UObject* Context, FFeedbackContext* Warn, FName
CallingContext)
{
  auto NewObjectAsset = NewObject<UMyCustomAsset>(InParent,
  InClass, InName, Flags);
  return NewObjectAsset;
}
```

4. Compile your code, and open the editor.

5. Right-click in **Content Browser**, and under the **Miscellaneous** tab of the **Create Advanced Asset** section, you should see your new class, and be able to create instances of your new custom type.

How it works...

1. The first class is the actual object that can exist in the game at runtime. It's your texture, data file, or curve data, whatever you require.

2. For the purpose of this recipe, the simplest example is an asset that has an `FString` property to contain a name.

3. The property is marked as `UPROPERTY` so that it remains in memory, and additionally marked as `EditAnywhere` so that it is editable on both, the default object and on instances of it.

4. The second class is `Factory`. Unreal uses the `Factory` design pattern to create instances of assets.

5. This means that there is a generic base `Factory` that uses virtual methods to declare the interface of object creation, and then `Factory` subclasses are responsible for creating the actual object in question.

6. The advantage of this approach is that the user-created subclass can potentially instantiate one of its own subclasses if required; it hides the implementation details regarding deciding which object to create away from the object requesting the creation.

7. With `UFactory` as our base class, we include the appropriate header.

8. The constructor is overridden, because there are a number of properties that we want to set for our new factory after the default constructor has run.

9. `bCreateNew` signifies that the factory is currently able to create a new instance of the object in question from scratch.

10. `bEditAfterNew` indicates that we would like to edit the newly created object immediately after creation.

11. The `SupportedClass` variable is an instance of `UClass` containing reflection information about the type of object the factory will create.

12. The most significant function of our `UFactory` subclass is the actual factory method—`FactoryCreateNew`.

13. `FactoryCreateNew` is responsible for determining the type of object that should be created, and using `NewObject` to construct an instance of that type. It passes the following parameters through to the `NewObject` call.

14. `InClass` is the class of object that will be constructed.

15. `InParent` is the object that should be containing the new object that will be created. If this isn't specified, the object is assumed to go into the transient package, which means that it won't be automatically saved.

16. `Name` is the name of the object to be created.

17. `Flags` is a bitmask of creation flags that control things such as making the object visible outside of the package it is contained in.

18. Within `FactoryCreateNew`, decisions can be made regarding which subclass should be instantiated. Other initialization can also be performed; for example, if there are sub-objects that require manual instantiation or initialization, they can be added here.

19. An example from the engine code for this function is as follows:

```
UObject* UCameraAnimFactory::FactoryCreateNew(UClass*
Class,UObject* InParent,FName Name,EObjectFlags
Flags,UObject* Context,FFeedbackContext* Warn)
{
   UCameraAnim* NewCamAnim =
   NewObject<UCameraAnim>(InParent, Class, Name, Flags);
   NewCamAnim->CameraInterpGroup =
   NewObject<UInterpGroupCamera>(NewCamAnim);
   NewCamAnim->CameraInterpGroup->GroupName = Name;
   return NewCamAnim;
}
```

20. As can be seen here, there's a second call to `NewObject` to populate the `CameraInterpGroup` member of the `NewCamAnim` instance.

See also

▶ The *Editing class properties in different places in the editor* recipe earlier in this chapter gives more context to the `EditAnywhere` property specifier

Creating custom context menu entries for Assets

Custom Asset types commonly have special functions you wish to be able to perform on them. For example, converting images to sprites is an option you wouldn't want to add to any other Asset type. You can create custom context menu entries for specific Asset types in order to make those functions accessible to users.

How to do it...

1. Create a new class based on `FAssetTypeActions_Base`. You'll need to include `AssetTypeActions_Base.h` in the header file.

2. Override the following virtual functions in the class:

```
virtual bool HasActions(const TArray<UObject*>& InObjects)
const override;
virtual void GetActions(const TArray<UObject*>& InObjects,
FMenuBuilder& MenuBuilder) override;
virtual FText GetName() const override;
virtual UClass* GetSupportedClass() const override;

virtual FColor GetTypeColor() const override;
virtual uint32 GetCategories() override;
```

3. Declare the following function:

```
void MyCustomAssetContext_Clicked();
```

4. Implement the declared functions in the `.cpp` file:

```
bool FMyCustomAssetActions::HasActions(const
TArray<UObject*>& InObjects) const
{
   return true;
}

void FMyCustomAssetActions::GetActions(const
TArray<UObject*>& InObjects, FMenuBuilder& MenuBuilder)
{
   MenuBuilder.AddMenuEntry(
   FText::FromString("CustomAssetAction"),
   FText::FromString("Action from Cookbook Recipe"),
   FSlateIcon(FEditorStyle::GetStyleSetName(),
   "LevelEditor.ViewOptions"),
   FUIAction(
   FExecuteAction::CreateRaw(this,
   &FMyCustomAssetActions::MyCustomAssetContext_Clicked),
   FCanExecuteAction()));
}

uint32 FMyCustomAssetActions::GetCategories()
{
   return EAssetTypeCategories::Misc;
}
FText FMyCustomAssetActions::GetName() const
```

```
{
  return FText::FromString(TEXT("My Custom Asset"));
}
UClass* FMyCustomAssetActions::GetSupportedClass() const
{
  return UMyCustomAsset::StaticClass();
}


FColor FMyCustomAssetActions::GetTypeColor() const
{
  return FColor::Emerald;
}
voidFMyCustomAssetActions::MyCustomAssetContext_Clicked()
{
  TSharedRef<SWindow> CookbookWindow = SNew(SWindow)
  .Title(FText::FromString(TEXT("Cookbook Window")))
  .ClientSize(FVector2D(800, 400))
  .SupportsMaximize(false)
  .SupportsMinimize(false);

  IMainFrameModule& MainFrameModule =
  FModuleManager::LoadModuleChecked<IMainFrameModule>
  (TEXT("MainFrame"));

  if (MainFrameModule.GetParentWindow().IsValid())
  {
    FSlateApplication::Get().AddWindowAsNativeChild
    (CookbookWindow, MainFrameModule.GetParentWindow()
    .ToSharedRef());
  }
  else
  {
    FSlateApplication::Get().AddWindow(CookbookWindow);
  }
};
```

5. Within your editor module, add the following code to the `StartupModule()` function:

```
IAssetTools& AssetTools =
FModuleManager::LoadModuleChecked<FAssetToolsModule>("Asset
Tools").Get();

auto Actions =MakeShareable(new FMyCustomAssetActions);
AssetTools.RegisterAssetTypeActions(Actions);
CreatedAssetTypeActions.Add(Actions);
```

6. Add the following inside the module's `ShutdownModule()` function:

```
IAssetTools& AssetTools =
FModuleManager::LoadModuleChecked<FAssetToolsModule>("Asset
Tools").Get();

for (auto Action : CreatedAssetTypeActions)
{
  AssetTools.UnregisterAssetTypeActions
  (Action.ToSharedRef());
}
```

7. Compile your project, and launch the editor.

8. Create an instance of your custom Asset inside **Content Browser**.

9. Right-click on your new Asset to see our custom command in the context menu.

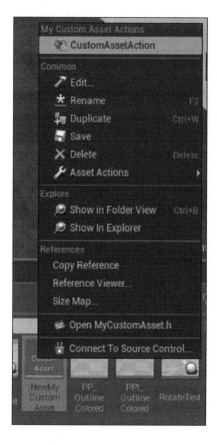

10. Select the **CustomAssetAction** command to display a new blank editor window.

How it works...

1. The base class for all asset type-specific context menu commands is `FAssetTypeActions_Base`, so we need to inherit from that class.

2. `FAssetTypeActions_Base` is an abstract class that defines a number of virtual functions that allow for extending the context menu. The interface which contains the original information for these virtual functions can be found in `IAssetTypeActions.h`.

3. We also declare a function which we bind to our custom context menu entry.

4. `IAssetTypeActions::HasActions ( const TArray<UObject*>& InObjects )` is the function called by the engine code to see if our `AssetTypeActions` class contains any actions that can be applied to the selected objects.

5. `IAssetTypeActions::GetActions(const TArray<UObject*>& InObjects, class FMenuBuilder& MenuBuilder)` is called if the `HasActions` function returns `true`. It calls functions on `MenuBuilder` to create the menu options for the actions that we provide.

6. `IAssetTypeActions::GetName()` returns the name of this class.

7. `IAssetTypeActions::GetSupportedClass()` returns an instance of `UClass` which our actions class supports.

8. `IAssetTypeActions::GetTypeColor()` returns the color associated with this class and actions.

9. `IAssetTypeActions::GetCategories()` returns a category appropriate for the asset. This is used to change the category under which the actions show in the context menu.

10. Our overridden implementation of `HasActions` simply returns `true` under all circumstances relying on filtering based on the results of `GetSupportedClass`.

11. Inside the implementation of `GetActions`, we can call some functions on the `MenuBuilder` object that we are given as a function parameter. The `MenuBuilder` is passed as a reference, so any changes that are made by our function will persist after it returns.

12. `AddMenuEntry` has a number of parameters. The first parameter is the name of the action itself. This is the name that will be visible within the context menu. The name is an `FText` so that it can be localized should you wish. For the sake of simplicity, we construct `FText` from a string literal and don't concern ourselves with multiple language support.

13. The second parameter is also `FText`, which we construct by calling `FText::FromString`. This parameter is the text displayed on a tooltip if the user hovers over our command for more than a small amount of time.

14. The next parameter is `FSlateIcon` for the command, which is constructed from the `LevelEditor.ViewOptions` icon within the editor style set.

15. The last parameter to this function is an `FUIAction` instance. The `FUIAction` is a wrapper around a delegate binding, so we use `FExecuteAction::CreateRaw` to bind the command to the `MyCustomAsset_Clicked` function on this very instance of `FMyCustomAssetActions`.

16. This means that when the menu entry is clicked, our `MyCustomAssetContext_Clicked` function will be run.

17. Our implementation of `GetName` returns the name of our Asset type. This string will be used on the thumbnail for our Asset if we don't set one ourselves, apart from being used in the title of the menu section that our custom Assets will be placed in.

18. As you'd expect, the implementation of `GetSupportedClass` returns `UMyCustomAsset::StaticClass()`, as this is the Asset type we want our actions to operate on.

19. `GetTypeColor()` returns the color that will be used for color coding in **Content Browser**—the color is used in the bar at the bottom of the asset thumbnail. I've used Emerald here, but any arbitrary color will work.

20. The real workhorse of this recipe is the `MyCustomAssetContext_Clicked()` function.

21. The first thing that this function does is create a new instance of `SWindow`.

22. `SWindow` is the Slate Window—a class from the Slate UI framework.

23. Slate Widgets are created using the `SNew` function, which returns an instance of the widget requested.

24. Slate uses the `builder` design pattern, which means that all the functions that are **chained** after `SNew` returns a reference to the object that was being operated on.

25. In this function, we create our new `SWindow`, then set the window title, its client size or area, and whether it can be maximized or minimized.

26. With our new Window ready, we need to get a reference to the root window for the editor so we can add our window to the hierarchy and get it displayed.

27. We do this using the `IMainFrameModule` class. It's a module, so we use the **Module Manager** to load it.

28. `LoadModuleChecked` will assert if we can't load the module, so we don't need to check it.

29. If the module was loaded, we check that we have a valid parent window. If that window is valid, then we use `FSlateApplication::AddWindowAsNativeChild` to add our window as a child of the top-level parent window.

30. If we don't have a top-level parent, the function uses `AddWindow` to add the new window without parenting it to another window within the hierarchy.

31. So now we have a class which will display custom actions on our custom Asset type, but we need to actually tell the engine that it should ask our class to handle custom actions for the type. In order to do that, we need to register our class with the Asset Tools module.

32. The best way to do this is to register our class when our editor module is loaded, and unregister it when it is shut down.

33. As a result, we place our code into the `StartupModule` and `ShutdownModule` functions.

34. Inside `StartupModule`, we load the Asset Tools module using **Module Manager**.

35. With the module loaded, we create a new shared pointer that references an instance of our custom Asset actions class.

36. All we then need to do is call `AssetModule.RegisterAssetTypeActions`, and pass in an instance of our actions class.

37. We then need to store a reference to that `Actions` instance so that we can unregister it later.

38. The sample code for this recipe uses an array of all the created asset actions in case we want to add custom actions for other classes as well.

39. Within `ShutdownModule`, we again retrieve an instance of the Asset Tools module.

40. Using a range-based for loop, we iterate over the array of `Actions` instances that we populated earlier, and call `UnregisterAssetTypeActions`, passing in our `Actions` class so it can be unregistered.

41. With our class registered, the editor has been instructed to ask our registered class if it can handle assets which are right-clicked on.

42. If the asset is of the Custom Asset class, then its `StaticClass` will match the one returned by `GetSupportedClass`. The editor will then call `GetActions`, and display the menu with the alterations made by our implementation of that function.

43. When the `CustomAssetAction` button is clicked, our custom `MyCustomAssetContext_Clicked` function will be called via the delegate that we created.

Creating new console commands

During development, console commands can be very helpful by allowing a developer or tester to easily bypass content, or disable the mechanics not relevant to the current test being run. The most common way to implement this is via console commands, which can invoke functions during runtime. The console can be accessed using the tilde key (~) or the equivalent in the upper-left area of the alphanumeric zone of your keyboard.

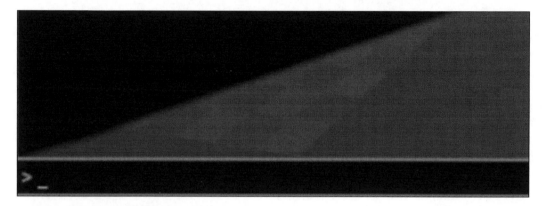

Getting ready

If you haven't already followed the *Creating a new editor module* recipe, do so, as this recipe will need a place to initialize and register the console command.

How to do it...

1. Open your editor module's header file, and add the following code:

```
IConsoleCommand* DisplayTestCommand;
IConsoleCommand* DisplayUserSpecifiedWindow;
```

2. Add the following within the implementation of `StartupModule`:

```
DisplayTestCommand =
IConsoleManager::Get().RegisterConsoleCommand(TEXT("Display
TestCommandWindow"), TEXT("test"),
FConsoleCommandDelegate::CreateRaw(this,
&FUE4CookbookEditorModule::DisplayWindow,
FString(TEXT("Test Command Window"))), ECVF_Default);
DisplayUserSpecifiedWindow=
IConsoleManager::Get().RegisterConsoleCommand(TEXT("Display
Window"), TEXT("test"),
FConsoleCommandWithArgsDelegate::CreateLambda(
    [&](const TArray< FString >& Args)
```

```
    {
      FString WindowTitle;
      for (FString Arg : Args)
      {
        WindowTitle +=Arg;
        WindowTitle.AppendChar(' ');
      }
      this->DisplayWindow(WindowTitle);
    }
  ), ECVF_Default);
```

3. Inside `ShutdownModule`, add this:

```
If (DisplayTestCommand)
{
  IConsoleManager::Get().UnregisterConsoleObject
  (DisplayTestCommand);
  DisplayTestCommand = nullptr;
}
If (DisplayUserSpecifiedWindow)
{
  IConsoleManager::Get().UnregisterConsoleObject
  (DisplayTestCommand);
  DisplayTestCommand = nullptr;
}
```

4. Implement the following function in the editor module:

```
void DisplayWindow(FString WindowTitle)
{
  TSharedRef<SWindow> CookbookWindow = SNew(SWindow)
  .Title(FText::FromString(WindowTitle))
  .ClientSize(FVector2D(800, 400))
  .SupportsMaximize(false)
  .SupportsMinimize(false);
  IMainFrameModule& MainFrameModule =
  FModuleManager::LoadModuleChecked<IMainFrameModule>
  (TEXT("MainFrame"));
  if (MainFrameModule.GetParentWindow().IsValid())
  {
    FSlateApplication::Get().AddWindowAsNativeChild
    (CookbookWindow, MainFrameModule.GetParentWindow()
    .ToSharedRef());
  }
  else
  {
    FSlateApplication::Get().AddWindow(CookbookWindow);
  }
}
```

5. Compile your code, and launch the editor.

6. Play the level, then hit the tilde key to bring up the console.

7. Type `DisplayTestCommandWindow`, and hit *Enter*.

8. You should see our tutorial window open up:

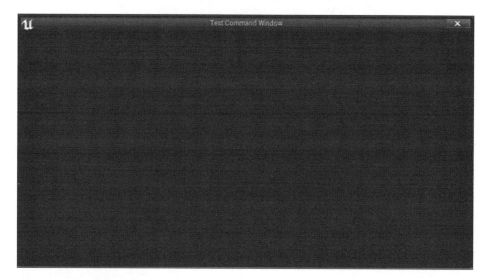

How it works...

1. Console commands are usually provided by a module. The best way to get the module to create the command when it is loaded is to place the code in the `StartupModule` method.

2. `IConsoleManager` is the module that contains the console functionality for the engine.

3. As it is a sub-module of the core module, we don't need to add any additional information to the build scripts to link in additional modules.

4. In order to call functions within the console manager, we need to get a reference to the current instance of `IConsoleManager` that is being used by the engine. To do so, we invoke the static `Get` function, which returns a reference to the module in a similar way to a singleton.

5. `RegisterConsoleCommand` is the function that we can use to add a new console command, and make it available in the console:

```
virtual IConsoleCommand* RegisterConsoleCommand(const
TCHAR* Name, const TCHAR* Help, const
FConsoleCommandDelegate& Command, uint32 Flags);
```

6. The parameters for the function are the following:

    1. `Name`: The actual console command that will be typed by users. It should not include spaces.

    2. `Help`: The tooltip that appears when users are looking at the command in the console. If your console command takes arguments, this is a good place to display usage information to users.

    3. `Command`: This is the actual function delegate that will be executed when the user types the command.

    4. `Flags`: These flags control visibility of the command in a shipping build, and are also used for console variables. `ECVF_Default` specifies the default behavior wherein the command is visible, and has no restrictions on availability in a release build.

7. To create an instance of the appropriate delegate, we use the `CreateRaw` static function on the `FConsoleCommand` delegate type. This lets us bind a raw C++ function to the delegate. The extra argument that is supplied after the function reference, the `FString` "Test Command Window", is a compile-time defined parameter that is passed to the delegate so that the end user doesn't have to specify the window name.

8. The second console command, `DisplayUserSpecifiedWindow`, is one that demonstrates the use of arguments with console commands.

9. The primary difference with this console command, aside from the different name for users to invoke it, is the use of `FConsoleCommandWithArgsDelegate` and the `CreateLambda` function on it in particular.

10. This function allows us to bind an anonymous function to a delegate. It's particularly handy when you want to wrap or adapt a function so its signature matches that of a particular delegate.

11. In our particular use case, the type of `FConsoleCommandWithArgsDelegate` specifies that the function should take a `const TArray` of FStrings. Our `DisplayWindow` function takes a single `FString` to specify the window title, so we need to somehow concatenate all the arguments of the console command into a single `FString` to use as our window title.

12. The lambda function allows us to do that before passing the `FString` onto the actual `DisplayWindow` function.

13. The first line of the function, `[&](const TArray<FString>& Args)`, specifies that this lambda or anonymous function wants to capture the context of the declaring function by reference by including the ampersand in the capture options `[&]`.

14. The second part is the same as a normal function declaration specifying that our lambda takes in `const Tarray` containing FStrings as a parameter called `Args`.

15. Within the lambda body, we create a new `FString`, and concatenate the strings that make up our arguments together, adding a space between them to separate them so that we don't get a title without spaces.

16. It uses a range-based `for` loop for brevity to loop over them all and perform the concatenation.

17. Once they're all concatenated, we use the `this` pointer (captured by the `&` operator mentioned earlier) to invoke `DisplayWindow` with our new title.

18. In order for our module to remove the console command when it is unloaded, we need to maintain a reference to the console command object.

19. To achieve this, we create a member variable in the module of type `IConsoleCommand*`, called `DisplayTestCommand`. When we execute the `RegisterConsoleCommand` function, it returns a pointer to the console command object that we can use as a handle later.

20. This allows us to enable or disable console commands at runtime based on gameplay or other factors.

21. Within `ShutdownModule`, we check to see if `DisplayTestCommand` refers to a valid console command object. If it does, we get a reference to the `IConsoleManager` object, and call `UnregisterConsoleCommand` passing in the pointer that we stored earlier in our call to `RegisterConsoleCommand`.

22. The call to `UnregisterConsoleCommand` deletes the `IConsoleCommand` instance via the passed-in pointer, so we don't need to `deallocate` the memory ourselves, just reset `DisplayTestCommand` to `nullptr` so we can be sure the old pointer doesn't dangle.

23. The `DisplayWindow` function takes in the window title as an `FString` parameter. This allows us to either use a console command that takes arguments to specify the title, or a console command that uses payload parameters to hard-code the title for other commands.

24. The function itself uses a function called `SNew()` to allocate and create an `SWindow` object.

25. `SWindow` is a Slate Window, a top-level window using the Slate UI framework.

26. Slate uses the `Builder` design pattern to allow for easy configuration of the new window.

27. The `Title`, `ClientSize`, `SupportsMaximize`, and `SupportsMinimize` functions used here, are all member functions of `SWindow`, and they return a reference to an `SWindow` (usually, the same object that the method was invoked on, but sometimes, a new object constructed with the new configuration).

28. The fact that all these member methods return a reference to the configured object allows us to chain these method invocations together to create the desired object in the right configuration.

29. The functions used in `DisplayWindow` create a new top-level Window that has a title based on the function parameter. It is 800x400 pixels wide, and cannot be maximized or minimized.

30. With our new Window created, we retrieve a reference to the main application frame module. If the top-level window for the editor exists and is valid, we add our new window instance as a child of that top-level window.

31. To do this, we retrieve a reference to the Slate interface, and call `AddWindowAsNativeChild` to insert our window in the hierarchy.

32. If there isn't a valid top-level window, we don't need to add our new window as a child of anything, so we can simply call `AddWindow`, and pass in our new window instance.

See also

▶ Refer to *Chapter 5, Handling Events and Delegates*, to learn more about delegates. It explains payload variables in greater detail.

▶ For more information on Slate, refer to *Chapter 9, User Interface*.

Creating a new graph pin visualizer for Blueprint

Within the Blueprint system, we can use instances of our `MyCustomAsset` class as variables, provided we mark that class as a `BlueprintType` in its `UCLASS` macro.

However, by default, our new asset is simply treated as `UObject`, and we can't access any of its members:

For some types of assets, we might wish to enable in-line editing of literal values in the same way that classes such as `FVector` support the following:

In order to enable this, we need to use a **Graph Pin** visualizer. This recipe will show you how to enable in-line editing of an arbitrary type using a custom widget defined by you.

How to do it...

1. Create a new header file called `MyCustomAssetPinFactory.h`.

2. Inside the header, add the following code:

```
#pragma once
#include "EdGraphUtilities.h"
#include "MyCustomAsset.h"
#include "SGraphPinCustomAsset.h"

struct UE4COOKBOOKEDITOR_API FMyCustomAssetPinFactory :
public FGraphPanelPinFactory
```

```
{
  public:
  virtual TSharedPtr<class SGraphPin> CreatePin(class
  UEdGraphPin* Pin) const override
  {
    if (Pin->PinType.PinSubCategoryObject ==
    UMyCustomAsset::StaticClass())
    {
      return SNew(SGraphPinCustomAsset, Pin);
    }
    else
    {
      return nullptr;
    }
  };
};
```

3. Create another header file called SGraphPinCustomAsset:

```
#pragma once
#include "SGraphPin.h"

class UE4COOKBOOKEDITOR_API SGraphPinCustomAsset : public
SGraphPin
{
  SLATE_BEGIN_ARGS(SGraphPinCustomAsset) {}
  SLATE_END_ARGS()
  void Construct(const FArguments& InArgs, UEdGraphPin*
  InPin);
  protected:
  virtual FSlateColor GetPinColor() const override { return
  FSlateColor(FColor::Black); };
  virtual TSharedRef<SWidget> GetDefaultValueWidget()
  override;
  void ColorPicked(FLinearColor SelectedColor);
};
```

4. Implement SGraphPinCustomAsset in the .cpp file:

```
#include "UE4CookbookEditor.h"
#include "SColorPicker.h"
#include "SGraphPinCustomAsset.h"

void SGraphPinCustomAsset::Construct(const FArguments& InArgs,
UEdGraphPin* InPin)
{
  SGraphPin::Construct(SGraphPin::FArguments(), InPin);
```

```
}
TSharedRef<SWidget>
SGraphPinCustomAsset::GetDefaultValueWidget()
{
   return SNew(SColorPicker)
   .OnColorCommitted(this,
   &SGraphPinCustomAsset::ColorPicked);
}

void SGraphPinCustomAsset::ColorPicked(FLinearColor
SelectedColor)
{
   UMyCustomAsset* NewValue = NewObject<UMyCustomAsset>();
   NewValue->ColorName =
   SelectedColor.ToFColor(false).ToHex();
   GraphPinObj->GetSchema()
   ->TrySetDefaultObject(*GraphPinObj, NewValue);
}
```

5. Add `#include "Chapter8/MyCustomAssetDetailsCustomization.h"` to the UE4Cookbook editor module implementation file.

6. Add the following member to the editor module class:

```
TSharedPtr<FMyCustomAssetPinFactory> PinFactory;
```

7. Add the following to `StartupModule()`:

```
PinFactory = MakeShareable(new FMyCustomAssetPinFactory());
FEdGraphUtilities::RegisterVisualPinFactory(PinFactory);
```

8. Also add the following code to `ShutdownModule()`:

```
FEdGraphUtilities::UnregisterVisualPinFactory(PinFactory);
PinFactory.Reset();
```

9. Compile your code, and launch the editor.

10. Create a new **Function** inside the Level Blueprint by clicking on the plus symbol beside **Functions** within the **My Blueprint** panel:

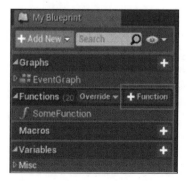

11. Add an input parameter.

12. Set its type to `MyCustomAsset` (**Reference**):

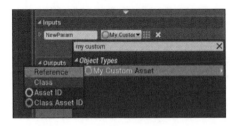

13. In the Level Blueprint's Event graph, place an instance of your new function, and verify that the input pin now has a custom visualizer in the form of a color picker:

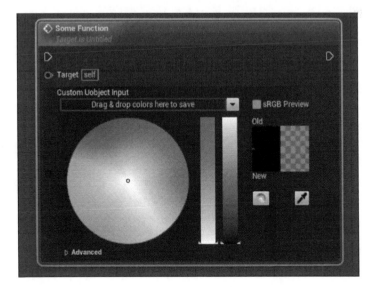

How it works...

1. Customizing how objects appear as literal values on Blueprint pins is done using the `FGraphPanelPinFactory` class.

2. This class defines a single virtual function:

    ```
    virtual TSharedPtr<class SGraphPin> CreatePin(class
    UEdGraphPin* Pin) const
    ```

3. The function of `CreatePin`, as the name implies, is to create a new visual representation of the graph pin.

4. It receives a `UEdGraphPin` instance. `UEdGraphPin` contains information about the object that the pin represents so that our factory class can make an informed decision regarding which visual representation we should be displaying.

5. Within our implementation of the function, we check that the pin's type is our custom class.

6. We do this by looking at the `PinSubCategoryObject` property, which contains a `UClass`, and comparing it to the `UClass` associated with our custom asset class.

7. If the pin's type meets our conditions, we return a new shared pointer to a Slate Widget, which is the visual representation of our object.

8. If the pin is of the wrong type, we return a null pointer to indicate a failed state.

9. The next class, `SGraphPinCustomAsset`, is the Slate Widget class, which is a visual representation of our object as a literal.

10. It inherits from `SGraphPin`, the base class for all graph pins.

11. The `SGraphPinCustomAsset` class has a `Construct` function, which is called when the widget is created.

12. It also implements some functions from the parent class: `GetPinColor()` and `GetDefaultValueWidget()`.

13. The last function defined is `ColorPicked`, a handler for when a user selects a color in our custom pin.

14. In the implementation of our custom class, we initialize our custom pin by calling the default implementation of `Construct`.

15. The role of `GetDefaultValueWidget` is to actually create the widget that is the custom representation of our class, and return it to the engine code.

16. In our implementation, it creates a new `SColorPicker` instance—we want the user to be able to select a color, and store the hex-based representation of that color inside the `FString` property in our custom class.

17. This `SColorPicker` instance has a property called `OnColorCommitted`— this is a slate event that can be assigned to a function on an object instance.

18. Before returning our new `SColorPicker`, we link `OnColorCommitted` to the `ColorPicked` function on this current object, so it will be called if the user selects a new color.

19. The `ColorPicked` function receives the selected color as an input parameter.

20. Because this widget is used when there's no object connected to the pin we are associated with, we can't simply set the property on the associated object to the desired color string.

21. We need to create a new instance of our custom asset class, and we do that by using the `NewObject` template function.

22. This function behaves similarly to the `SpawnActor` function discussed in other chapters, and initializes a new instance of the specified class before returning a pointer to it.

23. With a new instance in hand, we can set its `ColorName` property. `FLinearColors` can be converted to `FColor` objects, which define a `ToHex()` function that returns an `FString` with the hexadecimal representation of the color that was selected on the new widget.

24. Finally, we need to actually place our new object instance into the graph so that it will be referenced when the graph is executed.

25. To do this, we need to access the graph pin object that we represent, and use the `GetSchema` function. This function returns the Schema for the graph that owns the node that contains our pin.

26. The Schema contains the actual values that correspond to graph pins, and is a key element during graph evaluation.

27. Now that we have access to the Schema, we can set the default value for the pin that our widget represents. This value will be used during graph evaluation if the pin isn't connected to another pin, and acts like a default value provided during a function definition in C++.

28. As with all the extensions we've made in this chapter, there has to be some sort of initialization or registration to tell the engine to defer to our custom implementation before using its default inbuilt representation.

29. In order to do this, we need to add a new member to our editor module to store our `PinFactory` class instance.

30. During `StartupModule`, we create a new shared pointer that references an instance of our `PinFactory` class.

31. We store it inside the editor module's member so it can be unregistered later. Then we call `FEdGraphUtilities::RegisterVisualPinFactory(PinFactory)` to tell the engine to use our `PinFactory` to create the visual representation.

32. During `ShutdownModule`, we unregister the pin factory using `UnregisterVisualPinFactory`.

33. Finally, we delete our old `PinFactory` instance by calling `Reset()` on the shared pointer that contains it.

Inspecting types with custom Details panels

By default, `UObject`-derived UAssets open in the generic property editor. It looks like the following screenshot:

However, at times you may wish for custom widgets to allow editing of properties on your class. To facilitate this, Unreal supports **Details Customization**, which is the focus of this recipe.

How to do it...

1. Create a new header file called `MyCustomAssetDetailsCustomization.h`.

2. Add the following includes to the header:

```
#include "MyCustomAsset.h"
#include "DetailLayoutBuilder.h"
#include "IDetailCustomization.h"
#include "IPropertyTypeCustomization.h"
```

3. Define our customization class as follows:

```
class FMyCustomAssetDetailsCustomization : public
IDetailCustomization
{
  public:
  virtual void CustomizeDetails(IDetailLayoutBuilder&
  DetailBuilder) override;
  void ColorPicked(FLinearColor SelectedColor);
  static TSharedRef<IDetailCustomization>
  FMyCustomAssetDetailsCustomization::MakeInstance()
  {
    return MakeShareable(new
    FMyCustomAssetDetailsCustomization);
  }
  TWeakObjectPtr<class UMyCustomAsset> MyAsset;
};
```

4. In the implementation file, create an implementation for
`CustomizeDetails`:

```
void
FMyCustomAssetDetailsCustomization::CustomizeDetails(IDetai
lLayoutBuilder& DetailBuilder)
{
  const TArray< TWeakObjectPtr<UObject>>& SelectedObjects =
  DetailBuilder.GetDetailsView().GetSelectedObjects();
  for (int32 ObjectIndex = 0; !MyAsset.IsValid() &&
  ObjectIndex < SelectedObjects.Num(); ++ObjectIndex)
  {
    const TWeakObjectPtr<UObject>& CurrentObject =
    SelectedObjects[ObjectIndex];
    if (CurrentObject.IsValid())
    {
      MyAsset = Cast<UMyCustomAsset>(CurrentObject.Get());
    }
  }
  DetailBuilder.EditCategory("CustomCategory",
  FText::GetEmpty(), ECategoryPriority::Important)
  .AddCustomRow(FText::GetEmpty())
  [
    SNew(SVerticalBox)
    + SVerticalBox::Slot()
    .VAlign(VAlign_Center)
    [
      SNew(SColorPicker)
```

```
        .OnColorCommitted(this,
        &FMyCustomAssetDetailsCustomization::ColorPicked)
    ]
  ];
}
```

5. Also create a definition for `ColorPicked`:

```
void
FMyCustomAssetDetailsCustomization::ColorPicked(FLinearColo
r SelectedColor)
{
  if (MyAsset.IsValid())
  {
    MyAsset.Get()->ColorName =
    SelectedColor.ToFColor(false).ToHex();
  }
}
```

6. Lastly, add the following includes in the `.cpp` file:

```
#include "UE4CookbookEditor.h"
#include "IDetailsView.h"
#include "DetailLayoutBuilder.h"
#include "DetailCategoryBuilder.h"
#include "SColorPicker.h"
#include "SBoxPanel.h"
#include "DetailWidgetRow.h"
#include "MyCustomAssetDetailsCustomization.h"
```

7. In our editor module header, add the following to the implementation of `StartupModule`:

```
FPropertyEditorModule& PropertyModule =
FModuleManager::LoadModuleChecked<FPropertyEditorModule>("P
ropertyEditor");
PropertyModule.RegisterCustomClassLayout(UMyCustomAsset::St
aticClass()->GetFName(),
FOnGetDetailCustomizationInstance::CreateStatic(&FMyCustomA
ssetDetailsCustomization::MakeInstance));
```

8. Add the following to `ShutdownModule`:

```
FPropertyEditorModule& PropertyModule =
FModuleManager::LoadModuleChecked<FPropertyEditorModule>("P
ropertyEditor");
PropertyModule.UnregisterCustomClassLayout(UMyCustomAsset::
StaticClass()->GetFName());
```

9. Compile your code, and launch the editor. Create a new copy of `MyCustomAsset` via the content browser.

10. Double-click on it to verify that the default editor now shows your custom layout:

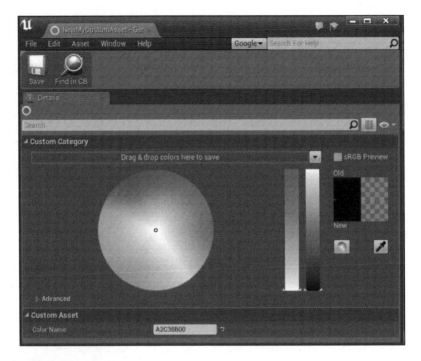

How it works...

1. Details Customization is performed through the `IDetailCustomization` interface, which developers can inherit from when defining a class which customizes the way assets of a certain class are displayed.

2. The main function that `IDetailCustomization` uses to allow for this process to occur is the following:

```
virtual void CustomizeDetails(IDetailLayoutBuilder&
DetailBuilder) override;
```

3. Within our implementation of this function, we use methods on `DetailBuilder` passed in as a parameter to get an array of all selected objects. The loop then scans those to ensure that at least one selected object is of the correct type.

4. Customizing the representation of a class is done by calling methods on the `DetailBuilder` object. We create a new category for our details view by using the `EditCategory` function.

5. The first parameter of the `EditCategory` function is the name of the category we are going to manipulate.

6. The second parameter is optional, and contains a potentially localized display name for the category.

7. The third parameter is the priority of the category. Higher priority means it is displayed further up the list.

8. `EditCategory` returns a reference to the category itself as `CategoryBuilder`, allowing us to chain additional method calls onto an invocation of `EditCategory`.

9. As a result, we call `AddCustomRow()` on `CategoryBuilder`, which adds a new key-value pair to be displayed in the category.

10. Using the Slate syntax, we then specify that the row will contain a Vertical Box with a single center-aligned slot.

11. Inside the slot, we create a color picker control, and bind its `OnColorCommitted` delegate to our local `ColorPicked` event handler.

12. Of course, this requires us to define and implement `ColourPicked`. It has the following signature:

```
void
FMyCustomAssetDetailsCustomization::ColorPicked
(FLinearColor SelectedColor)
```

13. Inside the implementation of `ColorPicked`, we check to see if one of our selected assets was of the correct type, because if at least one selected asset was correct, then `MyAsset` will be populated with a valid value.

14. Assuming we have a valid asset, we set the `ColorName` property to the hex string value corresponding to the color selected by the user.

9
User Interfaces – UI and UMG

In this chapter, we will cover the following topics:

- ▶ Drawing using Canvas
- ▶ Adding Slate Widgets to the screen
- ▶ Creating screen size-aware scaling for the UI
- ▶ Displaying and hiding a sheet of UMG elements in-game
- ▶ Attaching function calls to Slate events
- ▶ Using Data Binding with Unreal Motion Graphics
- ▶ Controlling widget appearance with Styles
- ▶ Creating a custom `SWidget/UWidget`

Introduction

Displaying feedback to the player is one of the most important elements within game design, and this will usually involve some sort of HUD, or at least menus, within your game.

In previous versions of Unreal, there was simple HUD support, which allowed you to draw simple shapes and text to the screen. However, it was somewhat limited in terms of aesthetics, and so, solutions such as **Scaleform** became common to work around the limitations. Scaleform leveraged Adobe's Flash file format to store vector images and UI scripts. It was not without its own cons for developers, though, not least the cost—it was a third-party product requiring an (at times expensive) license.

As a result, Epic developed Slate for the Unreal 4 editor and the in-game UI framework. Slate is a collection of widgets (UI elements) and a framework allowing a cross-platform interface for the Editor. It is also usable in-game to draw widgets, such as sliders and buttons, for menus and HUDs.

Slate uses declarative syntax to allow an xml-style representation of user interface elements in their hierarchy in native C++. It accomplishes this by making heavy use of macros and operator overloading.

That said, not everybody wants to ask their programmers to design the game's HUD. One of the significant advantages of using Scaleform within Unreal 3 was the ability to develop the visual appearance of game UIs using the Flash visual editor, so visual designers didn't need to learn a programming language. Programmers could then insert the logic and data separately. This is the same paradigm espoused by the **Windows Presentation Framework** (**WPF**), for example.

In a similar fashion, Unreal provides **Unreal Motion Graphics** (**UMG**). UMG is a visual editor for Slate widgets that allows you to visually style, layout, and animate user interfaces. UI widgets (or controls if you've come from a Win32 background) can have their properties controlled by either Blueprint code (written in the Graph view of the UMG window) or from C++. This chapter primarily deals with displaying UI elements, creating widget hierarchies, and creating base `SWidget` classes that can be styled and used within UMG.

Drawing using Canvas

Canvas is a continuation of the simple HUD implemented within Unreal 3. While it isn't so commonly used within shipping games, mostly being replaced by Slate/UMG, it's simple to use, especially when you want to draw text or shapes to the screen. Canvas drawing is still used extensively by console commands used for debugging and performance analysis such as the `stat game` and other `stat` commands. Refer to *Chapter 8, Integrating C++ and the Unreal Editor,* for the recipe for creating your own console commands.

How to do it...

1. Open your `<Module>.build.cs` file, and uncomment/add the following line:

```
PrivateDependencyModuleNames.AddRange(new string[] {
"Slate", "SlateCore" });
```

2. Create a new `GameMode` called `CustomHUDGameMode` using the editor class wizard. Refer to *Chapter 4, Actors and Components,* if you need a refresher on doing this.

3. Add a constructor to the class:

```
ACustomHUDGameMode();
```

4. Add the following to the constructor implementation:

```
ACustomHUDGameMode::ACustomHUDGameMode()
:AGameMode()
{
   HUDClass = ACustomHUD::StaticClass();
}
```

5. Create a new HUD subclass called `CustomHUD`, again using the wizard.

6. Add the `override` keyword to the following function:

```
public:
virtual void DrawHUD() override;
```

7. Now implement the function:

```
voidACustomHUD::DrawHUD()
{
   Super::DrawHUD();
   Canvas->DrawText(GEngine->GetSmallFont(), TEXT("Test
   string to be printed to screen"), 10, 10);
   FCanvasBoxItemProgressBar(FVector2D(5, 25),
   FVector2D(100, 5));
   Canvas->DrawItem(ProgressBar);
   DrawRect(FLinearColor::Blue, 5, 25, 100, 5);
}
```

8. **Compile** your code, and launch the editor.

9. Within the editor, open the **World Settings** panel from the **Settings** drop-down menu:

10. In the **World Settings** dialog, select `CustomHUDGameMode` from the list under **GameMode Override**:

11. Play and verify that your custom HUD is drawing to the screen:

How it works...

1. All the UI recipes here will be using Slate for drawing, so we need to add a dependency between our module and the Slate framework so that we can access the classes declared in that module.

2. The best place to put custom Canvas draw calls for a game HUD is inside a subclass of `AHUD`.

3. In order to tell the engine to use our custom subclass, though, we need to create a new `GameMode`, and specify the type of our custom class.

4. Within the constructor of our custom Game Mode, we assign the `UClass` for our new HUD type to the `HUDClass` variable. This `UClass` is passed onto each player controller as they spawn in, and the controller is then responsible for the `AHUD` instance that it creates.

5. With our custom `GameMode` loading our custom HUD, we need to actually create the said custom HUD class.

6. `AHUD` defines a virtual function called `DrawHUD()`, which is invoked in every frame to allow us to draw elements to the screen.

7. As a result, we override that function, and perform our drawing inside the implementation.

8. The first method used is as follows:

```
floatDrawText(constUFont* InFont, constFString&InText,
float X, float Y, float XScale = 1.f, float YScale = 1.f,
constFFontRenderInfo&RenderInfo = FFontRenderInfo());
```

9. `DrawText` requires a font to draw with. The default font used by `stat` and other HUD drawing commands in the engine code is actually stored in the `GEngine` class, and can be accessed by using the `GetSmallFont` function, which returns an instance of the `UFont` as a pointer.

10. The remaining arguments that we are use are the actual text that should be rendered, as well as the offset, in pixels, at which the text should be drawn.

11. `DrawText` is a function that allows you to directly pass in the data that is to be displayed.

12. The general `DrawItem` function is a Visitor implementation that allows you to create an object that encapsulates the information about the object to be drawn and reuse that object on multiple draw calls.

13. In this recipe, we create an element that can be used to represent a progress bar. We encapsulate the required information regarding the width and height of our box into an `FCanvasBoxItem`, which we then pass to the `DrawItem` function on our Canvas.

14. The third item that we draw is a filled rectangle. This function uses convenience methods defined in the HUD class rather than on the Canvas itself. The filled rectangle is placed at the same location as our `FCanvasBox` so that it can represent the current value inside the progress bar.

Adding Slate Widgets to the screen

The previous recipe used the `FCanvas` API to draw to the screen. However, `FCanvas` suffers from a number of limitations, for example, animations are difficult to implement, and drawing graphics on the screen involves creating textures or materials. `FCanvas` also doesn't implement anything in the way of widgets or window controls, making data entry or other forms of user input more complex than it needs to be. This recipe will show you how to begin creating HUD elements onscreen using Slate, which provides a number of built-in controls.

Getting ready

Add `Slate` and `SlateCore` to your module's dependencies if you haven't done so already (see recipe *Drawing using Canvas* for how to do this).

How to do it...

1. Create a new `PlayerController` subclass, `ACustomHUDPlayerController`.

2. Override the `BeginPlay` virtual method within your new subclass:

```
public:
virtual void BeginPlay() override;
```

3. Add the following code for your overridden `BeginPlay()` inside the subclass' implementation:

```
void ACustomHUDPlayerController::BeginPlay()
{
  Super::BeginPlay();
  TSharedRef<SVerticalBox> widget = SNew(SVerticalBox)
  + SVerticalBox::Slot()
  .HAlign(HAlign_Center)
  .VAlign(VAlign_Center)
  [
    SNew(SButton)
    .Content()
    [
      SNew(STextBlock)
      .Text(FText::FromString(TEXT("Test button")))
    ]
  ];
  GEngine->GameViewport
  ->AddViewportWidgetForPlayer(GetLocalPlayer(),
  widget, 1);
}
```

4. If you try to compile now, you'll get some errors regarding classes not being defined. This is because we need to include their headers:

```
#include "SlateBasics.h"
#include "SButton.h"
#include "STextBlock.h"
```

5. Create a new `GameMode` called `SlateHUDGameMode`:

6. Add a constructor inside the Game Mode:

```
ASlateHUDGameMode();
```

7. Implement the constructor with the following code:

```
ASlateHUDGameMode::ASlateHUDGameMode()
:Super()
{
  PlayerControllerClass =
  ACustomHUDPlayerController::StaticClass();
}
```

8. Add the following includes to the implementation file:

```
#include "CustomHudPlayerController.h"
```

9. After adding the include to the implementation file, compile your game.

10. Within the Editor, open **World Settings** from the toolbar:

11. Inside **World Settings**, override the level's Game Mode to be our `SlateHUDGameMode`.

12. Play the level, and see your new UI displayed on the screen:

How it works...

1. In order for us to reference Slate classes or functions in our code, our module must link with the `Slate` and `SlateCore` modules, so we add those to the module dependencies.

2. We need to instantiate our UI in one of the classes that loads when the game runs, so for this recipe, we use our custom `PlayerController`, in the `BeginPlay` function, as the place to create our UI.

3. Inside the `BeginPlay` implementation, we create a new `SVerticalBox` using the `SNew` function. We add a slot for a widget to our box, and set that slot to both horizontal and vertical centering.

4. Inside the slot, which we access using square brackets, we create a button that has `Textblock` inside it.

5. In `Textblock`, we set the `Text` property to a string literal value.

6. With the UI now created, we call `AddViewportWidgetForPlayer` to display this widget on the local player's screen.

7. With our custom `PlayerController` ready, we now need to create a custom `GameMode` to specify that it should use our new `PlayerController`.

8. With the custom `PlayerController` being loaded at the start of the game, when `BeginPlay` is called, our UI will be shown.

9. The UI is very small at this screen size. Refer to the next recipe for information on how to scale it appropriately for the resolution of the game window.

Creating screen size-aware scaling for the UI

If you have followed the previous recipe, you will notice that when you use **Play In Editor**, the button that loads is unusually small.

The reason for this is UI Scaling, a system that allows you to scale the user interface based on the screen size. User interface elements are represented in terms of pixels, usually in absolute terms (the button should be 10 pixels tall).

The problem with this is that if you use a higher-resolution panel, 10 pixels might be much smaller, because each pixel is smaller in size.

Getting ready

The UI scaling system in Unreal allows you to control a global scale modifier, which will scale all the controls on the screen based on the screen resolution. Given the earlier example, you might wish to adjust the size of the button so that its apparent size is unchanged when viewing your UI on a smaller screen. This recipe shows two different methods for altering the scaling rates.

How to do it...

1. Create a custom `PlayerController` subclass. Call it `ScalingUIPlayerController`.

2. Inside the class, override `BeginPlay`:

```
virtual void BeginPlay() override;
```

3. Add the following code in the implementation of that function:

```
Super::BeginPlay();
TSharedRef<SVerticalBox> widget = SNew(SVerticalBox)
+ SVerticalBox::Slot()
.HAlign(HAlign_Center)
.VAlign(VAlign_Center)
[
  SNew(SButton)
  .Content()
  [
    SNew(STextBlock)
    .Text(FText::FromString(TEXT("Test button")))
  ]
];
GEngine->GameViewport
->AddViewportWidgetForPlayer(GetLocalPlayer(), widget, 1);
```

4. Create a new `GameMode` subclass called `ScalingUIGameMode`, and give it a default constructor:

```
ScalingUIGameMode();
```

5. Within the default constructor, set the default player controller class to `ScalingUIPlayerController`:

```
AScalingUIGameMode::AScalingUIGameMode()
:AGameMode()
{
    PlayerControllerClass =
    ACustomHUDPlayerController::StaticClass();
}
```

6. This should give you a user interface like the one from the previous recipe. Note that the UI is very tiny if you use Play In Editor:

7. To alter the rate at which the UI scales down or up, we need to change the scaling curve. We can do that through two different methods.

The In-Editor method

1. Launch Unreal, then open the **Project Settings** dialog through the **Edit** menu:

2. Under the **User Interface** section, there is a curve that can be used to alter the UI scaling factor based on the short dimension of your screen:

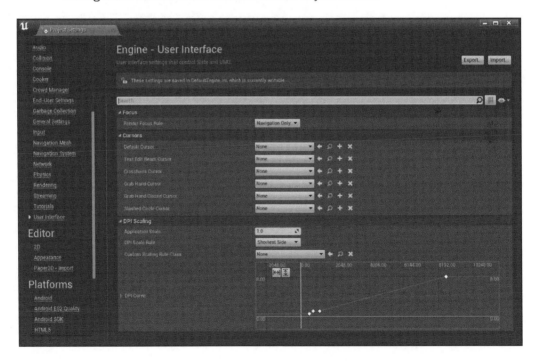

3. Click on the second dot, or keypoint, on the graph.

4. Change its output value to 1.

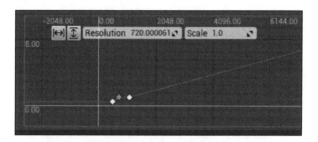

The Config file method

1. Browse to your project directory, and look inside the `Config` folder:

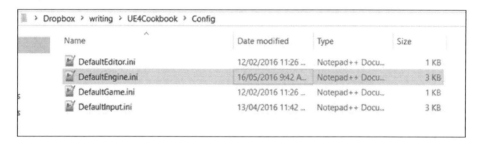

2. Open `DefaultEngine.ini` inside your text editor of choice.

3. Find the `[/Script/Engine.UserInterfaceSettings]` section:

```
[/Script/Engine.UserInterfaceSettings]
RenderFocusRule=NavigationOnly
DefaultCursor=None
TextEditBeamCursor=None
CrosshairsCursor=None
GrabHandCursor=None
GrabHandClosedCursor=None
SlashedCircleCursor=None
ApplicationScale=1.000000
UIScaleRule=ShortestSide
CustomScalingRuleClass=None
UIScaleCurve=(EditorCurveData=(PreInfinityExtrap=RCCE_Const
ant,PostInfinityExtrap=RCCE_Constant,Keys=((Time=480.000000,Value=
0.444000),(Time=720.000000,Value=1.000000),(Time=108
0.000000,Value=1.000000),(Time=8640.000000,Value=8.000000))
,DefaultValue=34028234663852885981170418348451692544 0.00000
0),ExternalCurve=None)
```

4. Look for a key called `UIScaleCurve` in that section.

5. In the value for that key, you'll notice a number of `(Time=x,Value=y)` pairs. Edit the second pair so that its `Time` value is `720.000000` and the `Value` is `1.000000`.

6. Restart the editor if you have it open.

7. Start the Play In Editor preview to confirm that your UI now remains readable at the **PIE** screen's resolution (assuming you are using a 1080p monitor so that the PIE window is running at 720p or thereabouts):

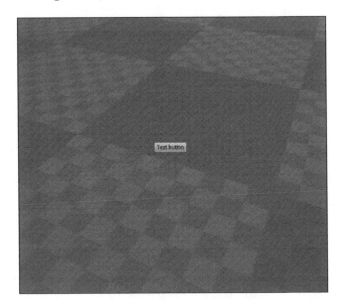

8. You can also see how the scaling works if you use a **New Editor Window** to preview your game.

9. To do so, click on the arrow to the right of **Play** on the toolbar.

10. Select **New Editor Window**.

11. Inside this window, you can use the console command `r.setreswidthxheight` to change the resolution, and observe the changes that result from doing so.

How it works...

1. As usual, when we want to use a custom `PlayerController`, we need a custom `GameMode` to specify which `PlayerController` to use.

2. We create both, a custom `PlayerController` and `GameMode`, and place some `Slate` code in the `BeginPlay` method of `PlayerController` so that some UI elements are drawn.

3. Because the main game viewport is usually quite small within the Unreal editor, the UI initially shows in a scaled-down fashion.

4. This is intended to allow for the game UI to take up less room on smaller resolution displays, but can have the side effect of making the text very difficult to read if the window isn't being stretched to fit the full screen.

5. Unreal stores the configuration data that should persist between sessions, but not necessarily be hard-coded into the executable inside config files.

6. Config files use an extended version of the `.ini` file format that has been commonly used with Windows software.

7. Config files store data using the following syntax:

    ```
    [Section Name]
    Key=Value
    ```

8. Unreal has a `UserInterfaceSettings` class, with a property called `UIScaleCurve` on it.

9. That `UPROPERTY` is marked as config, so Unreal serializes the value to the `.ini` file.

10. As a result, it stores the `UIScale` data in the `DefaultEngine.ini` file, in the `Engine.UserInterfaceSettings` section.

11. The data is stored using a text format, which contains a list of key points. Editing the `Time`, `Value` pairs alters or adds new key points to the curve.

12. The **Project Settings** dialog is a simple frontend for directly editing the `.ini` files yourself, and for designers, it is an intuitive way to edit the curve. However, having the data stored textually allows for programmers to potentially develop build tools that modify properties such as `UIScale` without having to recompile their game.

13. `Time` refers to the input value. In this case, the input value is the narrower dimension of the screen (usually, the height).

14. `Value` is the universal scaling factor applied to the UI when the screen's narrow dimension is approximately the height of the value in the `Time` field.

15. So, to set the UI to remain normal-sized at a 1280x720 resolution, set the time/input factor to 720, and the scale factor to 1.

See also

▶   You can refer to the UE4 documentation for more information regarding config files

Displaying and hiding a sheet of UMG elements in-game

So we have already discussed how to add a widget to the viewport, which means that it will be rendered on the player's screen.

However, what if we want to have UI elements that are toggled based on other factors, such as proximity to certain Actors, or a player holding a key down, or if we want a UI that disappears after a specified time?

How to do it...

1. Create a new `GameMode` class called `ToggleHUDGameMode`.

2. Override `BeginPlay` and `EndPlay`.

3. Add the following `UPROPERTY`:

```
UPROPERTY()
FTimerHandle HUDToggleTimer;
```

4. Lastly add this member variable:

```
TSharedPtr<SVerticalBox> widget;
```

5. Implement `BeginPlay` with the following code in the method body:

```
void AToggleHUDGameMode::BeginPlay()
{
  Super::BeginPlay();
  widget = SNew(SVerticalBox)
  + SVerticalBox::Slot()
  .HAlign(HAlign_Center)
  .VAlign(VAlign_Center)
  [
    SNew(SButton)
    .Content()
    [
      SNew(STextBlock)
      .Text(FText::FromString(TEXT("Test button")))
    ]
  ];
  GEngine->GameViewport
  ->AddViewportWidgetForPlayer(GetWorld()
  ->GetFirstLocalPlayerFromController(),
  widget.ToSharedRef(), 1);

  GetWorld()->GetTimerManager().SetTimer(HUDToggleTimer,
  FTimerDelegate::CreateLambda
  ([this]
```

```
  {
    if (this->widget->GetVisibility().IsVisible())
    {
      this->widget->SetVisibility(EVisibility::Hidden);
    }
    else
    {
      this->widget->SetVisibility(EVisibility::Visible);
    }
  }), 5, true);
}
```

6. Implement `EndPlay`:

```
void AToggleHUDGameMode::EndPlay(constEEndPlayReason::Type
EndPlayReason)
{
  Super::EndPlay(EndPlayReason);
  GetWorld->GetTimerManager().ClearTimer(HUDToggleTimer);
}
```

7. **Compile** your code, and start the editor.

8. Within the Editor, open **World Settings** from the toolbar:

9. Inside **World Settings**, override the level's **Game Mode** to be our `AToggleHUDGameMode`:

10. Play the level, and verify that the UI toggles its visibility every 5 seconds.

How it works...

As with most of the other recipes in this chapter, we are using a custom GameMode class to display our single-player UI on the player's viewport for convenience:

1. We override BeginPlay and EndPlay so that we can correctly handle the timer that will be toggling our UI on and off for us.

2. To make that possible, we need to store a reference to the timer as a UPROPERTY to ensure it won't be garbage collected.

3. Within BeginPlay, we create a new VerticalBox using the SNew macro, and place a button in its first slot.

4. Buttons have Content, which can be some other widget to host inside them, such as SImage or STextBlock.

5. In this instance, we place a STextBlock into the Content slot. The contents of the text block are irrelevant as long as they are long enough for us to be able to see our button properly.

6. Having initialized our widget hierarchy, we add the root widget to the player's viewport so that it can be seen by them.

7. Now we set up a timer to toggle the visibility of our widget. We are using a timer to simplify this recipe rather than having to implement user input and input bindings, but the principle is the same.

8. To do this, we get a reference to the game world, and its associated timer manager.

9. With the Timer manager in hand, we can create a new timer.

10. However, we need to actually specify the code to run when the timer expires. One simple way to do this is to use a lambda function for our toggle the hud function.

11. Lambdas are anonymous functions. Think of them as literal functions.

12. To link a lambda function to the timer, we need to create a timer delegate.

13. The FTimerDelegate::CreateLambda function is designed to convert a lambda function into a delegate, which the timer can call at the specified interval.

14. The lambda needs to access the this pointer from its containing object, our GameMode, so that it can change properties on the widget instance that we have created.

15. To give it the access it needs, we begin our lambda declaration with the [] operators, which enclose variables that should be captured into the lambda, and accessible inside it.

16. The curly braces then enclose the function body in the same way they would with a normal function declaration.

17. Inside the function, we check if our widget is visible. If it is visible, then we hide it using `SWidget::SetVisibility`.

18. If the widget isn't visible, then we turn it on using the same function call.

19. In the rest of the call to `SetTimer`, we specify the interval (in seconds) to call the timer, and set the timer to loop.

20. One thing we need to be careful of, though, is the possibility of our object being destroyed between two timer invocations, potentially leading to a crash if a reference to our object is left dangling.

21. In order to fix this, we need to remove the timer.

22. Given that we set the timer during `BeginPlay`, it makes sense to clear the timer during `EndPlay`.

23. `EndPlay` will be called whenever `GameMode` either ends play or is destroyed, so we can safely cancel the timer during its implementation.

24. With `GameMode` set as the default game mode, the UI is created when the game begins to play, and the timer delegate executes every 5 seconds to switch the visibility of the widgets between `true` and `false`.

25. When you close the game, `EndPlay` clears the timer reference, avoiding any problems.

Attaching function calls to Slate events

While creating buttons is all well and fine, at the moment, any UI element you add to the player's screen just sits there without anything happening even if a user clicks on it. We don't have any event handlers attached to the Slate elements at the moment, so events such as mouse clicks don't actually cause anything to happen.

Getting ready

This recipe shows you how to attach functions to these events so that we can run custom code when they occur.

How to do it...

1. Create a new `GameMode` subclass called `AClickEventGameMode`.

2. Add the following `private` members to the class:

```
private:
TSharedPtr<SVerticalBox> Widget;
TSharedPtr<STextBlock> ButtonLabel;
```

3. Add the following `public` functions, noting the override for `BeginPlay()`:

```
public:
virtual void BeginPlay() override;
FReplyButtonClicked();
```

4. Within the `.cpp` file, add the implementation for `BeginPlay`:

```
void AClickEventGameMode::BeginPlay()
{
  Super::BeginPlay();
  Widget = SNew(SVerticalBox)
  + SVerticalBox::Slot()
  .HAlign(HAlign_Center)
  .VAlign(VAlign_Center)
  [
    SNew(SButton)
    .OnClicked(FOnClicked::CreateUObject(this,
    &AClickEventGameMode::ButtonClicked))
    .Content()
    [
      SAssignNew(ButtonLabel, STextBlock)
      .Text(FText::FromString(TEXT("Click me!")))
    ]
  ];
  GEngine->GameViewport
  ->AddViewportWidgetForPlayer(GetWorld()
  ->GetFirstLocalPlayerFromController(),
  Widget.ToSharedRef(), 1);
  GetWorld()->GetFirstPlayerController()->bShowMouseCursor
  = true;
  GEngine->GetFirstLocalPlayerController(GetWorld())->
  SetInputMode(FInputModeUIOnly()
  .SetLockMouseToViewport(false)
  .SetWidgetToFocus(Widget));
}
```

5. Also add an implementation for `ButtonClicked()`:

```
FReplyAClickEventGameMode::ButtonClicked()
{
  ButtonLabel->SetText(FString(TEXT("Clicked!")));
  returnFReply::Handled();
}
```

6. **Compile** your code, and launch the editor.

7. Override the game mode in **World Settings** to be `AClickEventGameMode`:

8. Preview in the editor, and verify that the UI shows a button that changes from **Click Me!** to **Clicked!** when you use the mouse cursor to click on it.

How it works...

1. As with most of the recipes in this chapter, we use `GameMode` to create and display our UI to minimize the number of classes extraneous to the point of the recipe that you need to create.

2. Within our new game mode, we need to retain references to the Slate Widgets that we create so that we can interact with them after their creation.

3. As a result, we create two shared pointers as member data within our `GameMode`—one to the overall parent or root widget of our UI, and the other to the label on our button, because we're going to be changing the label text at runtime later.

4. We override `BeginPlay`, as it is a convenient place to create our UI after the game has started, and we will be able to get valid references to our player controller.

5. We also create a function called `ButtonClicked`. It returns `FReply`, a struct indicating if an event was handled. The function signature for `ButtonClicked` is determined by the signature of `FOnClicked`, a delegate which we will be using in a moment.

6. Inside our implementation of `BeginPlay`, the first thing we do is call the implementation we are overriding to ensure that the class is initialized appropriately.

7. Then, as usual, we use our `SNew` function to create `VerticalBox`, and we add a slot to it which is centered.

8. We create a new `Button` inside that slot, and we add a value to the `OnClicked` attribute that the button contains.

9. `OnClicked` is a delegate property. This means that the `Button` will broadcast the `OnClicked` delegate any time a certain event happens (as the name implies in this instance, when the button is clicked).

10. To subscribe or listen to the delegate, and be notified of the event that it refers to, we need to assign a delegate instance to the property.

11. We do that using the standard delegate functions such as `CreateUObject`, `CreateStatic`, or `CreateLambda`. Any of those will work—we can bind `UObject` member functions, static functions, lambdas, and other functions.

 Check *Chapter 5, Handling Events and Delegates,* to learn more on delegates to see about the other types of function that we can bind to delegates.

12. `CreateUObject` expects a pointer to a class instance, and a pointer to the member function defined in that class to call.

13. The function has to have a signature that is convertible to the signature of the delegate:

    ```
    /** The delegate to execute when the button is clicked */
    FOnClickedOnClicked;
    ```

14. As can be seen here, `OnClicked` delegate type is `FOnClicked`—this is why the `ButtonClicked` function that we declared has the same signature as `FOnClicked`.

15. By passing in a pointer to this, and the pointer to the function to invoke, the engine will call that function on this specific object instance when the button is clicked.

16. After setting up the delegate, we use the `Content()` function, which returns a reference to the single slot that the button has for any content that it should contain.

17. We then use `SAssignNew` to create our button's label, using the `TextBlock` widget.

18. `SAssignNew` is important, because it allows us to use Slate's declarative syntax, and yet assigns variables to point to specific child widgets in the hierarchy.

19. `SAssignNew` first argument is the variable that we want to store the widget in, and the second argument is the type of that widget.

20. With `ButtonLabel` now pointing at our button's `TextBlock`, we can set its `Text` attribute to a static string.

21. Finally, we add the widget to the player's viewport using `AddViewportWidgetForPlayer`, which expects, as parameters, `LocalPlayer` to add the widget to, the widget itself, and a depth value (higher values to the front).

22. To get the `LocalPlayer` instance, we assume we are running without split screen, and so, the first player controller will be the only one, that is, the player's controller. The `GetFirstLocalPlayerFromController` function is a convenience function that simply fetches the first player controller, and returns its local player object.

23. We also need to focus the widget so the player can click on it, and display a cursor so that the player knows where their mouse is on the screen.

24. We know from the previous step that we can assume the first local player controller is the one we're interested in, so we can access it and change its `ShowMouseCursor` variable to `true`. This will cause the cursor to be rendered on screen.

25. `SetInputMode` allows us to focus on a widget so that the player can interact with it amongst other UI-related functionality, such as locking the mouse to the game's viewport.

26. It uses an `FInputMode` object as its only parameter, which we can construct with the specific elements that we wish to include by using the `builder` pattern.

27. The `FInputModeUIOnly` class is a `FInputMode` subclass that specifies that we want all input events to be redirected to the UI layer rather than the player controller and other input handling.

28. The `builder` pattern allows us to chain the method calls to customize our object instance before it is sent into the function as the parameter.

29. We chain `SetLockMouseToViewport(false)` to specify that the player's mouse can leave the boundary of the game screen with `SetWidgetToFocus(Widget)`, which specifies our top-level widget as the one that the game should direct player input to.

30. Finally, we have our actual implementation for `ButtonClicked`, our event handler.

31. When the function is run due to our button being clicked, we change our button's label to indicate it has been clicked.

32. We then need to return an instance of `FReply` to the caller to let the UI framework know that the event has been handled, and to not continue propagating the event back up the widget hierarchy.

33. `FReply::Handled()` returns `FReply` set up to indicate this to the framework.

34. We could have used `FReply::Unhandled()`, but this would have told the framework that the click event wasn't actually the one we were interested in, and it should look for other objects that might be interested in the event instead.

Use Data Binding with Unreal Motion Graphics

So far, we've been assigning static values to the attributes of our UI widgets. However, what if we want to be more dynamic with widget content, or parameters such as border color? We can use a principle called data binding to dynamically link properties of our UI with variables in the broader program.

Unreal uses the Attribute system to allow us to bind the value of an attribute to the return value from a function, for example. This means that changing those variables will automatically cause the UI to change in response, according to our wishes.

How to do it...

1. Create a new `GameMode` subclass called `AAtributeGameMode`.

2. Add the following `private` member to the class:
   ```
   private:
   TSharedPtr<SVerticalBox> Widget;
   ```

3. Add the following `public` functions, noting the override for `BeginPlay()`:
   ```
   public:
   virtual void BeginPlay() override;
   FTextGetButtonLabel() const ;
   ```

4. Add the implementation for `BeginPlay` within the `.cpp` file:

```
voidAClickEventGameMode::BeginPlay()
{
  Super::BeginPlay();
  Widget = SNew(SVerticalBox)
  + SVerticalBox::Slot()
  .HAlign(HAlign_Center)
  .VAlign(VAlign_Center)
  [
    SNew(SButton)
    .Content()
    [
      SNew(STextBlock)
      .Text( TAttribute<FText>::Create(TAttribute<FText>
      ::FGetter::CreateUObject(this,
      &AAttributeGameMode::GetButtonLabel)))
    ]
  ];
  GEngine->GameViewport
  ->AddViewportWidgetForPlayer(GetWorld()
  ->GetFirstLocalPlayerFromController(),
  Widget.ToSharedRef(), 1);
}
```

5. Also, add an implementation for `GetButtonLabel()`:

```
FTextAAttributeGameMode::GetButtonLabel() const
{
  FVectorActorLocation = GetWorld()
  ->GetFirstPlayerController()->GetPawn()
  ->GetActorLocation();
  returnFText::FromString(FString::Printf(TEXT("%f, %f,
  %f"),
  ActorLocation.X, ActorLocation.Y, ActorLocation.Z));
}
```

6. **Compile** your code, and launch the editor.

7. Override the game mode in **World Settings** to be `AAttributeGameMode`.

8. Note that in a Play In Editor session, the value on the UI's button changes as the player moves around the scene.

1. Just like almost all other recipes in this chapter, the first thing we need to do is create a game mode as a convenient host for our UI. We create the UI in the same fashion as in the other recipes, by placing `Slate` code inside the `BeginPlay()` method of our game mode.

2. The interesting feature of this recipe concerns how we set the value of our button's label text:

```
.Text(
TAttribute<FText>::Create(TAttribute<FText>::FGetter::Creat
eUObject(this, &AAttributeGameMode::GetButtonLabel)))
```

3. The preceding syntax is unusually verbose, but what it is actually doing is comparatively simple. We assign something to the `Text` property, which is of the type `FText`. We can assign `TAttribute<FText>` to this property, and the `TAttribute` `Get()` method will be called whenever the UI wants to ensure that the value of `Text` is up to date.

4. To create `TAttribute`, we need to call the static `TAttribute<VariableType>::Create()` method.

5. This function expects a delegate of some description. Depending on the type of delegate passed to `TAttribute::Create`, `TAttribute::Get()` invokes a different type of function to retrieve the actual value.

6. In the code for this recipe, we invoke a member function of `UObject`. This means we know we will be calling the `CreateUObject` function on some delegate type.

 We can use `CreateLambda`, `CreateStatic`, or `CreateRaw` to invoke a lambda, a `static`, or a `member` function respectively on a raw C++ class. This will give us the current value for the attribute.

7. But what delegate type do we want to create an instance of? Because we're templating the `TAttribute` class on the actual variable type that the attribute will be associated with, we need a delegate that is also templated on the variable type as its return value.

8. That is to say, if we have `TAttribute<FText>`, the delegate connected to it needs to return an `FText`.

9. We have the following code within `TAttribute`:

```
template<typenameObjectType>
classTAttribute
{
  public:
  /**
   * Attribute 'getter' delegate
   *
   * ObjectTypeGetValue() const
   *
   * @return The attribute's value
   */
  DECLARE_DELEGATE_RetVal(ObjectType, FGetter);
  (...)
}
```

10. The `FGetter` delegate type is declared inside the `TAttribute` class, so its return value can be templated on the `ObjectType` parameter of the `TAttribute` template.

11. This means that `TAttribute<Typename>::FGetter` automatically defines a delegate with the correct return type of `Typename`.

12. So we need to create a `UObject`-bound delegate of type and signature for `TAttribute<FText>::FGetter`.

13. Once we have that delegate, we can call `TAttribute::Create` on the delegate to link the delegate's return value to our `TextBlock` member variable `Text`.

14. With our UI defined and a binding between the `Text` property, a `TAttribute<FText>`, and a delegate returning `FText`, we can now add the UI to the player's screen so that it's visible.

15. Every frame, the game engine checks all properties to see if they are linked to `TAttributes`.

16. If there's a connection, then the `TAttribute Get()` function is called, invoking the delegate, and returning the delegate's return value so that Slate can store it inside the widget's corresponding member variable.

17. For our demonstration of the process, `GetButtonLabel` retrieves the location of the first player pawn in the game world.

18. We then use `FString::Printf` to format the location data into a human readable string, and wrap that in an `FText` so that it can be stored as the `TextBlock` text value.

Controlling widget appearance with Styles

So far in this chapter, we've been creating UI elements that use the default visual representation. This recipe shows you how to create a Style in C++ that can be used as a common look-and-feel across your whole project.

How to do it...

1. Create a new class header in your project. Name the file "CookbookStyle.h".

2. Add the following code to the file:

```
#pragma once
#include "SlateBasics.h"
#include "SlateExtras.h"
classFCookbookStyle
{
  public:
  static void Initialize();
  static void Shutdown();
  static void ReloadTextures();
  staticconstISlateStyle& Get();
  staticFNameGetStyleSetName();
  private:
  staticTSharedRef<class FSlateStyleSet> Create();
  private:
  staticTSharedPtr<class
  FSlateStyleSet>CookbookStyleInstance;
};
```

3. Create a corresponding implementation cpp file for this class, and add the following code to it:

```
#include "UE4Cookbook.h"
#include "CookbookStyle.h"
#include "SlateGameResources.h"
TSharedPtr<FSlateStyleSet>FCookbookStyle::CookbookStyleInst
ance = NULL;
voidFCookbookStyle::Initialize()
{
  if (!CookbookStyleInstance.IsValid())
  {
    CookbookStyleInstance = Create();
    FSlateStyleRegistry::RegisterSlateStyle
    (*CookbookStyleInstance);
  }
```

```
}

voidFCookbookStyle::Shutdown()
{
  FSlateStyleRegistry::UnRegisterSlateStyle
  (*CookbookStyleInstance);
  ensure(CookbookStyleInstance.IsUnique());
  CookbookStyleInstance.Reset();
}
FNameFCookbookStyle::GetStyleSetName()
{
  staticFNameStyleSetName(TEXT("CookbookStyle"));
  returnStyleSetName;
}
#define IMAGE_BRUSH(RelativePath, ... ) FSlateImageBrush(
FPaths::GameContentDir() / "Slate"/ RelativePath +
TEXT(".png"), __VA_ARGS__ )
#define BOX_BRUSH(RelativePath, ... ) FSlateBoxBrush(
FPaths::GameContentDir() / "Slate"/ RelativePath +
TEXT(".png"), __VA_ARGS__ )
#define BORDER_BRUSH(RelativePath, ... ) FSlateBorderBrush(
FPaths::GameContentDir() / "Slate"/ RelativePath +
TEXT(".png"), __VA_ARGS__ )
#define TTF_FONT(RelativePath, ... ) FSlateFontInfo(
FPaths::GameContentDir() / "Slate"/ RelativePath +
TEXT(".ttf"), __VA_ARGS__ )
#define OTF_FONT(RelativePath, ... ) FSlateFontInfo(
FPaths::GameContentDir() / "Slate"/ RelativePath +
TEXT(".otf"), __VA_ARGS__ )

TSharedRef<FSlateStyleSet>FCookbookStyle::Create()
{
  TSharedRef<FSlateStyleSet>StyleRef =
  FSlateGameResources::New
  (FCookbookStyle::GetStyleSetName(), "/Game/Slate",
  "/Game/Slate");
  FSlateStyleSet& Style = StyleRef.Get();
  Style.Set("NormalButtonBrush",
  FButtonStyle().
  SetNormal(BOX_BRUSH("Button",
  FVector2D(54,54),FMargin(14.0f/54.0f))));
  Style.Set("NormalButtonText",
  FTextBlockStyle(FTextBlockStyle::GetDefault())
  .SetColorAndOpacity(FSlateColor(FLinearColor(1,1,1,1))));
  returnStyleRef;
}
```

```
#undef IMAGE_BRUSH
#undef BOX_BRUSH
#undef BORDER_BRUSH
#undef TTF_FONT
#undef OTF_FONT

voidFCookbookStyle::ReloadTextures()
{
  FSlateApplication::Get().GetRenderer()
  ->ReloadTextureResources();
}
constISlateStyle&FCookbookStyle::Get()
{
  return *CookbookStyleInstance;
}
```

4. Create a new Game Mode subclass, `StyledHUDGameMode`, and add the following code to its declaration:

```
#pragma once
#include "GameFramework/GameMode.h"
#include "StyledHUDGameMode.generated.h"
/**
 *
 */
UCLASS()
class UE4COOKBOOK_API AStyledHUDGameMode : public AGameMode
{
  GENERATED_BODY()
  TSharedPtr<SVerticalBox> Widget;
  public:
  virtual void BeginPlay() override;
};
```

5. Likewise, implement `GameMode`:

```
#include "UE4Cookbook.h"
#include "CookbookStyle.h"
#include "StyledHUDGameMode.h"
voidAStyledHUDGameMode::BeginPlay()
{
  Super::BeginPlay();
  Widget = SNew(SVerticalBox)
  + SVerticalBox::Slot()
  .HAlign(HAlign_Center)
  .VAlign(VAlign_Center)
```

```
    [
        SNew(SButton)
        .ButtonStyle(FCookbookStyle::Get(),
        "NormalButtonBrush")
        .ContentPadding(FMargin(16))
        .Content()
        [
            SNew(STextBlock)
            .TextStyle(FCookbookStyle::Get(), "NormalButtonText")
            .Text(FText::FromString("Styled Button"))
        ]
    ];
    GEngine->GameViewport
    ->AddViewportWidgetForPlayer(GetWorld()
    ->GetFirstLocalPlayerFromController(),
    Widget.ToSharedRef(), 1);
}
```

6. Lastly, create a 54x54 pixel png file with a border around it for our button. Save it to the Content | Slate folder with the name Button.png:

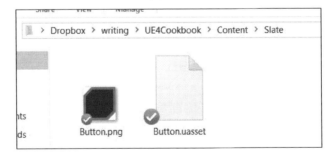

7. Finally, we need to set our game's module to properly initialize the style when it is loaded. In your game module's implementation file, ensure it looks like this:

```
class UE4CookbookGameModule : public FDefaultGameModuleImpl
{
    virtual void StartupModule() override
    {
        FCookbookStyle::Initialize();
    };
```

```
      virtual void ShutdownModule() override
      {
        FCookbookStyle::Shutdown();
      };
  };
```

8. **Compile** code, and set your game mode override to the new game mode as we've done in the other recipes this chapter.

9. When you play the game, you will see that your custom border is around the button, and the text is white rather than black.

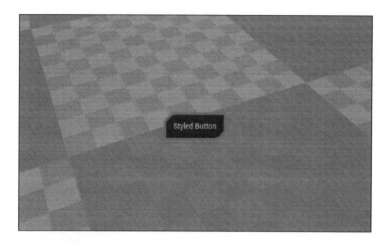

How it works...

1. In order for us to create styles that can be shared across multiple Slate widgets, we need to create an object to contain the styles and keep them in scope.

2. Epic provides the FSlateStyleSet class for this purpose. FSlateStyleSet contains a number of styles that we can access within Slate's declarative syntax to skin widgets.

3. However, it's inefficient to have multiple copies of our StyleSet object scattered through the program. We really only need one of these objects.

4. Because FSlateStyleSet itself is not a singleton, that is, an object that can only have one instance, we need to create a class that will manage our StyleSet object and ensure that we only have the single instance.

5. This is the reason we have the FCookbookStyle class.

6. It contains an Initialize() function, which we will call in our module's startup code.

7. In the `Initialize()` function, we check if we have an instance of our `StyleSet`.

8. If we do not have a valid instance, we call the private `Create()` function to instantiate one.

9. We then register the style with the `FSlateStyleRegistry` class.

10. When our module is unloaded, we will need to reverse this registration process, then erase the pointer so it does not dangle.

11. We now have an instance of our class, created during module initialization by calling `Create()`.

12. You'll notice that `Create` is wrapped by a number of macros that all have similar form.

13. These macros are defined before the function, and undefined after it.

14. These macros make it easier for us to simplify the code required within the `Create` function by eliminating the need to specify a path and extension for all the image resources that our Style might want to use.

15. Within the `Create` function, we create a new `FSlateStyleSet` object using the function `FSlateGameResources::New()`.

16. `New()` needs a name for the style, and the folder paths that we want to search for in this Style Set.

17. This allows us to declare multiple Style Sets pointing to different directories, but using the same names for the images. It also allows us to skin or restyle the whole UI simply by switching to a Style Set in one of the other base directories.

18. `New()` returns a shared reference object, so we retrieve the actual `FStyleSet` instance using the `Get()` function.

19. With this reference in hand, we can create the styles we want this set to contain.

20. To add styles to a set, we use the `Set()` method.

21. Set expects the name of the style, and then a style object.

22. Style objects can be customized using the `builder` pattern.

23. We first add a style called `"NormalButtonBrush"`. The name can be arbitrary.

24. Because we want to use this style to change the appearance of buttons, we need to use `FButtonStyle` for the second parameter.

25. To customize the style to our requirements, we use the Slate builder syntax, chaining whatever method calls that we need to set properties on our style.

26. For the first style in this set, we just change the visual appearance of the button when it isn't being clicked or is in a non-default state.

27. That means we want to change the brush used when the button is in the normal state, and so the function we use is `SetNormal()`.

28. Using the `BOX_BRUSH` macro, we tell Slate that we want to use `Button.png`, which is an image of 54x54 pixel size, and that we want to keep the 14 pixels in each corner unstretched for the purposes of nine-slice scaling.

[For a more visual explanation of the nine-slice scaling functionality, take a look at `SlateBoxBrush.h` in the engine source.]

29. For the second style in our Style Set, we create a style called `"NormalButtonText"`. For this style, we don't want to change everything from defaults in the style; we just want to alter one property.

30. As a result, we access the default text style, and clone it using the copy constructor.

31. With our fresh copy of the default style, we then change the color of the text to white, first creating a linear color of R=1 G=1 B=1 A=1, then converting that to a Slate color object.

32. With our Style Set configured with our two new styles, we can then return it to the calling function, which is `Initialize`.

33. `Initialize` stores our Style Set reference, and eliminates the need for us to create further instances.

34. Our style container class also has a `Get()` function, which is used to retrieve the actual `StyleSet` for use in Slate.

35. Because `Initialize()` has already been called at the module startup, `Get()` simply returns the `StyleSet` instance that was created within that function.

36. Within the game module, we add the code which actually calls `Initialize` and `Shutdown`. This ensures that while our module is loaded, we will always have a valid reference to our Slate Style.

37. As always, we create a Game Mode as the host for our UI, and we override `BeginPlay` so that we can create the UI when the game starts.

38. The syntax for creating the UI is exactly the same as we've used in previous recipes—creating a `VerticalBox` using `SNew`, and then using Slate's declarative syntax to populate the box with other widgets.

39. It is important to note the two following lines:

```
.ButtonStyle(FCookbookStyle::Get(), "NormalButtonBrush")
.TextStyle(FCookbookStyle::Get(), "NormalButtonText")
```

40. The preceding lines are part of the declarative syntax for our button, and the text that makes its label.

41. When we set the style for our widgets using a `<Class>Style()` method, we pass in two parameters.

42. The first parameter is our actual Style Set, retrieved using `FCookbookStyle::Get()`, and the second is a string parameter with the name of the style that we want to use.

43. With these minor changes, we override the styling of the widgets to use our custom styles so that when we add the widgets to the player's viewport, they display our customizations.

Create a custom SWidget/UWidget

The recipes in this chapter so far have shown you how to create UIs using the existing primitive widgets.

Sometimes, it is convenient for developers to use composition to collect a number of UI elements together, for example, to define a button class that automatically has a `TextBlock` as a label rather than manually specifying the hierarchy every time they are declared.

Furthermore, if you are manually specifying the hierarchy in C++, rather than declaring a compound object consisting of subwidgets, you won't be able to instantiate those widgets as a group using UMG.

Getting ready

This recipe shows you how to create a compound `SWidget` that contains a group of widgets and exposes new properties to control elements of those subwidgets. It will also show you how to create a `UWidget` wrapper, which will expose the new compound `SWidget` class to UMG for use by designers.

How to do it...

1. We need to add the UMG module to our module's dependencies.

2. Open up `<YourModule>.build.cs`, and add UMG to the following:
```
PrivateDependencyModuleNames.AddRange(new string[] {
"Slate", "SlateCore", "UMG" });
```

3. Create a new class called `CustomButton`, and add the following code to its declaration:
```
#pragma once
#include "SCompoundWidget.h"
class UE4COOKBOOK_API SCustomButton : public
SCompoundWidget
{
  SLATE_BEGIN_ARGS(SCustomButton)
```

```
      : _Label(TEXT("Default Value"))
      , _ButtonClicked()
      {}
      SLATE_ATTRIBUTE(FString, Label)
      SLATE_EVENT(FOnClicked, ButtonClicked)
      SLATE_END_ARGS()
      public:
      void Construct(constFArguments&InArgs);
      TAttribute<FString> Label;
      FOnClickedButtonClicked;
};
```

4. Implement the class with the following in the corresponding cpp file:

```cpp
#include "UE4Cookbook.h"
#include "CustomButton.h"
voidSCustomButton::Construct(constFArguments&InArgs)
{
  Label = InArgs._Label;
  ButtonClicked = InArgs._ButtonClicked;
  ChildSlot.VAlign(VAlign_Center)
  .HAlign(HAlign_Center)
  [SNew(SButton)
  .OnClicked(ButtonClicked)
  .Content()
  [
  SNew(STextBlock)
  .Text_Lambda([this] {return
  FText::FromString(Label.Get()); })
  ]
  ];
}
```

5. Create a second class, this time based on `UWidget`, called `UCustomButtonWidget`.

6. Add the following includes:

```cpp
#include "Components/Widget.h"
#include "CustomButton.h"
#include "SlateDelegates.h"
```

7. Declare the following delegates before the class declaration:

```cpp
DECLARE_DYNAMIC_DELEGATE_RetVal(FString, FGetString);
DECLARE_DYNAMIC_MULTICAST_DELEGATE(FButtonClicked);
```

8. Add the following protected members:

```
protected:
TSharedPtr<SCustomButton>MyButton;
virtualTSharedRef<SWidget>RebuildWidget() override;
```

9. Also add the following public members:

```
public:
UCustomButtonWidget();
UPROPERTY(BlueprintAssignable)
FButtonClickedButtonClicked;
FReplyOnButtonClicked();
UPROPERTY(BlueprintReadWrite, EditAnywhere)
FString Label;
UPROPERTY()
FGetStringLabelDelegate;
virtual void SynchronizeProperties() override;
```

10. Now create the implementation for UCustomButtonWidget:

```
#include "UE4Cookbook.h"
#include "CustomButtonWidget.h"
TSharedRef<SWidget>UCustomButtonWidget::RebuildWidget()
{
  MyButton = SNew(SCustomButton)
  .ButtonClicked(BIND_UOBJECT_DELEGATE(FOnClicked,
  OnButtonClicked));
  returnMyButton.ToSharedRef();
}
UCustomButtonWidget::UCustomButtonWidget()
:Label(TEXT("Default Value"))
{
}

FReplyUCustomButtonWidget::OnButtonClicked()
{
  ButtonClicked.Broadcast();
  returnFReply::Handled();
}
voidUCustomButtonWidget::SynchronizeProperties()
{
  Super::SynchronizeProperties();
  TAttribute<FString>LabelBinding =
  OPTIONAL_BINDING(FString, Label);
  MyButton->Label = LabelBinding;
}
```

11. Create a new Widget Blueprint by right-clicking on the **Content Browser**, selecting **User Interface**, and then **Widget Blueprint**:

12. Open your new **Widget Blueprint** by double-clicking on it.

13. Find the **Custom Button Widget** in the Widget Palette:

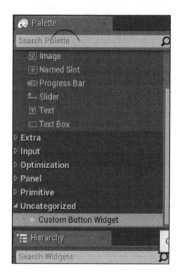

14. Drag an instance of it out into the main area.

15. With the instance selected, change the **Label** property in the **Details** panel:

16. Verify that your button has changed its label.

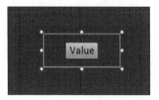

17. Now we will create a binding to demonstrate that we can link arbitrary blueprint functions to the label property on our widget, which, in turn, drives the Widget's textblock label.

18. Click on **Bind** to the right of the **Label** property, and select **Create Binding**:

19. Within the graph that is now displayed, place a **Get Game Time in Seconds** node:

20. Link the return value from the Get Game Time node to the **Return Value** pin in the function:

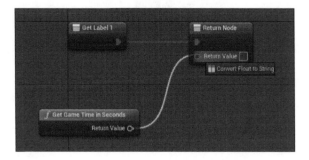

21. A convert float to string node will be automatically inserted for you:

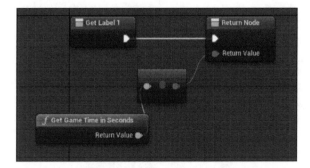

22. Next, open the **Level Blueprints** by clicking on the **Blueprints** button on the taskbar, then selecting **Open Level Blueprint**:

23. Place a construct widget node into the graph:

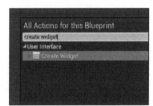

24. Select the class of widget to spawn as the new Widget Blueprint that we created a moment ago within the editor:

25. Click and drag away from the **Owning Player** pin on the create widget node, and place a **Get Player Controller** node:

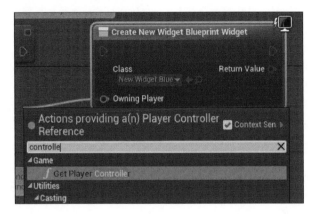

26. Likewise, drag away from the return value of the create widget node, and place a **Add to Viewport** node.

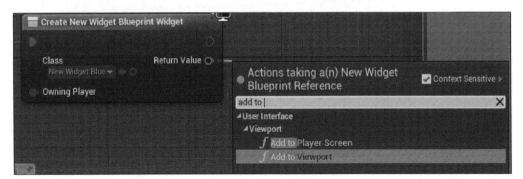

27. Lastly, link the `BeginPlay` node to the execution pin on the create widget node.

28. Preview your game, and verify that the widget we've displayed onscreen is our new custom button with its label bound to the number of seconds that have elapsed since the game started:

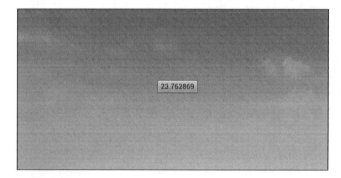

How it works...

1. In order to use the `UWidget` class, our module needs to include the UMG module as one of its dependencies, because `UWidget` is defined inside the UMG module.

2. The first class that we need to create, however, is our actual `SWidget` class.

3. Because we want to aggregate two widgets together into a compound structure, we create our new widget as a `CompoundWidget` subclass.

4. `CompoundWidget` allows you to encapsulate a widget hierarchy as a widget itself.

5. Inside the class, we use the `SLATE_BEGIN_ARGS` and `SLATE_END_ARGS` macros to declare an internal `struct` called `FArguments` on our new `SWidget`.

6. Within `SLATE_BEGIN_ARGS` and `SLATE_END_ARGS`, the `SLATE_ATTRIBUTE` and `SLATE_EVENT` macros are used.

7. `SLATE_ATTRIBUTE` creates `TAttribute` for the type we give it.

8. In this class, we declare `TAttribute` called `_Label`, which is more specifically a `TAttribute<FString>`.

9. `SLATE_EVENT` allows us to create member delegates that we can broadcast when something happens internally to the widget.

10. In `SCustomButton`, we declare a delegate with the signature `FOnClicked`, called `ButtonClicked`.

11. `SLATE_ARGUMENT` is another macro, unused in this recipe, which creates an internal variable with the type and name you provide, appending an underscore to the start of the variable name.

12. `Construct()` is the function that widgets implement to self-initialize when they are being instantiated.

13. You'll notice we also create a `TAttribute` and a `FOnClicked` instance ourselves, without the underscores. These are the actual properties of our object into which the arguments that we declared earlier will be copied.

14. Inside the implementation of `Construct`, we retrieve the arguments that were passed to us in the `FArgumentsstruct`, and store them inside our actual member variables for this instance.

15. We assign `Label` and `ButtonClicked` based on what was passed in, then we actually create our widget hierarchy.

16. We use the same syntax as usual for this with one thing to note, namely, the use of `Text_Lambda` to set the text value of our internal text block.

17. We use a `lambda` function to retrieve the value of our `Label TAttribute` using `Get()`, then convert it to `FText`, and store it as our text block's `Text` property.

18. Now that we have our `SWidget` declared, we need to create a wrapper `UWidget` object that will expose this widget to the UMG system so that designers can use the widget within the **WYSIWYG** editor.

19. This class will be called `UCustomButtonWidget`, and it inherits from `UWidget` rather than `SWidget`.

20. The `UWidget` object needs a reference to the actual `SWidget` that it owns, so we place a protected member in the class that will store it as a shared pointer.

21. A constructor is declared, so is a `ButtonClicked` delegate that can be set in blueprint. We also mirror a `Label` property that is marked as `BlueprintReadWrite` so that it can be set in the UMG editor.

22. Because we want to be able to bind our button's label to a delegate, we add the last of our member variables, which is a delegate that returns a `String`.

23. The `SynchronizeProperties` function applies properties that have been mirrored in our `UWidget` class across to the `SWidget` that we are linked with.

24. `RebuildWidget` reconstructs the native widget this `UWidget` is associated with. It uses `SNew` to construct an instance of our `SCustomButton` widget, and uses the Slate declarative syntax to bind the UWidget's `OnButtonClicked` method to the `ButtonClicked` delegate inside the native widget.

25. This means that when the native widget is clicked, the `UWidget` will be notified by having `OnButtonClicked` called.

26. `OnButtonClicked` re-broadcasts the clicked event from the native button via the UWidget's `ButtonClicked` delegate.

27. This means that UObjects and the UMG system can be notified of the button being clicked without having a reference to the native button widget themselves. We can bind to `UCustomButtonWidget::ButtonClicked` to be notified about it.

28. `OnButtonClicked` then returns `FReply::Handled()` to indicate that the event does not need to propagate further.

29. Inside `SynchronizeProperties`, we call the parent method to ensure that any properties in the parent are also synchronized properly.

30. We use the `OPTIONAL_BINDING` macro to link the `LabelDelegate` delegate in our `UWidget` class to `TAttribute`, and in turn, the native button's label. It is important to note that the `OPTIONAL_BINDING` macro expects the delegate to be called `NameDelegate` based on the second parameter to the macro.

31. `OPTIONAL_BINDING` allows for the value to be overridden by a binding made via UMG, but only if the UMG binding is valid.

32. This means that when `UWidget` is told to update itself, for example, because the user customizes a value in the **Details** panel within UMG, it will recreate the native `SWidget` if necessary, then copy the values set in Blueprint/UMG via `SynchronizeProperties` so that everything continues to work as expected.

AI for Controlling NPCs

10

The role of **Artificial Intelligence** (**AI**) in your game is quite important. In this chapter, we'll cover the following recipes for controlling your **NPC** characters with a bit of AI:

- ▶ Laying down a Navigation Mesh
- ▶ Following behavior
- ▶ Connecting a Behavior Tree to a Character
- ▶ Constructing Task nodes
- ▶ Using Decorators for conditions
- ▶ Using periodic services
- ▶ Using Composite nodes – Selectors, Sequences, and Simple Parallel
- ▶ AI for a Melee Attacker

Introduction

AI includes many aspects of a game's NPC as well as player behavior. The general topic of AI includes pathfinding and NPC behavior. Generally, we term the selection of what the NPC does for a period of time within the game as behavior.

AI in UE4 is well supported. A number of constructs exist to allow basic AI programming from within the editor. If the AI provided inside the engine doesn't suit your needs, custom AI programming from C++ can also be used.

Laying down a Navigation Mesh

A Navigation Mesh (also known as a **Nav Mesh**) is basically a definition of areas that an AI-controlled unit considers passable (that is, areas which the "AI-controlled" unit is allowed to move into or across). A Nav Mesh does not include geometry that would block the player if the player tried to move through it.

Getting ready

Constructing a Nav Mesh based on your scene's geometry is fairly easy in UE4. Start with a project that has some obstacles around it, or one that uses a terrain.

How to do it...

To construct your Nav Mesh, simply perform the following steps:

1. Go to **Modes | Volumes**.
2. Drag **Nav Mesh Bounds Volume** onto your viewport.

> Press the *P* key to view your Nav Mesh.

3. Scale the Nav Mesh out to cover the area that the actors that use the Nav Mesh should be allowed to navigate and pathfind in.

How it works...

A Nav Mesh doesn't block the player pawn (or other entities) from stepping on certain geometry, but it serves to guide AI-controlled entities regarding where they can and cannot go.

Following behavior

The most basic AI-controlled follow behavior is available as a simple function node. All you have to do is perform the steps that follow to get one AI-controlled unit to follow a unit or object.

Getting ready

Have a UE4 project ready with a simple landscape or set of geometry on the ground— ideally, with a *cul-de-sac* somewhere in the geometry for testing out AI movement functions. Create a Nav Mesh over this geometry so that the `AIMoveTo` function will work as described in the previous recipe.

How to do it...

1. Create a Nav Mesh for your level's geometry as described in the preceding recipe, *Laying down a Navigation Mesh*.

2. Create a Blueprint class deriving from `Character` by finding the `Character` class in the **Class Viewer**, right-clicking on it, and selecting **Create Blueprint Class...**

3. Name your Blueprint class `BP_Follower`.

4. Double-click on the `BP_Follower` class to edit its Blueprint.

5. In the `Tick` event, add an `AIMoveTo` node, which moves towards the player pawn (or any other unit) as follows:

How it works...

The `AIMoveTo` node will automatically use a Nav Mesh if one is available. If a Nav Mesh is not available, then the NPC unit won't move.

If you do not want the unit to move with pathfinding using the Nav Mesh, then simply use a **Move To Location or Actor** node.

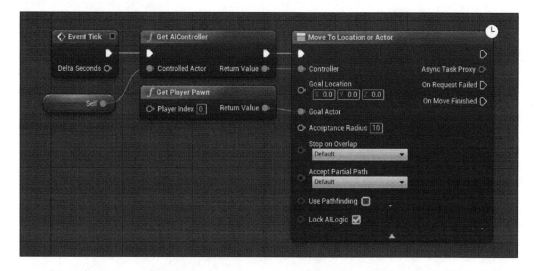

A **Move To Location or Actor** node works even without a Nav Mesh on the geometry.

Connecting a Behavior Tree to a Character

A `BehaviorTree` chooses a behavior to be exhibited by an AI-controlled unit at any given moment in time. Behavior Trees are relatively simple to construct, but there is a lot of setting up to do to get one running. You also have to be familiar with the components available for constructing your **Behavior Tree** to do so effectively.

A Behavior Tree is extremely useful for defining NPC behavior that is more varied than simply moving towards an opponent (as shown in the previous recipe with `AIMoveTo`).

Getting ready

The process of setting up a Behavior Tree to control a character is fairly complicated. The first thing we need is a Blueprint of a `Character` class derivative to control. We then need to create a custom AI Controller object that will run our Behavior Tree to control our Melee attacker character. The `AIController` class inside our Blueprint will run our Behavior Tree.

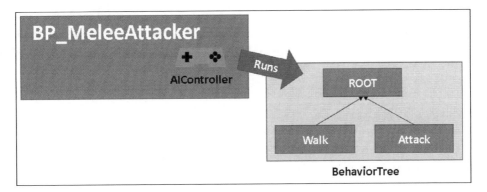

The Behavior Tree itself contains a very important data structure called a **Blackboard**. The Blackboard is like a chalkboard for containing variable values for the Behavior Tree.

A Behavior Tree hosts six different types of node, which are as follows:

1. **Task**: Task nodes are the purple nodes in the Behavior Tree that contain Blueprint code to run. It's something that the AI-controlled unit has to do (code-wise). Tasks must return either `true` or `false`, depending on whether the task succeeded or not (by providing a `FinishExecution()` node at the end).

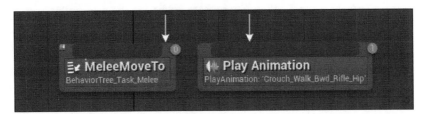

2. **Decorator**: A decorator is just a Boolean condition for the execution of a node. It checks a condition, and is typically used within a Selector or Sequence block.

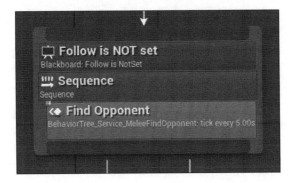

3. **Service**: Runs some Blueprint code when it ticks. The tick interval for these nodes is adjustable (can run slower than a per-frame tick, for example, every 10 seconds). You can use these to query the scene for updates, or a new opponent to chase, or things like that. The Blackboard can be used to store queried information. Service nodes do not have a `FinishExecute()` call at the end. There is an example Service node in the Sequence node in the preceding diagram.

4. **Selector**: Runs all subtrees from left to right until it encounters a success. When it encounters a success, execution returns back up the tree.

5. **Sequence**: Runs subtrees from left to right until it encounters a failure. When a failure is encountered, execution goes back up the tree.

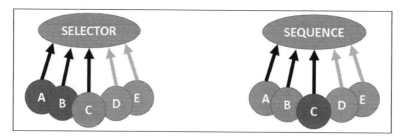

Selector nodes attempt to execute nodes until success (after which it returns), while Sequence nodes execute all until a failure is encountered (after which it returns).

Keep in mind that if your Tasks do not call `FinishExecute()`, neither Selectors nor Sequences will be able to run more than one of them in succession.

6. **Simple Parallel**: Runs a single task (purple) in parallel with a subtree (gray).

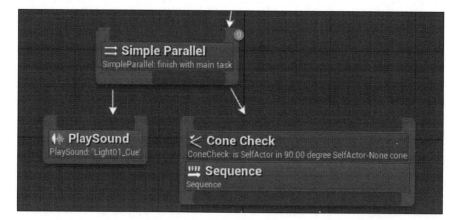

How to do it...

1. Begin by creating a Blueprint for your Melee unit inside UE4. You should do so by deriving a custom Blueprint from `Character`. To do so, go to the **Class Viewer**, type `Character`, and right-click. Select **Create Blueprint...** from the context menu that appears and name your Blueprint class `BP_MeleeCharacter`.

2. To use a Behavior Tree, we need to start by setting up a custom AI Controller for our `Character` class derivative. Go to **Content Browser** and derive a Blueprint from the `AIController` class—be sure to turn off **Filters | Actors only** first!

 Non-actor class derivatives are not shown by default in the **Class Viewer**! To make the `AIController` class show, you need to go to the **Filters** menu and uncheck the **Actors only** menu option.

3. Create your Behavior Tree and Blackboard objects by right-clicking in **Content Browser** and selecting **Artificial Intelligence | Behavior Tree** and **Artificial Intelligence | Blackboard**.

4. Open the **Behavior Tree** object, and under **Blackboard Asset** in the **Details** panel, select the Blackboard that you've created. Blackboards contain keys and values (named variables) for your Behavior Tree to use.

5. Open your `BP_AIMeleeController` class derivative and go to the Event Graph. Under **Event BeginPlay**, select and add a **Run Behavior Tree** node to the graph. Under BTAsset, be sure to select your `BehaviorTree_FFA_MeleeAttacker` asset.

How it works...

A Behavior Tree is connected to an AI Controller, which in turn is connected to a Blueprint of a Character. We will control the behavior of `Character` through the Behavior Tree by entering Task and Service nodes to the diagram.

Constructing Task nodes

Task nodes are like function blocks. Each Task node you construct will allow you to bundle up some Blueprint code for execution when certain conditions in your Behavior Tree are met.

Tasks have three distinct events: Receive Tick (with AI version), Receive Execute (AI), and Receive Abort (AI). You can respond to any of these three events in the Task's Blueprint. Usually, you should respond to the Receive Execute (AI version) of the Task.

Getting ready

To create a Task node, you should already have a Behavior Tree ready and attached to an appropriate AI Controller and Blueprinted Character (see previous recipe).

How to do it...

1. To construct a Task node with an executable Blueprint code inside it, you must select **New Task** from the menu bar from our **Behavior Tree** Blueprint editor. From the drop-down menu that appears, select to base your **New Task** on `BTTask_BlueprintBase`.

Unlike Behavior Tree or Blackboard creation, there isn't a way to create a **New Task** directly from the **Content Browser**.

2. Double-click and open the Behavior Tree task that you've just created to edit it. Override any of the available events (listed in the **Functions** subheading under the **My Blueprint** tab):

    1. **Receive Tick AI**: The AI version of the `Tick` event for the Behavior Tree Task. You should override this function when you need your task to `Tick` with the actor that contains it. Do not override this function if you only want your task to execute when it is called by the Behavior Tree (not when the game engine ticks).

    2. **Receive Execute AI**: The main function that you want to override. Receive Execute AI allows you to run some Blueprint code whenever the Task node is invoked from the Behavior Tree diagram.

    3. **Receive Abort AI**: An abortion on a Behavior Tree task is called when the task is being aborted (by a `FinishAbort()` node call from the Blueprints diagram).

> There are non-AI versions of the preceding functions, which have just differing arguments: In the `*AI` version, the owner object is cast as a `Pawn`, and there is an Owner Controller passed along to the event call.

Using Decorators for conditions

Decorators are nodes that allow you to enter a conditional expression on evaluation of another node. They are fairly oddly named, but they are called Decorators because they tend to *dress up* execution nodes with conditions for execution. For example, in the following diagram, the `MoveTo` function is only executed when the Decorators condition is met:

There are several pre-packaged Decorators that come with UE4, including Blackboard (variable checks), **Compare Blackboard Entries**, **Cone Check**, **Cooldown**, **Does Path Exist**, and so on. In this recipe, we explore the use of some of these conditionals to control the execution of different branches of a Behavior Tree.

Getting ready

The ability to create a Decorator is only available from the menu bar of an existing **Behavior Tree**.

 The **New Decorator** button is in the Menu bar of an existing **Behavior Tree**, so to find it, you must have an existing **Behavior Tree** open.

How to do it...

1. In the Menu bar of an existing **Behavior Tree**, select **New Decorator**. Base it on the existing Blueprint, `BTDecorator_BlueprintBase`.

2. Assemble your Blueprints diagram determining whether or not the Decorator's condition is successful under the `PerformConditionCheck` function override.

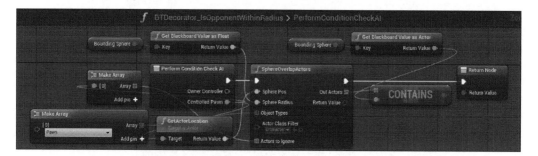

3. Internals of a Decorator checking if the follow target from the Blackboard is inside a bounding sphere of certain radius. Return `true` if the Decorator's condition is met (and the block dependent on the Decorator executes), or return `false` if the Decorator's condition is not met (and the block dependent on the Decorator does not execute).

How it works...

Decorators are just like `if` statements; the only difference is that they place a condition to execute the node directly beneath them in a Behavior Tree.

Using periodic services

Services are nodes that contain Blueprint code to be executed periodically. Services are a lot like Tasks, but they do not have a `FinishExecute()` call at the end.

Getting ready

Adding Services to your Behavior Tree is essential for periodic checks of things such as if there are any new enemy units within range, or if your current target left focus. You can create your own Services. In this recipe, we'll assemble a Service that will check if the opponent you are following is still the closest within a visibility cone. If not, then the opponent changes.

There are four main events for a Service node (other than Tick):

1. **Receive Activation AI**: Triggers when the Behavior Tree starts and the node is first activated.

2. **Receive Search Start AI**: Triggers when the Behavior Tree enters the underlying branch.

3. **Receive Tick AI**: Triggers each frame where the Service is invoked. The bulk of the work is performed here.

4. **Receive Deactivation AI**: Triggers when the Behavior Tree closes and the node is deactivated.

How to do it...

1. First, add a **New Service** to your **Behavior Tree** via the **New Service** button in the **Behavior Tree** Menu Bar:

2. Name your Service something that describes what it does, such as `BehaviorTree_Service_CheckTargetStillClosest`.

3. Double-click on your Service to begin editing its Blueprint.

4. In the editor, add a Receive Tick AI node, and perform any updates to the Blackboard that you need.

How it works...

Service nodes execute some Blueprint code at some regularly spaced time-intervals (with the option of deviation). Inside a Service node, you will usually update your Blackboard.

Using Composite nodes – Selectors, Sequences, and Simple Parallel

Composite nodes form tree nodes inside the Behavior Tree, and contain more than one thing to execute within them. There are three types of Composite nodes:

▶ **Selectors**: Go through children from left to right looking for a successful node. If a node fails, it tries the next one. When successful, the node is completed and we can go back up the tree.

▶ **Sequence**: Execute from left to right, until a node fails. If the node is successful, do the next one. If the node fails, go back up the tree.

▶ **Simple Parallel**: Single task (purple) in parallel with some subtree (gray).

Getting ready

Using composite nodes is fairly straightforward. You only need a Behavior Tree to get started with them.

How to do it...

1. Right-click anywhere on the blank space in your Behavior Tree diagram.

2. Select **Composites | Selector or Composites | Sequence**.

   ❑ **Selectors**: Will execute all tasks in series until one succeeds

   ❑ **Sequence**: Will execute all tasks in series until one fails

3. Append to the node a chain of Tasks or other Composite nodes, as desired.

AI for a Melee Attacker

We can use a Behavior Tree to construct an NPC with melee attack behavior. The Melee Attacker will have the following behavior:

1. Search for the best opponent to attack every 10 seconds. The best opponent to attack is going to be the closest opponent within a `SearchRadius`. We will achieve this using a Service. Chalk the opponent we are attacking into the Melee Attacker's Behavior Tree Blackboard.

2. Move towards the opponent we are attacking (indicated by the Blackboard).

3. If we are within `AttackRadius` units of the opponent, damage the opponent we are attacking every `AttackCooldown` seconds.

>
> This is just one way to attack an opponent using a `BehaviorTree`. You will find you can also attack inside an attack animation for the Melee Attacker, in which case you could just indicate to Play Animation when within `AttackRadius` of the opponent.

Getting ready

Have a Blueprint of a Melee Attacker Character ready. I called mine `BP_Melee`. Prepare the `BP_Melee` Character's AI Controller to use a new Behavior Tree that we will create next.

How to do it...

1. From the root, we want a node that returns immediately if it fails. Create a new Sequence node with a Service called `BehaviorTree_Service_FindOpponent` inside it. Put the interval at 10 seconds for the node.

2. Build out the `BehaviorTree_Service_FindOpponent` node as follows:

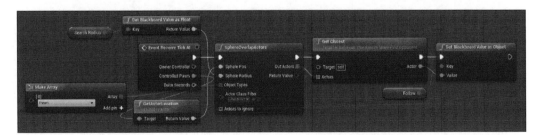

3. Inside another Behavior Tree node, indicate a per-frame motion towards the follow target:

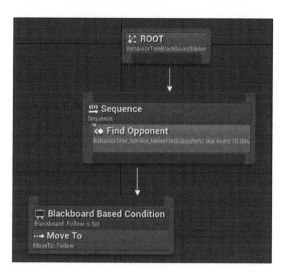

4. Finally, we'd like to damage the opponent when in `AttackRadius` of him. When the player is within `AttackRadius`, you can begin playing the attack animation (which could kick off damage events to the opponent), run a Damage Service (every `AttackCooldown` seconds), or simply **Cooldown** and **Damage Opponent** as shown in the following screenshot:

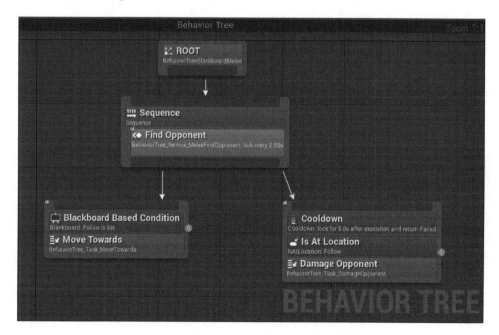

11
Custom Materials and Shaders

Material definition and creation tools in UE4 are fantastic, not to mention its real-time rendering performance. When you see your first glittering gold shader, you will be amazed at UE4's Material shading capabilities, which are possible with a bit of math. We will show you how to use these tools through the following recipes:

- Modifying color using a basic Material
- Modifying position using a Material
- Shader code via Custom node
- The Material function
- Shader parameters and Material instances
- Glimmer
- Leaves and Wind
- Reflectance dependent on the viewing angle
- Randomness – Perlin noise
- Shading a Landscape

Introduction

In computer graphics, a **shader** is used to color something. Traditionally, shaders were so called since they defined the shade that an object got based on its original color and light source position.

Nowadays, shaders aren't really thought of as providing shading to an object as much as a textured, final color.

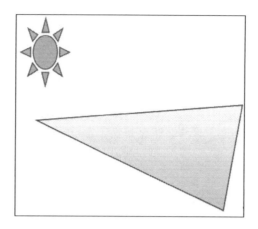

 Shaders are about determining the final color of an object given the light source, geometric positions, and initial colors (including textures, and more expensively, material properties).

There are two flavors of shader: vertex shaders and pixel shaders.

- ► **Vertex shaders**: Color at the vertex (point in the mesh), and smoothly shade from one 3-space point to another 3-space point.

- ► **Pixel shaders**: Color at the pixel (point on the screen). The 3-space physical location of a pixel (aka fragment) is calculated using some simple math.

In UE4, we just call a shader a Material. Materials abstract the vertex and fragment processing pipelines into block-programmable functions, so you don't have to think about the GPU or code to get the graphical output you desire. You simply think in terms of blocks and pictures. You can construct Materials and build GPU shading functionality without ever writing a line of **High Level Shading Language** (**HLSL**), **OpenGL Shading Language** (**GLSL**), or Cg (C for graphics) code!

 You will commonly hear of three major GPU programming languages: HLSL, GLSL, and Cg. GLSL is OpenGL's GPU programming language, while HLSL is Microsoft's offering. After battling it out for popularity through the 90s and the first decade of the twenty-first century, Cg was born in an attempt to unify all GPU programming under it. Cg is still popular, but GLSL and HLSL also remain in popular use.

Modifying color using a basic Material

The primary usage of Materials is to make surfaces appear in the color you want them. In your scene, you will have light sources and surfaces. Surfaces are coated in materials that reflect and refract the light, which you then see using the camera's eye. The basic thing to do with a material is to modify the color of a surface.

> Do not ignore the importance of tuning your light sources to make materials look as you wish them to look!

Getting used to the Material Editor takes some practice, but once you get used to it, you can do amazing things with it. In this recipe, we'll just use some of the very basic functionality to construct a wooden textured material.

> Texture versus Material: Keep in mind that there is a big difference between the terms texture and material. A texture is just an image file (such as a photograph of some `wood.png`); a material, on the other hand, is a combination of textures, colors, and mathematical formulae for describing how a surface appears under light. Materials will account for surface properties, such as color absorption, reflectance, and shininess, while a texture is just a group of colored pixels (or texels, as the GPU calls them).

Shaders are programmed just like normal C++ code, only far more restricted. There are several parameter types you can choose from. Most of them will be floats or packages of floats arranged in a vector format (`float`, `float2`, `float3`, `float4`). For things such as positions and colors, you'll use `float3` or `float4`; for things such as texture coordinates, you'll use `float2`.

Getting ready

You need a clean UE4 project into which you want to place your new material. Install the **GameTexture Materials** pack from the UE4 Marketplace (Epic Games Launcher Application) in your UE4 project. It contains some required textures that we'll need for this recipe. You also need a piece of simple geometry to show the results of your shader.

How to do it...

1. To create a basic material, right-click in the **Content Browser,** and create a **Material** (available from the top four Basic Asset elements).

2. Name your material (for example, `GoldenMaterial`), then double-click on it to edit it.

3. Welcome to the Material Editor:

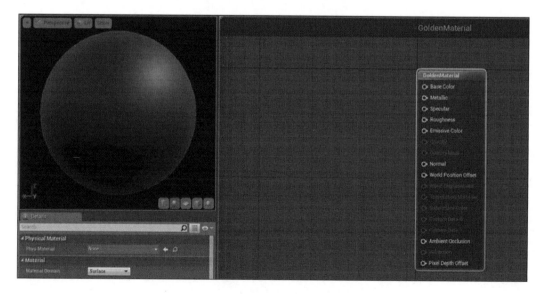

4. You can tell it is the Material Editor because of the presence of the Material output node on the right. To the left is a 3D rendered sphere demonstrating what your material looks like. Materials start out as a kind of coal-ish black semi-shiny material. We can adjust all the material parameters, believe it or not, to make anything from a material that emits light like the Sun, to water, or to the texture of a unit's armor. Let us begin by adjusting the output colors of the material to create a gold-colored metallic material.

1. Change the **Base Color** to yellow by right-clicking on any blank spot in the Material Editor window and choosing a **Constant3Vector** (which represents an RGB color). Adjust the color by double-clicking on the node and dragging around the value of the color swatches. Connect the output of the Constant3Vector to **Base Color,** and wait for the 3D picture on the left to reload with your new material's appearance. Connect the output of the Constant3Vector to the **Base Color** to give the material a yellow appearance as shown in the following screenshot:

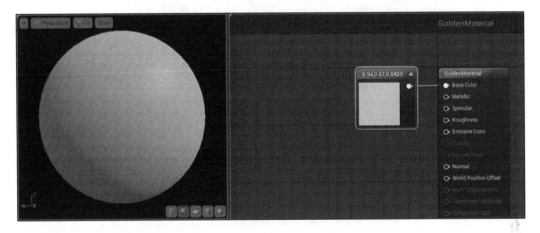

2. Select a metallicness level for all channels by attaching a constant value to the **Metallic** input, and setting it to 1. 1 is very metallic, and 0 is not metallic at all (and so will look plasticy, like the material shown in the next screenshot).

3. Choose a **Specular** value for the material, again between 0 and 1. **Specular** materials are shiny, while non-specular ones are not.

4. Choose a **Roughness** value for the material. **Roughness** refers to how spread out the specular highlight is. If **Roughness** is high (near 1.0), then the surface is clay-like, with almost specular highlight. The specular highlight appears fat and wide near the values 0.7 or 0.8. When roughness is near 0, then the specular highlight is very sharp and thin (extremely shiny/mirror-like surface).

 The material on the left has roughness = 0, and the material on the right has roughness = 1.

5. Apply your material to an object in your scene by clicking and dragging the material onto the model mesh that you want the material to apply to. Alternatively, select a model mesh component, and the new material that you have created by name in the **Details** panel.

6. Finally, create a light in the scene to examine your material's response properties further. Without a light, every material appears black (unless its an emissive material). Add a light via **Modes | Lights**.

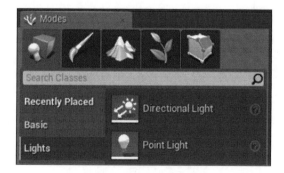

Chapter 11

Modifying position using a Material

A less common thing to do is to use a Material to modify an object's position. This is commonly done in things such as water shaders. We do it using the **World Position Offset** node inside the Material's output.

We can modulate the output position of a vertex using some GPU math. This lightens the load of rendering realistic water on the CPU by a significant amount.

Getting ready

Create a piece of geometry in your world. Construct a new shader called Bob, which we'll edit to produce a simple bobbing motion for objects rendered with the material.

How to do it...

1. In your new Material (named Bob), right-click and add **Texcoord** and **Time Input** nodes.

2. Cascade the sum of the **Texcoord** (for spatial) and **Time Input** nodes through a sin() function call to create some wavy displacement. Multiply the output of the sin() function, and pass as Z-inputs to **World Displacement**.

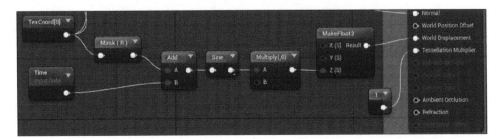

Part of the simple water shader given in the code of `Chapter11` that produces the displacement.

3. Select **PN Triangles** under **Tessellation | D3D11Tessellation Mode**, and set **Tessellation Multiplier** in the material to 1.0.

 Normally, specularity and translucency cannot be combined in UE4 shaders. However, the Surface Perpixel (experimental, limited features) Lighting Mode does allow you to enable both. In addition to selecting this lighting mode, you must remember to ensure to press ` and type `r.ForwardLighting 1` in the Stats console window.

Shader code via Custom node

If you prefer code to diagrammatic blocks, you're in luck. You can write your own HLSL code to deploy to the GPU for the shading of some vertices in your project. We can construct **Custom** nodes that simply contain math code working on named variables to perform some generic computation. In this recipe, we'll write a custom math function to work with.

Getting ready

You need a material shader, and a general mathematical function to implement. As an example, we'll write a **Custom** node that returns the square of all inputs.

How to do it...

1. In order to create a custom material expression, simply right-click anywhere on the canvas, and select **Custom**.

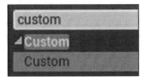

2. With your new **Custom** block selected, go to the **Details** panel on the left side of your Material Editor window (choose **Window | Details** if your **Details** panel is not displayed).

3. Under **Description**, name your **Custom** block. For example, Square3, because we plan to square three float inputs and return a float3.

4. Click the **+** icon as many times you need to generate as many inputs as you need to serve. In this case, we're going to serve three float inputs.

5. Name each input. We've named ours *x, y,* and *z* in the diagram that follows. To use each input in the calculation, you must name it.

6. Select the output type. Here we chose to output a float3.

7. Enter the computation in the **Code** section at the top using the named variables you have created. The code we return here is as follows:

```
return float3( x*x, y*y, z*z );
```

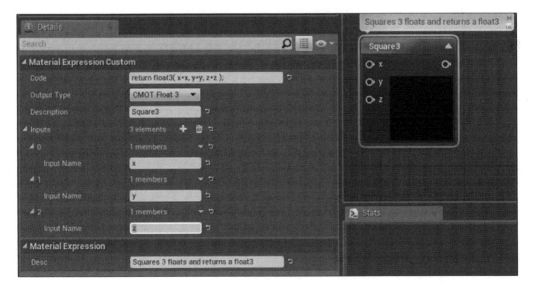

> What this does is construct a 3-float vector, and return the square of *X* in the x value, the square of *Y* in the y value, and the square of *Z* in the z value.
>
> To return different values for *X*, *Y*, *Z* components of a vector type, we had to return a call to a `float3` or `float4` constructor. If you're not returning a vector type, you can just use a `return` statement (without calling a `float` constructor).

How it works...

A custom node is really just a bit of HLSL code. Any valid HLSL code can be used in the code text field. A vertex or pixel shader program has several standard inputs in it. These standard inputs have been defined for a very long time, and they are the parameters you can use to change the way your geometry renders.

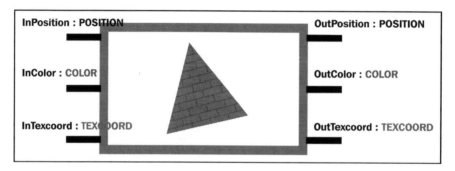

HLSL and Cg have a concept called semantics, which attaches a kind of concrete typing to a float. This is done so that the external program calling the shader knows where to put which input when calling your vertex or pixel shading program.

In the following Cg function signature, in addition to being a `float` variable, `inPosition` is semantically a `POSITION` typed variable `inTexcoord` a `TEXCOORD` typed variable, and `inColor` a `COLOR` typed variable. Inside the shader, you can use the variables for anything you want, the semantics are simply for routing the correct input to the correct variable (to make sure that the color comes in on the `COLOR` typed variable—otherwise, we'd have to do something like track the order in which the parameters are specified or something!)

The output parameters of the function specify how the output of the shader is to be interpreted. Interpretation is only for the recipient of the output data of your program (the next step in the rendering pipeline). Inside your shader program you know you are just writing out a bunch of floats to the shader pipeline. There's nothing that forbids you from mixing different types of semantics inside the shader. A `COLOR` semantic variable can be multiplied by a `POSITION` semantic input, and sent out as a `TEXCOORD` semantic output if you so desired.

The Material function

As always, **modularity** is one of the best practices in programming. Material shaders are no exception: it is far better if your shader blocks are modular, and can be boxed out and identified as named functions. This way, not only are your shader blocks clearer, but they can also be reused in multiple Material shaders, or even exported to your local UE4 library for future use in other projects.

Getting ready

A reusable or repeatable block of shader functionality can be factored out of your custom material shader program. In this example, we'll write a simple function series—`Square`, `Square2`, `Square3`, and `Square4`—that squares input values. Get ready to perform the work in this recipe by opening a UE4 project and navigating to the **Content Browser**.

How to do it...

1. Right-click in the **Content Browser,** and select **Materials & Textures | Material Function**.

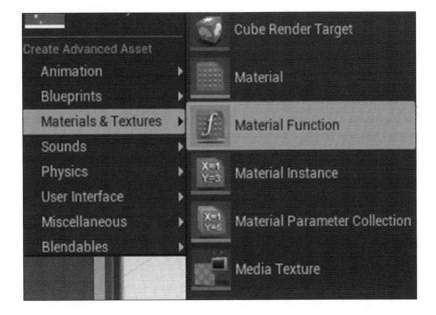

2. Name your **Material Function** `Square`.
3. Double-click on **Material Function**.

4. As soon as you open **Material Function**, deselect the **Output Result** node by left-clicking anywhere in the blank canvas space of the Material Editor. Take a look at the **Details** panel, and note that the Function's exposure to the UE4 library is optionally available:

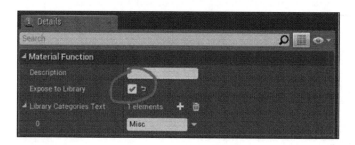

5. The **Expose to Library** checkbox appears in the **Details** panel when no nodes are selected in the **Material Function** Editor screen.

6. Right-click anywhere in the blank space in the **Material Function** editor, and select **Input**. Name your input. Notice how **Input** nodes are only available in the **Material Functions** editor, not in the normal Material editing view.

7. From any regular Material, invoke your function by doing one of the following:

    1. Right-click in the blank space, and select `MaterialFunction`, then select your `MaterialFunction` from the drop-down menu.

    2. Right-click and type the name of your **Material Function** (this requires you to have exposed your **Material Function** previously).

8. If you don't want to expose your **Material Function** to the UE4 library, then you have to use a `MaterialFunction` block to call your custom function.

9. Right-click anywhere in the **Material Function** editor, and select **Output**.

How it works...

Material Functions are some of the most useful blocks you can create. With them, you can modularize your shader code to be much more neat, compact, and reusable.

There's more...

Migrating your functionality to the shader library is a good idea. You can make your custom function appear in the function library by choosing **Expose to Library** in the root of the shader (provided you have nothing selected in the Material Editor window).

When developing a **Material Function**, sometimes, it's helpful to change the Material Preview node to a node other than the output node. Preview a specific node's output by right-clicking the output jack for any node and selecting **Start Previewing Node**.

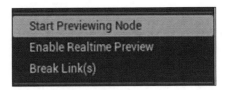

The window in the top-left corner of the Material Editor will now show the output of the node you are previewing. In addition, the text **Previewing** will be added to the node you are previewing (if it's not the final output node). Ensure that **Live Preview** is enabled in the menu bar at the top of the Material Editor. Typically, you would want the final output to be previewed.

Shader parameters and Material instances

A parameter to a shader is going to be a variable input to that shader. You can configure scalars or vectors to be used as input parameters to your shader. Some materials within UE4 come preprogrammed with material parameters exposed.

Getting ready

In order to set up a parameter to a shader, you first need a shader with something that you want to modify with a variable. A good thing to modify with a variable is the suit color of a character. We can expose the color of the suit as a shader parameter that we multiply suit color by.

How to do it...

1. Construct a new Material.

2. Within the Material, create a `VectorParameter`. Give the parameter a name, such as `Color`. Give it a default value, such as blue or black.

3. Close the Material.

4. In **Content Browser**, right-click on the Material with the parameter in it, and select **Create Material Instance**.

5. Double-click on your Material instance. Check the box beside your `VectorParameter` name, and voila! Your `VectorParameter` is customizable without further affecting the base functionality of the Material.

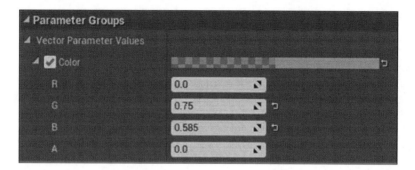

6. Further, if you change the base functionality of the Material, the Material instance will inherit those changes without needing any further configurations.

How it works...

Material Parameters allow you to edit the value of variables sent to a Material without editing the Material itself. In addition, you can also change a Material instance's values from C++ code quite easily. This is useful for things such as team colors, and the like.

Glimmer

Some shader functionality is easily accessible using the standard nodes inside the UE4 Material Editor. You can come up with some neat speckled effects, such as the glittering gold shader we show you how to construct in the following recipe. The purpose of this recipe is to familiarize you with the Material Editor's base functions so that you can learn to construct your own material shaders.

Getting ready

Create an asset (such as a treasure chest) that you want to glow, or open the the source code package of `Chapter11` to find the `treasureChest.fbx` model.

What we'll do is move a plane across the object of a certain thickness *W*. When the plane passes over the geometry, the emissive color channel is activated, and a glimmer effect is created across the treasure.

We expose several parameters to control the glimmer, including **Speed**, **Period** (time between glimmers), **Width**, **Gain**, **PlaneDirection**, and finally, **Color**.

How to do it...

1. Create a new Material by right-clicking in the **Content Browser,** and selecting **Material**.

2. Add input parameters to scale time as shown in the following image, pulling in a `Time` input, and making it periodic by calling `Fmod` with the period of time:

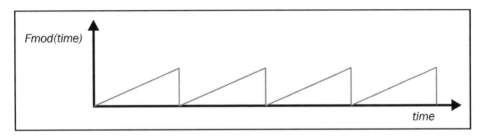

3. `Fmod` with period will make time follow a sawtooth pattern. The value of time read will not increase past the **Period**, because we will keep kicking it down to 0 using the `fmod` operation.

4. Provide the `OnPlane` function in a separate file. The `OnPlane` function uses the Plane Equation $Ax + By + Cz + D = 0$ to determine if an input point is on a plane or not. Pass the `LocalPosition` coordinates into the `OnPlane` function to determine if, in the given frame, this section should be highlighted with emissive glow in the geometry or not.

How it works...

An imaginary plane of light passes through the geometry at the speed specified by speed, once every **Period** seconds. The plane starts at the corner of a bounding box, in the direction specified by **PlaneDirection**. The plane always starts at the corner of the box where it will pass through the entire volume when the plane is shifted forward with time.

Leaves and Wind

In this recipe, we'll write a simple particle shader demonstrating how to create leaves in wind. We can do so using a **Particle Emitter** combined with a Material Shader that "shades" our leaves to give them the appearance of blowing in the wind.

Getting ready

To begin, you'll need a leaf texture as well as a scene in which to place the falling leaves. In the Chapter11 code package, you'll find a scene called LeavesAndTree that contains a deciduous tree that you can use.

How to do it...

1. Create a new particle emitter by right-clicking in the **Content Browser,** and choosing **Particle System**.

2. Construct a new Material shader by right-clicking in the **Content Browser** and choosing **Material**. Your leaf material should contain a texture of a leaf in the BaseColor component. We'll edit the **World Position** of the leaf in a later step to represent a jitter in motion represented by the wind.

3. Add a couple of parameters to modify the Leaves particle emitter:

    1. **Spawn** should have a nice high rate of about 100.

    2. **Initial Location** can be distributed in a cube of 100 units per side.

    3. **Lifetime** can be 4-5 seconds.

    4. **Initial Velocity** should be something like ranging from (-50,-50,-100) to (25,25,-10).

     5. **Initial Color** can be a distribution vector with values at green, yellow, and red.

     6. **Acceleration** can be (0,0,-20).

     7. **Initial Rotation Rate** can be 0.25 (max).

     8. An **Orbit** parameter can be added with distribution (0,0,0) to (0,10,10).

4. **Wind**: Create a **Material Parameter Collection** (**MPC**) by right-clicking anywhere in the blank space in **Content Browser** and selecting **New Material Parameter Collection**.

5. Double-click to edit your new Material Parameter Collection, and enter a new parameter `TheWind`. Give it initial values of `(1, 1, 1)`.

6. In your level Blueprint (**Blueprints | Level Blueprint**), create a client-side variable called `TheWind`. We will send this variable down to the GPU in each frame after we change it locally at the CPU. Initialize the `TheWind` variable to `(1, 1, 1)` in event `BeginPlay`.

7. In the Event `Tick`, modify the wind to your liking. In my version of the wind, I have multiplied the wind in each frame by a random vector with values between [-1,1] in three dimensions. This gives the wind a nice jittery look per-frame.

8. Send the wind variable update down to the GPU by choosing a **Set Vector Parameter Value** node immediately after you modify the wind vector. The **Set Vector Parameter Value** must reference a variable inside a Material Parameter Collection, so reference `TheWind` variable inside the Material Parameter Collection that we created in *STEP 4*.

9. Modify `WorldPositionOffset` by some multiple of `TheWind` each frame. Since `TheWind` variable varies slowly, the modification presented in each frame will be a slight variation of the modification presented in the last frame, producing a smooth leaf motion.

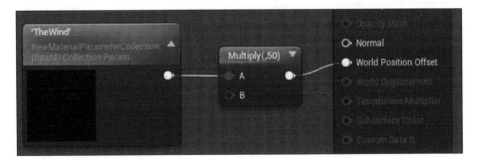

How it works...

The leaves fall at more or less a constant rate with additional light gravity, but they are pulled around by a constantly varying wind vector inside the shader.

Reflectance dependent on the viewing angle

The tendency of the reflectance of a material to depend on the viewing angle is called the **Fresnel** effect. A material may be more specular from a grazing angle than from a head-on angle.

 The Fresnel effect has magnitude at a grazing angle. This water material seen in the preceding screenshot has high specularity and opacity at a grazing angle due to use of the Fresnel effect.

UE4 has a specially built-in capability to account for this. We'll construct a water shader that has view-angle dependence for translucency to give an example of how to use the Fresnel effect realistically.

Getting ready

You need a new shader to which you want to add the Fresnel effect. Preferably, select a material that you want to look a bit different depending on the viewing angle.

How to do it...

1. Inside your material, drive a channel (either Opacity, Specularity, or a diffuse color) by the output of a Fresnel node.

2. The Fresnel node's parameters Exponent and Base Reflect Fraction can be adjusted as follows:

    1. **Exponent**: Describes how Fresnel the material is. Higher values here exaggerate the Fresnel effect.

    2. **Base Reflect Fraction**: Lower numbers exaggerate the Fresnel Effect. For a value of 1.0, the Fresnel effect will not manifest.

How it works...

There is a fair bit of math behind implementing the Fresnel effect, but using it to drive a component in a material is fairly easy, and can help you come up with some very beautiful looking materials.

Randomness – Perlin noise

Some shaders benefit from the ability to use random values. Each Material has a few nodes that can help add randomness to a shader. Randomness from a **Perlin** noise texture can be used to generate interesting-looking materials such as marbled materials. The noise can also be used to drive bump maps, height maps, and displacement fields for some neat effects.

Getting ready

Choose a material to which you'd like to add some randomness. Open the Material in the Material Editor, and follow the steps.

How to do it...

1. Insert a **Noise** node into your Material Editor window.
2. Normalize the coordinates of the object you're adding the noise to. You can use math such as the following to do so:

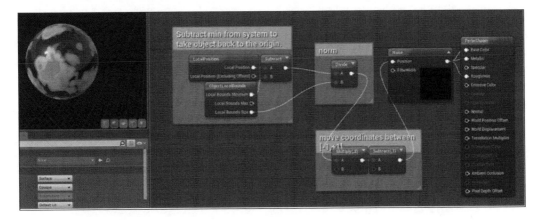

1. Subtract the minimum from each processed vertex in the system to take the object to sit at the origin.
2. Divide the vertex by the size of the object to put the object in a unit box.

3. Multiply the vertex value by 2 to expand the unit box from 1x1 to 2x2.

4. Subtract 1 from the vertex values to move the unit to being centered in the origin with values from *[-1,-1,-1]* to *[+1,+1,+1]*.

3. Select a value from which to draw noise. Keep in mind that noise works extremely well with input values between $-1 \leq x \leq +1$. Outside of this range, Perlin's noise starts to appear snowy when zoomed out (because there will be too much variation in the output values over your input x).

How it works...

Perlin's noise can help you produce some beautiful marbly textures and patterns. Besides using it in graphics, you can also use Perlin noise to drive motion and other phenomena in a natural looking way.

Shading a Landscape

Landscape shaders are relatively easy to construct. They allow you to specify multi-texturing for a very large custom piece of geometry called a Landscape.

Getting ready

Landscape objects are fantastic for use as a ground plane for your game world level. You can construct multiple landscapes in the same level using the Landscape tab. Access the Landscape palette in the **Modes** panel by clicking on the picture of a mountain, as shown in the following screenshot:

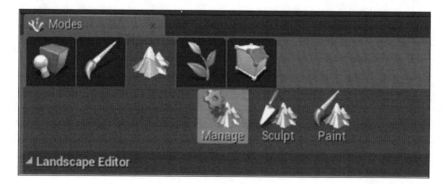

How to do it...

1. Construct a new Landscape object by clicking on **Modes** | Landscape. Under the **New Landscape** heading, select the **Create New** radio button. You will see a green wireframe overlay proposing the new landscape. You can adjust its size using the **Section Size** and **Sections Per Component** settings.

 The landscape will tile the textures we select for it **Section Size * Sections Per Component * Number of Components** times when we finally texture. You can keep note of this number if you want to make the landscape texture tile fewer times—simply divide the UV coordinates fed to the textures by the number computed in the preceding line.

2. Do not click on anything else in this dialog yet, as we still have to construct our Landscape Material. This is outlined in the following steps.

3. Navigate to **Content Browser** and create a new Material for use by your landscape. Call it `LandscapeMaterial`.

4. Edit your `LandscapeMaterial` by double-clicking on it. Right-click anywhere in the blank space and select a `LandscapeCoordinate` node to feed the UV coordinates through the textures that we're about to apply.

    ❏ To reduce the tiling on the Landscape, you'll need to divide the output of the `LandscapeCoordinate` node by the total size of the landscape (**Section Size * Sections Per Component * Number of Components**) (as described in a tip in *Step 1*)

5. Add a `LandscapeLayerBlend` node to the canvas. Lead the output of the node to the **Base Color** layer.

6. Click on the `LandscapeLayerBlend` node, and add a few Layers to the element in the **Details** tab. This will allow you to blend between the textures using **Texture Painting**. Name each, and select the method for blending from among the following options:

    ❏ By painted weight (LB Weight Blend).

    ❏ By alpha value inside the texture (LB Alpha Blend).

    ❏ By height (LB Height Blend).

7. Set other parameters for each `LandscapeLayer` you're adding as you desire.

8. Feed in the textures, one for each layer of Landscape blend.

9. Reduce the specularity of the landscape to 0 by adding a constant 0 input to the Specular input.

10. Save and close your material.

11. Go to the **Modes** | Landscape tab now, and select your newly created `LandscapeMaterial` in the drop-down menu.

12. Under the **Layers** section, click on the **+** icon beside each of the Landscape layers that are available. Create and save a Target Layer object for each Landscape layer that you have.

13. Finally, scroll down the Landscape tab, and click on the **Create** button.

14. Click on the Paint tab, select a brush size and a texture to paint with, and begin texture painting your landscape.

How it works...

Landscape materials can be blended either by height, or by manual artistry, as shown in this recipe.

12
Working with UE4 APIs

The **Application Programming Interface** (**API**) is the way in which you, as the programmer, instruct the engine, and so the PC, what to do. All of UE4's functionality is encapsulated into modules, including very basic and core functionality. Each module has an API for it. To use an API, there is a very important linkage step, where you must list all APIs that you will be using in your build in a `ProjectName.Build.cs` file, which is located in your **Solution Explorer** window.

 Do not name any of your UE4 projects the exact same name as one of the UE4 API names!

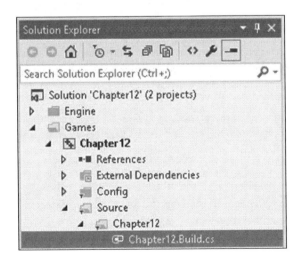

There are a variety of APIs inside the UE4 engine that expose functionality to various essential parts of it. Some of the interesting APIs that we'll explore in this chapter are as follows:

- Core/Logging API – Defining a custom log category
- Core/Logging API – `FMessageLog` to write messages to the **Message Log**
- Core/Math API – Rotation using `FRotator`
- Core/Math API – Rotation using `FQuat`
- Core/Math API – Rotation using `FRotationMatrix` to have one object face another
- Landscape API – Landscape generation with Perlin noise
- Foliage API – Adding trees procedurally to your level
- Landscape and Foliage APIs – Map generation using Landscape and Foliage APIs
- GameplayAbilities API – Triggering an actor's gameplay abilities with game controls
- GameplayAbilities API – Implementing stats with `AttributeSet`
- GameplayAbilities API – Implementing buffs with `GameplayEffect`
- GameplayTags API – Attaching `GameplayTags` to an actor
- GameplayTasks API – Making things happen with `GameplayTasks`
- HTTP API – Web request
- HTTP API – Progress bars

Introduction

The UE4 engine's base functionality available in the editor is quite broad. The functionality from C++ code is actually grouped out into little sections called APIs. There is a separate API module for each important functionality in the UE4 codebase. This is done to keep the codebase highly organized and modular.

 Using different APIs may require special linkage in your `Build.cs` file! If you are getting build errors, be sure to check that the linkage with the correct APIs is there!

The complete API listing is located in the following documentation: `https://docs.unrealengine.com/latest/INT/API/`.

Core/Logging API – Defining a custom log category

UE4 itself defines several logging categories, including categories such as `LogActor`, which has any log messages to do with the `Actor` class, and `LogAnimation`, which logs messages about Animations. In general, UE4 defines a separate logging category for each module. This allows developers to output their log messages to different logging streams. Each log steam's name is prefixed to the outputted message as shown in the following example log messages from the engine:

```
LogContentBrowser: Native class hierarchy updated for
'HierarchicalLODOutliner' in 0.0011 seconds. Added 1 classes and 2
folders.
LogLoad: Full Startup: 8.88 seconds (BP compile: 0.07 seconds)
LogStreaming:Warning: Failed to read file
'../../../Engine/Content/Editor/Slate/Common/Selection_16x.png'
error.
LogExternalProfiler: Found external profiler: VSPerf
```

The above are sample log messages from the engine, each prefixed with their log category. Warning messages appear in yellow and have **Warning** added to the front as well.

The example code you will find on the Internet tends to use `LogTemp` for a UE4 project's own messages, as follows:

```
UE_LOG( LogTemp, Warning, TEXT( "Message %d" ), 1 );
```

We can actually improve upon this formula by defining our own custom `LogCategory`.

Getting ready

Have a UE4 project ready in which you'd like to define a custom log. Open a header file that will be included in almost all files using this log.

How to do it...

1. Open the main header file for your project; for example, if your project's name is Pong, you'll open `Pong.h`. Add the following line of code after `#include Engine.h`:

```
DECLARE_LOG_CATEGORY_EXTERN( LogPong, Log, All ); // Pong.h
```

Defined in `AssertionMacros.h`, there are three arguments to this declaration, which are as follows:

- ❑ `CategoryName`: This is the log category name being defined (`LogPong` here)
- ❑ `DefaultVerbosity`: This is the default verbosity to use on log messages
- ❑ `CompileTimeVerbosity`: This is the verbosity to bake into compiled code

2. Inside the main `.cpp` file for your project, include the following line of code:

```
DEFINE_LOG_CATEGORY( LogPong ); // Pong.cpp
```

3. Use your log with the various display categories, as follows:

```
UE_LOG( LogPong, Display, TEXT( "A display message, log is
working" ) ); // shows in gray
UE_LOG( LogPong, Warning, TEXT( "A warning message" ) );
UE_LOG( LogPong, Error, TEXT( "An error message " ) );
```

```
LogCh12:Display: A display message, log is working
LogCh12:Warning: A warning message
```

How it works...

Logging works by outputting messages to the **Output Log** (**Window | Developer Tools | Output Log**) as well as a file. All information outputted to the **Output Log** is also mirrored to a simple text file that is located in your project's `/Saved/Logs` folder. The extension of the log files is `.log`, with the most recent one being named `YourProjectName.log`.

There's more...

You can enable or suppress log messages for a particular log channel from within the editor using the following console commands:

```
Log LogName off // Stop LogName from displaying at the output
Log LogName Log // Turn LogName's output on again
```

If you'd like to edit the initial values of the output levels of some of the built-in log types, you can use a C++ class to create changes to the `Engine.ini` config file. You can change the initial values in the `engine.ini` configuration file. See `https://wiki.unrealengine.com/Logs,_Printing_Messages_To_Yourself_During_Runtime` for more details.

▸ UE_LOG sends its output to **Output Window**. If you'd like to use the more specialized **Message Log** window in addition, you can alternatively use the FMessageLog object to write your output messages. FMessageLog writes to both the **Message Log** and the **Output Window**. See the next recipe for details.

Core/Logging API – FMessageLog to write messages to the Message Log

FMessageLog is an object that allows you to write output messages to the **Message Log** (**Window | Developer Tools | Message Log**) and **Output Log** (**Window | Developer Tools | Output Log**) simultaneously.

Getting ready

Have your project ready and some information to log to **Message Log**. Display **Message Log** in your UE4 Editor. The following screenshot is of the **Message Log**:

How to do it...

1. Add #define to your main header file (ProjectName.h) defining LOCTEXT_ NAMESPACE as something unique to your codebase:

   ```
   #define LOCTEXT_NAMESPACE "Chapter12Namespace"
   ```

   This #define is used by the LOCTEXT() macro, which we use to generate FText objects, but is not seen in output messages.

2. Declare your FMessageLog by constructing it somewhere very global. You can use extern in your ProjectName.h file. Consider the following piece of code as an example:

   ```
   extern FName LoggerName;
   extern FMessageLog Logger;
   ```

3. And then, create your `FMessageLog` by defining it in a `.cpp` file and registering it with `MessageLogModule`. Be sure to give your logger a clear and unique name on construction. It's the category of your log that will appear to the left of your log messages in **Output Log**. For example, `ProjectName.cpp`:

```cpp
#define FTEXT(x) LOCTEXT(x, x)
FName LoggerName( "Chapter12Log" );
FMessageLog CreateLog( FName name )
{
    FMessageLogModule& MessageLogModule =
    FModuleManager::LoadModuleChecked<FMessageLogModule>
    ("MessageLog");
    FMessageLogInitializationOptions InitOptions;
    InitOptions.bShowPages = true;// Don't forget this!
    InitOptions.bShowFilters = true;
    FText LogListingName = FTEXT( "Chapter 12's Log Listing"
    );
    MessageLogModule.RegisterLogListing( LoggerName,
    LogListingName, InitOptions );
}
// Somewhere early in your program startup
// (eg in your GameMode constructor)
AChapter12GameMode::AChapter12GameMode()
{
    CreateLogger( LoggerName );
    // Retrieve the Log by using the LoggerName.
    FMessageLog logger( LoggerName );
    logger.Warning(
    FTEXT( "A warning message from gamemode ctor" ) );
}
```

The KEY to LOCTEXT (first argument) must be unique or you will get a previously hashed string back. If you'd like, you can include a #define that repeats the argument to LOCTEXT twice, as we did earlier.

```cpp
#define FTEXT(x) LOCTEXT(x, x)
```

4. Log your messages using the following code:

```cpp
Logger.Info( FTEXT( "Info to log" ) );
Logger.Warning( FTEXT( "Warning text to log" ) );
Logger.Error( FTEXT( "Error text to log" ) );
```

This code utilizes the FTEXT() macro defined earlier. Be sure it is in your codebase.

 Constructing your message log again after initialization retrieves a copy of the original message log. For example, at any place in the code, you can write the following code:

```
FMessageLog( LoggerName ).Info( FTEXT( "An info
message"
) );
```

Core/Math API – Rotation using FRotator

Rotation in UE4 has such complete implementation that it can be hard to choose how to rotate your objects. There are three main methods—FRotator, FQuat, and FRotationMatrix. This recipe outlines the construction and use of the first of the three different methods for the rotation of objects—the FRotator. Using this, and the following two recipes, you can select at a glance a method to use to rotate your objects.

Getting ready

Have a UE4 project that has an object you can get a C++ interface with. For example, you can construct a C++ class Coin that derives from Actor to test out rotations with. Override the Coin::Tick() method to apply your rotations from the C++ code. Alternatively, you can call these rotation functions in the Tick event from Blueprints.

In this example, we will rotate an object at a rate of one degree per second. The actual rotation will be the accumulated time since the object was created. To get this value, we'll just call GetWorld()->TimeSeconds.

How to do it...

1. Create a custom C++ derivative of the Actor class called Coin.

2. In the C++ code, override the ::Tick() function of the Coin actor derivative. This will allow you to effect a change to the actor in each frame.

3. Construct your FRotator. FRotators can be constructed using a stock pitch, yaw, and roll constructor, as shown in the following example:

   ```
   FRotator( float InPitch, float InYaw, float InRoll );
   ```

4. Your FRotator will be constructed as follows:

   ```
   FRotator rotator( 0, GetWorld()->TimeSeconds, 0 );
   ```

5. The standard orientation for an object in UE4 is with Forward facing down the *+X* axis. Right is the *+Y* axis, and Up is *+Z*.

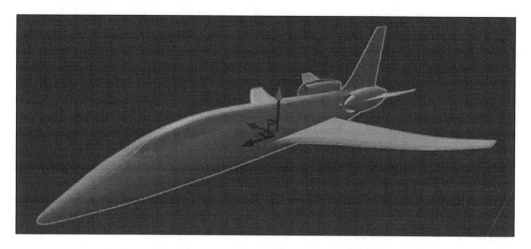

6. Pitch is rotation about the *Y* axis (across), yaw is rotation about the *Z* axis (up), and roll is rotation about the *X* axis. This is best understood in the following three points:

   ❑ **Pitch**: If you think of an airplane in UE4 standard coordinates, the *Y* axis goes along the wingspan (pitching tilts it forward and backward)

   ❑ **Yaw**: The *Z* axis goes straight up and down (yawing turns it left and right)

   ❑ **Roll**: The *X* axis goes straight along the fuselage of the plane (rolling does barrel rolls)

    You should note that in other conventions, the *X* axis is pitch, the *Y* axis is yaw, and the *Z* axis is roll.

7. Apply your `FRotator` to your actor using the `SetActorRotation` member function, as follows:

```
FRotator rotator( 0, GetWorld()->TimeSeconds, 0 );
SetActorRotation( rotation );
```

Core/Math API – Rotation using FQuat

Quaternions sound intimidating, but they are extremely easy to use. You may want to review the theoretical math behind them using the following videos:

▶ Fantastic Quaternions by Numberphile – `https://www.youtube.com/watch?v=3BR8tK-LuB0`

▶ Understanding Quaternions by Jim Van Verth – `http://gdcvault.com/play/1017653/Math-for-Game-Programmers-Understanding`

However, we won't cover the math background here! In fact, you don't need to understand much about the math background quaternions to use them extremely effectively.

Getting ready

Have a project ready and an `Actor` with an override `::Tick()` function that we can enter the C++ code into.

How to do it...

1. To construct a quaternion, the best constructor to use is as follows:

```
FQuat( FVector Axis, float AngleRad );
```

For example, to define a twisting rotation:

Quaternions have quaternion addition, quaternion subtraction, multiplication by a scalar, and division by a scalar defined for them, amongst other functions. They are extremely useful to rotate things at arbitrary angles, and point objects at one another.

How it works...

Quaterions are a bit strange, but using them is quite simple. If *v* is the axis around which to rotate, and θ is the magnitude of the angle of rotation, then we get the following equations for the components of a quaternion:

$$x = v_x \sin\left(\frac{\theta}{2}\right)$$

$$y = v_y \sin\left(\frac{\theta}{2}\right)$$

$$z = v_z \sin\left(\frac{\theta}{2}\right)$$

$$w = \cos\left(\frac{\theta}{2}\right)$$

So, for example, rotation about $v = (1,2,1) = \left(\frac{1}{\sqrt{5}}, \frac{2}{\sqrt{5}}, \frac{1}{\sqrt{5}} \right)$ by an angle of $\frac{\pi}{2}$ will have the following quaternion components:

$$\left(x, y, z, w \right) = \left(\frac{1}{\sqrt{10}}, \frac{2}{\sqrt{10}}, \frac{1}{\sqrt{10}}, \frac{1}{\sqrt{2}} \right)$$

Three of the four components of the quaternion (*x*, *y*, and *z*) define the axis around which to rotate (scaled by the sine of half the angle of rotation), while the fourth component (*w*) has only the cosine of half the angle to rotate with.

There's more...

Quaternions, being themselves vectors, can be rotated. Simply extract the (*x*, *y*, *z*) components of the quaternion, normalize, and then rotate that vector. Construct a new quaternion from that new unit vector with the desired angle of rotation.

Multiplying quaternions together represents a series of rotations that happen subsequently. For example, rotation of 45° about the *X* axis, followed by a rotation of 45° about the *Y* axis will be composed by the following:

```
FQuat ( FVector ( 1, 0, 0 ), PI/4.f ) *
FQuat ( FVector ( 0, 1, 0 ), PI/4.f );
```

Core/Math API – Rotation using FRotationMatrix to have one object face another

FRotationMatrix offers matrix construction using a series of ::Make* routines. They are easy to use and useful to get one object to face another. Say you have two objects, one of which is following the other. We want the rotation of the follower to always be facing what it is following. The construction methods of FRotationMatrix make this easy to do.

Getting ready

Have two actors in a scene, one of which should face the other.

How to do it...

1. In the follower's `Tick()` method, look into the available constructors under the `FRotationMatrix` class. Available are a bunch of constructors that will let you specify a rotation for an object (from stock position) by reorienting one or more of the *X, Y, Z* axes, named with the `FRotationMatrix::Make*()` pattern.

2. Assuming you have a default stock orientation for your actor (with Forward facing down the +*X* axis, and up facing up the +*Z* axis), find the vector from the follower to the object he is following, as shown in this piece of code:

```
FVector toFollow = target->GetActorLocation() -
GetActorLocation();
FMatrix rotationMatrix = FRotationMatrix::MakeFromXZ(
toTarget, GetActorUpVector() );
SetActorRotation( rotationMatrix.Rotator() );
```

How it works...

Getting one object to look at another, with a desired up vector, can be done by calling the correct function, depending on your object's stock orientation. Usually, you want to reorient the *X* axis (Forward), while specifying either the *Y* axis (Right) or *Z* axis (Up) vectors (`FRotationMatrix::MakeFromXY()`). For example, to make an actor look along a `lookAlong` vector, with its right side facing right, we'd construct and set `FRotationMatrix` for it as follows:

```
FRotationMatrix rotationMatrix = FRotationMatrix::MakeFromXY(
lookAlong, right );
actor->SetActorRotation( rotationMatrix.Rotator() );
```

Landscape API – Landscape generation with Perlin noise

If you use ALandscape in your scene, you may want to program the heights on it using code instead of manually brushing it in. To access the ALandscape object and its functions inside of your code, you must compile and link in the Landscape and LandscapeEditor APIs.

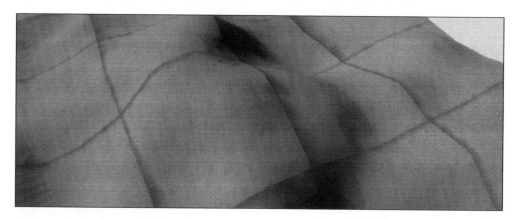

Getting ready

Generating a landscape is not terribly challenging. You need to link in both the Landscape and LandscapeEditor APIs, and also have a programmatic way to set the height values across the map. In this recipe, we'll show how to use the Perlin noise for this.

Previously, you may have seen Perlin noise used for coloration, but that is not all it is good for. It is excellent for terrain heights as well. You can sum multiple Perlin noise values to get beautiful fractal noise. It is worth a brief study of Perlin noise to understand how to get good outputs.

How to do it...

1. Retrieve the Perlin noise module from http://webstaff.itn.liu.se/~stegu/ aqsis/aqsis-newnoise/. The two files you'll need are noise1234.h and noise1234.cpp (or you can select another pair of noise generation files from this repository if you wish). Link these files into your project and be sure to #include YourPrecompiledHeader.h into noise1234.cpp.

2. Link in the Landscape and LandscapeEditor APIs in your Project.Build.cs file.

3. Construct an interface using UMG that allows you to click a **Generate** button to call a C++ function that will ultimately populate the current Landscape with Perlin noise values. You can do this as follows:

      ❏ Right-click on your **Content Browser** and select **User Interface | Widget Blueprint**.

      ❏ Populate **Widget Blueprint** with a single button that kicks off a single Gen() function. The Gen() function can be attached to your Chapter12GameMode derived class object as that is easy to retrieve from the engine. The Gen() function must be BlueprintCallable UFUNCTION(). (See the *Creating a UFUNCTION* section in *Chapter 2, Creating Classes*, for details on how to do so.)

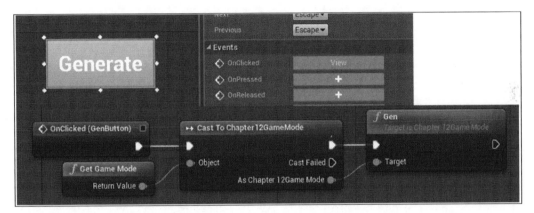

      ❏ Be sure to display your UI by creating it and adding it to the viewport in one of your booting Blueprints; for example, in your HUD's BeginPlay event.

4. Create a Landscape using the UE4 Editor. The landscape will be assumed to stay on screen. We will only modify its values using code.

5. Inside your map generation routine, modify your `ALandscape` object using code that does the following:

  ❑ Find the `Landscape` object in the level by searching through all objects in the `Level`. We do this using a C++ function that returns `TArray` of all `Landscape` instances in the level:

```
TArray<ALandscape*> AChapter12GameMode::GetLandscapes()
{
  TArray<ALandscape*> landscapes;
  ULevel *level = GetLevel();
  for( int i = 0; i < level->Actors.Num(); i++ )
  if( ALandscape* land = Cast<ALandscape>(level->Actors[i])
)
  landscapes.Push( land );
  return landscapes;
}
```

  ❑ Initialize the world's `ULandscapeInfo` objects for `ALandscape` editing using the very important line, which is as follows:

```
ULandscapeInfo::RecreateLandscapeInfo( GetWorld(), 1 );
```

The preceding line of code is extremely important. Without it, the `ULandscapeInfo` objects will not be initialized and your code will not work. Surprisingly, this is a static member function of the `ULandscapeInfo` class, and so it initializes all `ULandscapeInfo` objects within the level.

  ❑ Get extents of your `ALandscape` object so that we can compute the number of height values we will need to generate.

  ❑ Creates a set of height values to replace original values.

  ❑ Calls `LandscapeEditorUtils::SetHeightmapData( landscape, data );` to park new landscape height values into your `ALandscape` object.

  For example, use the following code:

```
// a) REQUIRED STEP: Call static function
// ULandscapeInfo::RecreateLandscapeInfo().
// What this does is populate the Landscape object with
// data values so you don't get nulls for your
// ULandscapeInfo objects on retrieval.
ULandscapeInfo::RecreateLandscapeInfo( GetWorld(), 1 );

// b) Assuming landscape is your landscape object pointer,
```

```
// get extents of landscape, to compute # height values
FIntRect landscapeBounds = landscape->GetBoundingRect();

// c) Create height values.
// LandscapeEditorUtils::SetHeightmapData() adds one to
// each dimension because the boundary edges may be used.
int32 numHeights = (rect.Width()+1)*(rect.Height()+1);
TArray<uint16> Data;
Data.Init( 0, numHeights );
for( int i = 0; i < Data.Num(); i++ ) {
    float nx = (i % cols) / cols; // normalized x value
    float ny = (i / cols) / rows; // normalized y value
    Data[i] = PerlinNoise2D( nx, ny, 16, 4, 4 );
}

// d) Set values in with call:
LandscapeEditorUtils::SetHeightmapData( landscape, Data );
```

> The initial values of `heightmap` will all be `32768` (SHRT_MAX (or
> USHRT_MAX/2+1)) when the map is completely flat. This is because the
> map uses unsigned shorts (`uint16`) for its values, making it incapable of
> taking on negative values. For the map to dip below z=0, the programmers
> made the default value half of the maximum value of `heightmap`.

How it works...

The Perlin noise function is used to generate a height value for (x, y) coordinate pairs. The
2D version of Perlin noise is used so that we can get a Perlin noise value based on 2-space
spatial coordinates.

There's more...

You can play with the Perlin noise functions with the spatial coordinates of the map, and
assign the heights of the maps to different combinations of the Perlin noise function. You will
want to use a sum of multiple octaves of the Perlin noise function to get more detail into the
landscape.

The `PerlinNoise2D` generation function looks as follows:

```
uint16 AChapter12GameMode::PerlinNoise2D( float x, float y,
    float amp, int32 octaves, int32 px, int32 py )
{
    float noise = 0.f;
    for( int octave = 1; octave < octaves; octave *= 2 )
```

```
{
    // Add in fractions of faster varying noise at lower
    // amplitudes for higher octaves. Assuming x is normalized,
    // WHEN octave==px  you get full period. Higher frequencies
    // will go out and also meet period.
    noise += Noise1234::pnoise( x*px*octave, y*py*octave, px, py )
    / octave;
}
    return USHRT_MAX/2.f + amp*noise;
}
```

The `PerlinNoise2D` function accounts for the fact that the mid-level value of the function (sea level or flat land) should have a value of `SHRT_MAX` (32768).

Foliage API – Adding trees procedurally to your level

The **Foliage** API is a great way to populate your level with trees using code. If you do it this way, then you can get some good results without having to manually produce a natural looking randomness by hand.

We will correlate the placement of foliage with the Perlin noise value so that the chance to place a tree at a given location is higher when the Perlin noise values are higher.

Getting ready

Before using the code interface to the Foliage API, you should try the in-editor feature to familiarize yourself with the feature. After that, we will discuss using the code interface to place the foliage in the level.

Important! Keep in mind that the material for a `FoliageType` object must have the **Used with Instanced Static Meshes** checkbox checked in its panel. If you do not do so, then the material cannot be used to shade a foliage material.

Be sure to check the **Used with Instanced Static Meshes** checkbox for your materials that you use on your `FoliageType`, otherwise your Foliage will appear gray.

How to do it...

Manually

1. From the **Modes** panel, select the picture of a small growing plant with leaves.

2. Click on the **+ Add Foliage Type** drop-down menu and select to construct a new `Foliage` object.

3. Save the `Foliage` object by whatever name you wish.

4. Double-click to edit your new `Foliage` object. Select Mesh from your project, preferably a tree-shaped object, to paint foliage into the landscape with.

5. Adjust Paint Brush Size and Paint Density to your liking. Left click to start painting in foliage.

6. *Shift* + click to erase foliage that you've put down. The Erase density value tells you how much foliage to leave behind when erasing.

Procedurally

If you would like the engine to distribute the foliage in the level for you, you have a few steps to cover before being able to do so from within the editor. These steps are as follows:

1. Go to the **Content Browser** and right-click to create a few `FoliageType` objects to distribute procedurally in the level.

2. Click **Edit | Editor Preferences**.

3. Click the **Experimental** tab.

4. Enable the **Procedural Foliage** checkbox. This allows you access to the **Procedural Foliage** classes from within the Editor.

5. Go back to **Content Browser**, right-click and create **Miscellaneous | Procedural Foliage Spawner**.

6. Double-click to open your **Procedural Foliage Spawner** and select-in the `FoliageTypes` that you created in step 1.

7. Drag your **Procedural Foliage Spawner** onto the level and size it such that it contains the area where you want your procedural foliage laid out.

8. From the Brushes menu, drag on a few Procedural Foliage Blocker volumes. Place a few of these inside the **Procedural Foliage Spawner** volume to block foliage from appearing in these areas.

9. Open the menus downwards and click **SIMULATE**. The **Procedural Foliage Spawner** should fill with foliage.

10. Experiment with the settings to get the foliage distributions that you like.

See also

▶ The preceding recipe generates foliage prior to gameplay start. If you're interested in procedural foliage spawning at runtime, see the next recipe, *Landscape and Foliage API – Map generation using Landscape and Foliage APIs*.

Landscape and Foliage API – Map generation using Landscape and Foliage APIs

We can use the earlier mentioned landscape generation code to create a landscape, and the procedural foliage functionality to randomly distribute some foliage on it.

Combining the capabilities of the Landscape API and Foliage API will allow you to procedurally generate complete maps. In this recipe, we will outline how this is done.

We will programmatically create a landscape and populate it with foliage using code.

Getting ready

To prepare to perform this recipe, we will need a UE4 project with a Generate button to kick off generation. You can see the *Landscape API – Landscape generation with Perlin noise* recipe for an example of how to do this. You simply need to create a small UMG UI widget that has a Generate button. Connect the OnClick event of your Generate button to a C++ UFUNCTION() inside any C++ global object, such as your Chapter12GameMode object, that will be used to generate your terrain.

How to do it...

1. Enter a loop that attempts to place *N* trees, where *N* is the number of trees to place randomly, which is specified in the UPROPERTY() of the Chapter12GameMode object.

2. Get random XY coordinates from within a 2D box bounding the landscape object.

3. Get the Perlin noise value @ (x, y). You may use a different Perlin noise formulation than the one used to determine landscape heights for foliage placement.

4. Generate a random number. If the number generated is within the range of units of the Perlin noise function there, then place a tree using the SpawnFoliageInstance function. Otherwise, do not place a tree there.

You should note that we are covering randomness in location using the underlying randomness in the spot we choose to test for tree placement. The actual chance to place a tree there depends on the Perlin noise value there, and whether it is within the range of units of PerlinTreeValue.

Very dense tree distributions will look like isocontours on the map then. The width of the isocontours is the range of units.

How it works...

Perlin noise works by generating smooth noise. For each location in an interval, (say *[-1, 1]*), there is a smoothly varying Perlin noise value.

Perlin noise values are sampled on a 2D texture. At each pixel (and even in between), we can get a very smoothly varying noise value.

Adding octaves (or integer multiples) to some variable that travels in distance across the Perlin noise function allows us to get jaggy-looking effects; for example, the tufts in clouds or crags in mountains are gotten by wider-spaced samples, which give faster varying noise.

To get cool-looking Perlin noise outputs, we will simply apply math functions to sampled Perlin noise values; for example, the sin and cos functions can generate some cool looking marble effects for you.

Perlin noise becomes periodic, that is, tileable, with the Perlin noise functions provided by the earlier linked implementation in this recipe. By default, Perlin noise is not periodic. If you need your Perlin noise to be periodic, be careful which library function you are calling.

The base Perlin noise function is a deterministic function that returns the same value every time you call it with the same value.

There's more...

You may also set up sliders inside your Chapter12GameMode object derivative to affect the foliage and landscape generation, including parameters such as the following:

▶   Amplitude of the landscape

▶   Density of the foliage

▶   Isocontour level for foliage

▶   Variance in foliage height or scale

GameplayAbilities API – Triggering an actor's gameplay abilities with game controls

The **GameplayAbilities** API can be used to attach C++ functions to invoke on certain button pushes, triggering the game unit to exhibit its abilities during play in response to keystroke events. In this recipe, we will show you how to do that.

Getting ready

Enumerate and describe your game character's abilities. You will need to know what your character does in response to key events to code in this recipe.

There are several objects that we need to use here; they are as follows:

▸ `UGameplayAbility` class—this is needed to derivate the C++ class instances of the `UGameplayAbility` class, one derivative class for each ability.

  ❑ Define what each ability does in `.h` and `.cpp` by overriding available functions, such as `UGameplayAbility::Acti vateAbility`, `UGameplayAbility::InputPressed`, `UGameplayAbility::CheckCost`, `UGameplayAbility::ApplyCost`, `UGameplayAbility::ApplyCooldown`, and so on

▸ `GameplayAbilitiesSet`—this is a `DataAsset` derivative object that contains a series of enum'd command values, and blueprints of the corresponding `UGameplayAbility` derivative classes that define the behavior for that particular input command. Each GameplayAbility is kicked off by a keystroke or mouse click, which is set in `DefaultInput.ini`.

How to do it...

In the following, we'll implement a `UGameplayAbility` derivative called `UGameplayAbility_Attack` for a `Warrior` class object. We'll attach this gameplay functionality to input command string `Ability1`, which we'll activate on the left-mouse button click.

1. Link the `GameplayAbilities` API in your `ProjectName.Build.cs` file.

2. Derive a C++ class from `UGameplayAbility`. For example, write a C++ UCLASS `UGameplayAbility_Attack`.

3. In the very least, you want to override the following:

   ❑ The `UGameplayAbility_Attack::CanActivateAbility` member function to indicate when the actor is allowed to invoke the ability.

   ❑ The `UGameplayAbility_Attack::CheckCost` function to indicate whether the player can afford to use ability or not. This is extremely important, because if this returns false, ability invocation should fail.

   ❑ The `UGameplayAbility_Attack::ActivateAbility` member function and write the code that the `Warrior` is to execute when his `Attack` ability is activated.

   ❑ The `UGameplayAbility_Attack::InputPressed` member function and to respond to the key input event assigned to the ability.

4. Derive a Blueprint class from your `UGameplayAbility_Attack` object inside the UE4 editor.

5. Inside the editor, navigate to **Content Browser** and create a
   `GameplayAbilitiesSet` object by:

   ❑ Right clicking on **Content Browser** and selecting **Miscellaneous | Data
   Asset**

   ❑ In the dialog box that follows, select `GameplayAbilitySet` for Data Asset
   Class

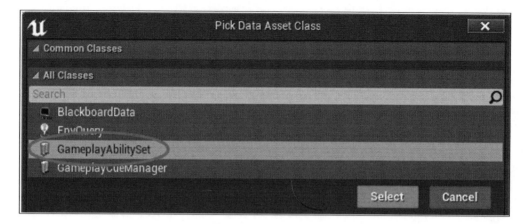

In fact, the `GameplayAbilitySet` object is a `UDataAsset` derivative.
It is located in `GameplayAbilitySet.h` and contains a single member
function, `GameplayAbilitySet::GiveAbilities()`, which I strongly
recommend you not to use for reasons listed in a later step.

6. Name your `GameplayAbilitySet` data asset something related to the
   `Warrior` object so we know to select it into the `Warrior` class (for example,
   `WarriorGameplayAbilitySet`).

7. Double-click to open and edit the new `WarriorAbilitySet` Data Asset. Stack in
   a list of `GameplayAbility` class derivative Blueprints by clicking **+** on the `TArray`
   object inside of it. Your `UGameplayAbility_Attack` object must appear in the
   dropdown.

8. Add UPROPERTY `UGameplayAbilitySet* gameplayAbilitySet` member to
   your `Warrior` class. Compile, run, and select-in `WarriorAbilitySet` as it sits
   in **Content Browser** (created in steps 5 to 7) of the abilities that this `Warrior` is
   capable of.

9. Ensure that your `Actor` class derivative also derives from the
   `UAbilitySystemInterface` interface. This is extremely important so
   that calls to `(Cast<IAbilitySystemInterface>(yourActor))-`
   `>GetAbilitySystemComponent()` succeed.

10. Sometime after the construction of your actor, call `gameplayAbilitySet->GiveAbilities( abilitySystemComponent )`; or enter a loop, as shown in the following step where you invoke `abilitySystemComponent->GiveAbility()` for each ability listed in your `gameplayAbilitySet`.

11. Write an override for `AWarrior::SetupPlayerInputComponent( UInputComponent* Input )` to connect the input controller to the Warrior's GameplayAbility activations. After doing so, iterate over each GameplayAbility listed in your GameplayAbilitySet's **Abilities** group.

> Do not use the `GameplayAbilitySet::GiveAbilities()` member function because it doesn't give you access to the set of `FGameplayAbilitySpecHandle` objects that you actually need to later bind and invoke the ability to an input component.

```
void AWarrior::SetupPlayerInputComponent( UInputComponent* Input )
{
  Super::SetupPlayerInputComponent( Input );
  // Connect the class's AbilitySystemComponent
  // to the actor's input component
  AbilitySystemComponent->BindToInputComponent( Input );

  // Go thru each BindInfo in the gameplayAbilitySet.
  // Give & try and activate each on the AbilitySystemComponent.
  for( const FGameplayAbilityBindInfo& BindInfo :
  gameplayAbilitySet->Abilities )
  {
    // BindInfo has 2 members:
    //   .Command (enum value)
    //   .GameplayAbilityClass (UClass of a UGameplayAbility)
    if( !BindInfo.GameplayAbilityClass )
    {
      Error( FS( "GameplayAbilityClass %d not set",
      (int32)BindInfo.Command ) );
      continue;
    }

    FGameplayAbilitySpec spec(
    // Gets you an instance of the UClass
    BindInfo.GameplayAbilityClass->
    GetDefaultObject<UGameplayAbility>(),
    1, (int32)BindInfo.Command ) ;
```

```
    // STORE THE ABILITY HANDLE FOR LATER INVOKATION
    // OF THE ABILITY
    FGameplayAbilitySpecHandle abilityHandle =
    AbilitySystemComponent->GiveAbility( spec );

    // The integer id that invokes the ability
    // (ith value in enum listing)
    int32 AbilityID = (int32)BindInfo.Command;

    // CONSTRUCT the inputBinds object, which will
    // allow us to wire-up an input event to the
    // InputPressed() / InputReleased() events of
    // the GameplayAbility.
    FGameplayAbiliyInputBinds inputBinds(
      // These are supposed to be unique strings that define
      // what kicks off the ability for the actor instance.
      // Using strings of the format
      // "ConfirmTargetting_Player0_AbilityClass"
      FS( "ConfirmTargetting_%s_%s", *GetName(),
        *BindInfo.GameplayAbilityClass->GetName() ),
      FS( "CancelTargetting_%s_%s", *GetName(),
        *BindInfo.GameplayAbilityClass->GetName() ),
      "EGameplayAbilityInputBinds", // The name of the ENUM that
      // has the abilities listing (GameplayAbilitySet.h).
      AbilityID, AbilityID
    );
    // MUST BIND EACH ABILITY TO THE INPUTCOMPONENT, OTHERWISE
    // THE ABILITY CANNOT "HEAR" INPUT EVENTS.
    // Enables triggering of InputPressed() / InputReleased()
    // events, which you can in-turn use to call
    // TryActivateAbility() if you so choose.
    AbilitySystemComponent->BindAbilityActivationToInputComponent(
      Input, inputBinds
    );

    // Test-kicks the ability to active state.
    // You can try invoking this manually via your
    // own hookups to keypresses in this Warrior class
    // TryActivateAbility() calls ActivateAbility() if
    // the ability is indeed invokable at this time according
    // to rules internal to the Ability's class (such as cooldown
    // is ready and cost is met)
    AbilitySystemComponent->TryActivateAbility(
      abilityHandle, 1 );
  }
}
```

How it works...

You must subclass and link in a set of `UGameplayAbility` objects to your actor's `UAbilitySystemComponent` object through a series of calls to `UAbilitySystemCompo nent::GiveAbility( spec )` with appropriately constructed `FGameplayAbilitySpec` objects. What this does is it decks out your actor with this bunch of `GameplayAbilities`. The functionality of each `UGameplayAbility`, its cost, cooldown, and activation is all neatly contained within the `UGameplayAbility` class derivative that you will construct.

There's more...

You'll want to carefully code in a bunch of the other functions that are available in the `GameplayAbility.h` header file, including implementations for the following:

- ► `SendGameplayEvent`: This is a function to notify GameplayAbility that some general gameplay event has happened.

- ► `CancelAbility`: This is a function to stop an ability's usage midway through, and giving the ability an interrupted state.

- ► Keep in mind that there are a bunch of existing `UPROPERTY` near the bottom of the `UGameplayAbility` class declaration that either activate or cancel the ability upon addition or removal of certain `GameplayTags`. See the following *GameplayTags API – Attaching GameplayTags to an actor* recipe for more details.

- ► A bunch more! Explore the API and implement those functions you find to be useful in your code.

See also

- ► The `GameplayAbilities` API is a rich and nicely interwoven series of objects and functions. Really explore `GameplayEffects`, `GameplayTags` and `GameplayTasks` and how they integrate with the `UGameplayAbility` class to fully explore the functionality the library has to offer.

GameplayAbilities API – Implementing stats with UAttributeSet

The `GameplayAbilities` API allows you to associate a set of attributes, that is, `UAttributeSet`, to an Actor. `UAttributeSet` describes properties appropriate for that Actor's in-game attributes, such as `Hp`, `Mana`, `Speed`, `Armor`, `AttackDamage`, and so on. You can either define a single game-wide set of attributes common to all Actors, or several different sets of attributes appropriate for the different classes of actors.

Getting ready

AbilitySystemComponent is the first thing you will need to add to your actors to equip them to use *GameAbilities API* and UAttributeSets. To define your custom UAttributeSet, you will simply derive from the UAttributeSet base class and extend the base class with your own series of UPROPERTY members. After that, you must register your custom AttributeSet with your Actor class' AbilitySystemComponent.

How to do it...

1. Link to the GameplayAbilities API in your ProjectName.Build.cs file.

2. In its own file, derive from the UAttributeSet class and deck the class out with a set of UPROPERTY that you want each Actor to have in their property set. For example, you might want to declare your UAttributeSet derivate class similar to the following piece of code:

```
#include "Runtime/GameplayAbilities/Public/AttributeSet.h"
#include "GameUnitAttributeSet.generated.h"

UCLASS(Blueprintable, BlueprintType)
class CHAPTER12_API UGameUnitAttributeSet : public
UAttributeSet
{
  GENERATED_BODY()
  public:
  UGameUnitAttributeSet( const FObjectInitializer& PCIP );
  UPROPERTY( EditAnywhere, BlueprintReadWrite, Category =
  GameUnitAttributes )  float Hp;
  UPROPERTY( EditAnywhere, BlueprintReadWrite, Category =
  GameUnitAttributes )  float Mana;
  UPROPERTY( EditAnywhere, BlueprintReadWrite, Category =
  GameUnitAttributes )  float Speed;
};
```

 If your code is networked, you might want to enable replication on each of the UPROPERTY with the replicated declaration in the UPROPERTY macro.

3. Connect GameUnitAttributeSet with your AbilitySystemComponent inside your Actor class by calling the following code:

```
AbilitySystemComponent->InitStats(
  UGameUnitAttributeSet::StaticClass(), NULL );
```

You can put this call somewhere in `PostInitializeComponents()`, or in code that is called later than that.

4. Once you have registered `UAttributeSet`, you can move on with the next recipe and apply `GameplayEffect` to some of the elements in the attribute set.

5. Be sure your `Actor` class object implements `IAbilitySystemInterface` by deriving from it. This is extremely important as the `UAbilitySet` object will attempt a cast to `IAbilitySystemInterface` to call `GetAbilitySystemComponent()` on it at various places in the code.

How it works...

`UAttributeSets` simply allow you to enumerate and define attributes of different actors. `GameplayEffects` will be your means to make changes to the attributes of a specific actor.

There's more...

You can code in definitions of `GameplayEffects`, which will be things that act on the AbilitySystemComponent's `AttributeSet` collections. You can also write `GameplayTasks` for generic functions that run at specific time or events, or even in response to tag addition (`GameplayTagResponseTable.cpp`). You can define `GameplayTags` to modify GameplayAbility behavior as well as select and match gameplay units during play.

GameplayAbilities API – Implementing buffs with GameplayEffect

A buff is just an effect that introduces a temporary, permanent, or recurring change to a game unit's attributes from its `AttributeSet`. Buffs can either be good or bad, supplying either bonuses or penalties. For example, you might have a hex buff that slows a unit to half speed, an angel wing buff that increases unit speed by 2x, or a cherub buff that recovers 5 hp every five seconds for three minutes. A `GameplayEffect` affects an individual gameplay attributes in the `UAttributeSet` attached to an `AbilitySystemComponent` of an Actor.

Getting ready

Brainstorm your game units' effects that happen during the game. Be sure that you've created an `AttributeSet`, shown in the previous recipe, with gameplay attributes that you'd like to affect. Select an effect to implement and follow the succeeding steps with your example.

You may want to turn `LogAbilitySystem` to a `VeryVerbose` setting by going to the **Output Log** and typing `` ` ``, and then `Log LogAbilitySystem All`.

This will display much more information from `AbilitySystem` in the **Output Log**, making it easier to see what's going on within the system.

How to do it...

In the following steps, we'll construct a quick `GameplayEffect` that heals 50 hp to the selected unit's `AttributeSet`:

1. Construct your `UGameplayEffect` class object using the `CONSTRUCT_CLASS` macro with the following line of code:

```
// Create GameplayEffect recovering 50 hp one time only to
unit
CONSTRUCT_CLASS( UGameplayEffect, RecoverHP );
```

2. Use the `AddModifier` function to change the `Hp` field of `GameUnitAttributeSet`, as follows:

```
AddModifier( RecoverHP,
GET_FIELD_CHECKED( UGameUnitAttributeSet, Hp ),
EGameplayModOp::Additive, FScalableFloat( 50.f ) );
```

3. Fill in the other properties of `GameplayEffect`, including fields such as `DurationPolicy` and `ChanceToApplyToTarget` or any other fields that you'd like to modify, as follows:

```
RecoverHP->DurationPolicy =
EGameplayEffectDurationType::HasDuration;
RecoverHP->DurationMagnitude = FScalableFloat( 10.f );
RecoverHP->ChanceToApplyToTarget = 1.f;
RecoverHP->Period = .5f;
```

4. Apply the effect to an `AbilitySystemComponent` of your choice. The underlying `UAttributeSet` will be affected and modified by your call, as shown in the following piece of code:

```
FActiveGameplayEffectHandle recoverHpEffectHandle =
AbilitySystemComponent->ApplyGameplayEffectToTarget(
RecoverHP,
AbilitySystemComponent, 1.f );
```

How it works...

GameplayEffects are simply little objects that effect changes to an actor's AttributeSet. GameplayEffects can occur once, or repeatedly, in intervals over a Period. You can program-in effects pretty quickly and the GameplayEffect class creation is intended to be inline.

There's more...

Once the GameplayEffect is active, you will receive an FActiveGameplayEffectHandle. You can use this handle to attach a function delegate to run when the effect is over using the OnRemovedDelegate member of the FActiveGameplayEffectHandle. For example, you might call:

```
FActiveGameplayEffectHandle recoverHpEffectHandle =
AbilitySystemComponent->ApplyGameplayEffectToTarget( RecoverHP,
AbilitySystemComponent, 1.f );
if( recoverHpEffectHandle ) {
  recoverHpEffectHandle->AddLambda( [] () {
    Info( "RecoverHp Effect has been removed." );
  } );
}
```

GameplayTags API – Attaching GameplayTags to an Actor

GameplayTags are just small bits of text that describes states (or buffs) for the player or attributes that can attach to things such as GameplayAbilities and also to describe GameplayEffects, as well as states that clear those effects. So, we can have GameplayTags, such as Healing or Stimmed, that trigger various GameplayAbilities or GameplayEffects to our liking. We can also search for things via GameplayTags and attach them to our AbilitySystemComponents if we choose.

How to do it...

There are several steps to getting `GameplayTags` to work correctly inside your engine build; they are as follows:

1. First, we will need to create a Data Table asset to carry all of our game's tag names. Right-click on **Content Browser** and select **Miscellaneous | Data Table**. Select a table class structure deriving from `GameplayTagTableRow`.

   List all tags available inside your game under that data structure.

2. Add `UPROPERTY()` `TArray<FString>` to your `GameMode` object to list the names of the `TagTableNames` that you want to load into the `GameplayTags` module manager:

   ```
   UPROPERTY( EditAnywhere, BlueprintReadWrite, Category =
   GameplayTags )
   TArray<FString> GameplayTagTableNames;
   ```

3. In your GameMode's `PostInitializeComponents` function, or later, load the tags in the tables of your choice using `GetGameplayTagsManager`:

   ```
   IGameplayTagsModule::Get().GetGameplayTagsManager().
   LoadGameplayTagTable( GameplayTagTableNames );
   ```

4. Use your `GameplayTags`. Inside each of your GameplayAbility objects, you can modify the blockedness, cancelability, and activation requirements for each GameplayAbility using tag attachment or removal.

You do have to rebuild your engine in order to get your tags to load within the editor. The patch to the engine source that is proposed allows you to hook in a call to `IGameplayTagsModule::Get().GetGameplayTagsManager().` `LoadGameplayTagTable( GameplayTagTableNames )`.

To get this call embedded into the editor's startup, you will need to edit the engine's source.

GameplayTasks API – Making things happen with GameplayTasks

`GameplayTasks` are used to wrap up some gameplay functionality in a reusable object. All you have to do to use them is derive from the `UGameplayTask` base class and override some of the member functions that you prefer to implement.

Getting ready

Go in the UE4 Editor and navigate to **Class Viewer**. Ensure that you have linked in the `GameplayTasks` API into your `ProjectName.Build.cs` file and search with **Actors Only** tickbox off for the `GameplayTask` object type.

How to do it...

1. Ensure that you have linked `GameplayTasks` API into your `ProjectName.Build. cs` file.

2. Click on **File | Add C++ Class...** Choose to derive from `GameplayTask`. To do so, you must first tick **Show All Classes**, and then type `gameplaytask` into the filter box. Click on **Next**, name your C++ class (something like `GameplayTask_TaskName` is the convention) then add the class to your project. The example spawns a particle emitter and is called `GameplayTask_CreateParticles`.

3. Once your `GameplayTask_CreateParticles.h` and `.cpp` pair are created, navigate to the `.h` file and declare a static constructor that creates a `GameplayTask_CreateParticles` object for you:

```
// Like a constructor.
UGameplayTask_CreateParticles* UGameplayTask_
CreateParticles::ConstructTask(
  TScriptInterface<IGameplayTaskOwnerInterface> TaskOwner,
  UParticleSystem* particleSystem,
  FVector location )
{
  UGameplayTask_CreateParticles* task =
  NewTask<UGameplayTask_CreateParticles>( TaskOwner );
  // Fill fields
```

```
    if( task )
    {
        task->ParticleSystem = particleSystem;
        task->Location = location;
    }
    return task;
}
```

4. Override the `UGameplayTask_CreateEmitter::Activate()` function, which contains code that runs when `GameplayTask` is effected, as follows:

```
void UGameplayTask_CreateEmitter::Activate()
{
    Super::Activate();
    UGameplayStatics::SpawnEmitterAtLocation( GetWorld(),
    ParticleSystem->GetDefaultObject<UParticleSystem>(),
    Location );
}
```

5. Add `GameplayTasksComponent` to your `Actor` class derivative, which is available in the **Components** dropdown of the **Components** tab in the Blueprint editor.

6. Create and add an instance of your `GameplayTask` inside your `Actor` derivative instance using the following code:

```
UGameplayTask_CreateParticles* task =
    UGameplayTask_CreateParticles::ConstructTask( this,
    particleSystem, FVector( 0.f, 0.f, 200.f ) );
if( GameplayTasksComponent )
{
    GameplayTasksComponent->AddTaskReadyForActivation( *task );
}
```

7. This code runs anywhere in your `Actor` class derivative, any time after `GameplayTasksComponent` is initialized (any time after `PostInitializeComponents()`).

How it works...

`GameplayTasks` simply register with the `GameplayTasksComponent` situated inside an `Actor` class derivative of your choice. You can activate any number of `GameplayTasks` at any time during gameplay to trigger their effects.

`GameplayTasks` can also kick off `GameplayEffects` to change attributes of `AbilitySystemsComponents` if you wish.

There's more...

You can derive `GameplayTasks` for any number of events in your game. What's more is that you can override a few more virtual functions to hook into additional functionality.

HTTP API – Web request

When you're maintaining scoreboards or other such things that require regular HTTP request access to servers, you can use the HTTP API to perform such web request tasks.

Getting ready

Have a server to which you're allowed to request data via HTTP. You can use a public server of any type to try out HTTP requests if you'd like.

How to do it...

1. Link to the HTTP API in your `ProjectName.Build.cs` file.

2. In the file in which you will send your web request, include the `HttpModule.h` header file, the `HttpManager.h` header file, and the `HttpRetrySystem.h` file, as shown in the following code snippet:

   ```
   #include "Runtime/Online/HTTP/Public/HttpManager.h"
   #include "Runtime/Online/HTTP/Public/HttpModule.h"
   #include "Runtime/Online/HTTP/Public/HttpRetrySystem.h"
   ```

3. Construct an `IHttpRequest` object from `FHttpModule` using the following code:

   ```
   TSharedRef<IHttpRequest>
   http=FHttpModule::Get().CreateRequest();
   ```

    `FHttpModule` is a singleton object. One copy of it exists for the entire program that you are meant to use for all interactions with the `FHttpModule` class.

4. Attach your function to run to the `IHttpRequest` object's `FHttpRequestCompleteDelegate`, which has a signature as follows:

   ```
   void HttpRequestComplete( FHttpRequestPtr request,
   FHttpResponsePtr response, bool success );
   ```

5. The delegate is found inside of the `IHttpRequest` object as `http->OnProcessRequestComplete()`:

```
FHttpRequestCompleteDelegate& delegate = http-
>OnProcessRequestComplete();
```

There are a few ways to attach a callback function to the delegate. You can use the following:

- A lambda using `delegate.BindLambda()`:

```
delegate.BindLambda(
    // Anonymous, inlined code function (aka lambda)
    [] ( FHttpRequestPtr request, FHttpResponsePtr response,
bool
    success ) -> void
    {
    UE_LOG( LogTemp, Warning, TEXT( "Http Response: %d, %s"
),
    request->GetResponse()->GetResponseCode(),
    *request->GetResponse()->GetContentAsString() );
});
```

- Any UObject's member function:

```
delegate.BindUObject( this,
&AChapter12GameMode::HttpRequestComplete );
```

 You cannot attach to `UFunction` directly here as the `.BindUFunction()` command requests arguments that are all UCLASS, USTRUCT or UENUM.

- Any plain old C++ object's member function using `.BindRaw`:

```
PlainObject* plainObject = new PlainObject();
delegate.BindRaw( plainObject, &PlainObject::httpHandler
);
// plainObject cannot be DELETED Until httpHandler gets
called..
```

 You have to ensure that your `plainObject` refers to a valid object in memory at the time the HTTP request completes. This means that you cannot use `TAutoPtr` on `plainObject`, because that will deallocate `plainObject` at the end of the block in which it is declared, but that may be before the HTTP request completes.

❑ A global C-style static function:

```
// C-style function for handling the HTTP response:
void httpHandler( FHttpRequestPtr request,
FHttpResponsePtr response, bool success )
{
   Info( "static: Http req handled" );
}
delegate.BindStatic( &httpHandler );
```

When using a delegate callback with an object, be sure that the object instance that you're calling back on lives on at least until the point at which the `HttpResponse` arrives back from the server. Processing the `HttpRequest` takes real time to run. It is a web request after all—think of waiting for a web page to load.

You have to be sure that the object instance on which you're calling the callback function has not deallocated on you between the time of the initial call and the invocation of your `HttpHandler` function. The object must still be in memory when the callback returns after the HTTP request completes.

You cannot simply expect that the `HttpResponse` function happens immediately after you attach the callback function and call `ProcessRequest()`! Using a reference counted `UObject` instance to attach the `HttpHandler` member function is a good idea to ensure that the object stays in memory until the HTTP request completes.

6. Specify the URL of the site you'd like to hit:

```
http->SetURL( TEXT( "http://unrealengine.com" ) );
```

7. Process the request by calling `ProcessRequest`:

```
http->ProcessRequest();
```

How it works...

The HTTP object is all you need to send off HTTP requests to a server and get HTTP responses. You can use the HTTP request/response for anything that you wish; for example, submitting scores to a high scores table or to retrieve text to display in-game from a server.

They are decked out with a URL to visit and a function callback to run when the request is complete. Finally, they are sent off via `FManager`. When the web server responds, your callback is called and the results of your HTTP response can be shown.

There's more...

You can set additional HTTP request parameters via the following member functions:

- ▶ `SetVerb()` to change whether you are using the `GET` or `POST` method in your HTTP request

- ▶ `SetHeaders()` to modify any general header settings you would like

HTTP API – Progress bars

The `IHttpRequest` object from HTTP API will report HTTP download progress via a callback on a `FHttpRequestProgressDelegate` accessible via `OnRequestProgress()`. The signature of the function we can attach to the `OnRequestProgress()` delegate is as follows:

```
HandleRequestProgress( FHttpRequestPtr request, int32
    sentBytes, int32 receivedBytes )
```

The three parameters of the function you may write include: the original `IHttpRequest` object, the bytes sent, and the bytes received so far. This function gets called back periodically until the `IHttpRequest` object completes, which is when the function you attach to `OnProcessRequestComplete()` gets called. You can use the values passed to your `HandleRequestProgress` function to advance a progress bar that you will create in UMG.

Getting ready

You will need an internet connection to use this recipe. We will be requesting a file from a public server. You can use a public server or your own private server for your HTTP request if you'd like.

In this recipe, we will bind a callback function to just the `OnRequestProgress()` delegate to display the download progress of a file from a server. Have a project ready where we can write a piece of code that will perform `IHttpRequest`, and a nice interface on which to display percentage progress.

How to do it...

1. Link to the UMG and HTTP APIs in your `ProjectName.Build.cs` file.

2. Build a small UMG UI with `ProgressBar` to display your HTTP request's progress.

3. Construct an `IHttpRequest` object using the following code:

```
TSharedRef<IHttpRequest> http =
HttpModule::Get().CreateRequest();
```

4. Provide a callback function to call when the request progresses, which updates a visual GUI element:

```
http->OnRequestProgress().BindLambda( [] ( FHttpRequestPtr
request, int32 sentBytes, int32 receivedBytes ) -> void
{
    int32 totalLen = request->GetResponse()-
    >GetContentLength();
    float perc = (float)receivedBytes/totalLen;
    if ( HttpProgressBar )
    HttpProgressBar->SetPercent ( perc );
} );
```

5. Process your request with `http->ProcessRequest()`.

How it works...

The `OnRequestProgress()` callback gets fired every so often with the bytes sent and bytes received HTTP progress. We will compute the total percent of the download that is complete by calculating `(float)receivedBytes/totalLen`, where `totalLen` is the HTTP response's total length in bytes. Using the lambda function we attached to the `OnRequestProgress()` delegate callback, we can call the UMG widget's `.SetPercent()` member function to reflect the download's progress.

Index

C

D

data binding
  using, with Unreal Motion Graphics 332-335
Decorators
  about 361
  creating 362
  using, for conditions 361
delegate
  about 140
  unregistering 143, 144
delegate, associated to UFUNCTION
  creating 140-143
delegate, taking input parameters
  creating 144-146
Destroy
  used, for destroying Actor 85
Details Customization 306

E

Epic 34
event handling
  implementing, via virtual functions 137-139
events
  creating, for implementing in
    Blueprint 236-239

F

Fantastic Quaternions by Numberphile
  reference 396
Feature 34
FMessageLog 393
FObjectFinder
  used, for loading assets into
    components 89-91
Foliage API
  map, generating with 406-408
  trees, adding manually to your level 405
  trees, adding procedurally to your
    level 404-406
FQuat
  used, for rotating objects 396, 397

Fresnel effect 384
FRotationMatrix
  about 398
  used, for rotating objects 398, 399
FRotator
  used, for rotating objects 395, 396
function calls
  attaching, to Slate Events 328-331
functions
  creating 232-235

G

gameplay
  implementing, framework used 408-413
GameplayAbilities API
  about 408
  buffs, implementing with
    GameplayEffect 415-417
  stats, implementing with
    UAttributeSet 413-415
GameplayTags
  attaching, to Actor 417-419
GameplayTags API 417
GameplayTasks API
  working with 419, 420
garbage collection
  forcing 71
garbage collector 66
glimmer
  about 380
  controlling 381
graph pin visualizer 300
grok 15

H

HTTP API
  about 421
  progress bars 424
  web request 421-423

I

Ignore class
about 173
used, for lettings objects pass through one
    another 173, 174
In-Editor method 321, 322
inheritance
Actor functionality, implementing by 92-94
InventoryComponent
creating, for RPG 114-125
Issue Tracker
about 28
using 28-31

K

Kanban 31
Killable interface 194

L

landscape
shading 386-388
Landscape API
about 400
landscape generation, with Perlin
    noise 400-403
map, generating with 406-408
leaves
creating, in wind 382, 383
Lerp 235

M

malloc()
about 62
using 62, 63
managed memory
about 65
ConstructObject< >, using 65-67
memory, deallocating 67
NewObject< >, using 65, 66
smart pointers, using 68, 69

map
generating, with Foliage API 406-408
generating, with Landscape API 406-408
Markdown
about 29
reference link 30
Material function 377, 378
Material instances 379, 380
Material Parameter Collection (MPC) 383
Melee Attacker 365, 366
memory management 62
Message Log
messages writing to, FMessageLog
    used 393-395
modularity 377
mouse UI input handling [UMG] 171, 172
multicast delegate
creating 148-150
multi-cast delegates
exposing, to Blueprint 240-248

N

native UInterface functions
calling, from C++ 189-193
Navigation Mesh (Nav Mesh)
about 354
constructing 354
new Asset type
creating 283-287
new console commands
creating 294-299
new editor module
creating 266-269
new editor window
creating 280-283
new graph pin visualizer
creating, for Blueprint 300-305
new Menu entries
creating 278, 279
NewObject< >()
using 65, 66
new operator
about 64
using 64

Made in the USA
San Bernardino, CA
22 November 2016